Myth
and
Southern
History

Myth and Southern History

The Old South

Edited by **PATRICK GERSTER**
and **NICHOLAS CORDS**

LAKEWOOD COMMUNITY COLLEGE

 RAND McNALLY COLLEGE PUBLISHING COMPANY • Chicago

For
Mark, Jennifer, Jason
James and John

Acknowledgments

As is the case with any project based on secondary sources, we have incurred many debts. Because this work is thematic, we are indebted to all those historians whose works have contributed either directly or indirectly to our developing interest in the relationship between myth and history. The work being regional in focus, we are particularly indebted to southern historians' contributions, and most particularly to those whose works are included herein. We are impressed that they represent the historical profession at its finest. We also extend our thanks to Lawrence Malley, Robert Erhart, and Margaret L. Boberschmidt of Rand McNally; to Neil R. McMillen for strategic aid and valuable suggestions; and to our typist, Mrs. Van Johnson. Finally, we express deep gratitude to our wives and families for their support and forebearance.

It's all *now* you see. Yesterday won't be over until tomorrow and tomorrow began ten thousand years ago. For every Southern boy fourteen years old, not once but whenever he wants it, there is the instant when it's still not yet two o'clock on that July afternoon in 1863, the brigades are in position behind the rail fence, the guns are laid and ready in the woods and the furled flags are already loosened to break out and Pickett himself with his long oiled ringlets and his hat in one hand probably and his sword in the other looking up the hill waiting for Longstreet to give the word and it's all in the balance, it hasn't happened yet, it hasn't even begun yet, it not only hasn't begun yet but there is still time for it not to begin against that position and those circumstances which made more men than Garnett and Kemper and Armstead and Wilcox look grave yet it's going to begin, we all know that, we have come too far with too much at stake and that moment doesn't even need a fourteen-year-old boy to think *This time. Maybe this time* with all this much to lose and all this much to gain: Pennsylvania, Maryland, the world, the golden dome of Washington itself to crown with desperate and unbelievable victory the desperate gamble, the cast made two years ago; or to anyone who ever sailed even a skiff under a quilt sail, the moment in 1492 when somebody thought *This is it:* the absolute edge of no return, to turn back now and make home or sail irrevocably on and either find land or plunge over the world's roaring rim.

WILLIAM FAULKNER, *Intruder in the Dust*

Contents

Introduction

Students of the southern past have long sought to identify a central theme in southern history. It was out of such a concern, for example, that historian Ulrich B. Phillips spoke of the sustained southern commitment to white supremacy; journalist Wilbur J. Cash sought to tap the inner workings of "the mind" of the South; and others have concluded the inner logic of southern history to be climate, geography, or its seemingly distinctive economic, political, social, or religious patterns. Indeed the debate over the central theme of southern history is a continuing one, with the only consensus being that there does exist a common thread of experience somewhere in the deep recesses of the southern past.

In 1964, while in pursuit of this central theme, George B. Tindall isolated "mythology" as a "new frontier" in southern history.[1] Acknowledging the work of earlier historians such as Francis Pendelton Gaines (*The Southern Plantation: A Study in the Development and Accuracy of a Tradition,* 1925), and anticipating the verdict of southern historians to come, Tindall's essay enthusiastically endorsed mythology as a tool for analyzing the rather blatant ambiguities, ironies, and paradoxes inherent in the southern past. The lens of myth had indeed been applied to the South before Professor Tindall's seminal work, but it was left for him to suggest that such an approach might well result in a new synthesis and a perspective worthy of sustained application. In short, Tindall's article posed the question: Is myth indeed one of the more important psychological determinants of southernism?

To what extent George B. Tindall's suggested approach to southern history will withstand the long-term erosion of historical scholarship is a question only future generations of scholars can answer with any full degree of certitude. It is the opinion of the editors, however, that an affirmative yet tentative judgment is now possible given the body of historical literature which has arisen clearly vindicating the Tindall thesis. An impressive array of southern scholars prior to and since Tindall's seminal essay have sought to determine the parameters of myth within what C. Vann Woodward has labeled "that twilight zone between living memory and written history." This volume brings together a sampling of their findings. Such scholars

---

[1] George B. Tindall, "Mythology: A New Frontier in Southern History," in *The Idea of the South: Pursuit of a Central Theme,* ed. Frank E. Vandiver (Chicago, 1964).

are representative of an expanding and distinguished group of American historians who have come to see important distinctions between what might be termed "history as actuality" and "history as perceived."[2]

But perhaps further clarification and explanation are needed before this work can indeed provide the measure of historical insight which the "new frontier of mythology" potentially holds. The term "myth," as presented in this set of readings, is viewed in two ways. In the first instance, some of the authors seem to have Thomas A. Bailey's definition in mind as they speak of the myths of southern history: "a historical myth is . . . an account or belief that is demonstrably untrue, in whole or substantial part."[3] Those reflecting this definition tend to emphasize the negative aspects of myth, to isolate, and when the occasion warrants to debunk the results of misguided scholarship. Second, others appear more consistent with Henry Nash Smith's view of myth as "an intellectual construction that fuses concept and emotion into an image."[4] Briefly stated, one school seeks to emphasize historical inaccuracies while the other approaches the problem from the vantage point of social psychology. One sees myth as the by-product of historical scholarship (or lack of it), while the other shows a marked concern for the ways in which myth serves the decidedly positive function of unifying experience providing, in the words of Mark Schorer, "a large controlling image that gives philosophical meaning to the facts of ordinary life. . . ."[5] Certainly, at times both definitions are present—on occasion they tend to blend to the point of becoming almost indistinguishable. Both notions of myth are germane to the South and its history.

It is also important to note that the existence of a southern mythology in no way sets the South apart as distinctive or unique. It has been demonstrated in other quarters that much behavior and belief based on myth survives, and in fact thrives, in the contemporary world. The preeminent mythic scholar, Mircea Eliade, has observed that "certain aspects and functions of mythical thought are constituents of the human being."[6] Fundamental to the "human condition," myths in their infinite variety and complexity serve a supportive role to the dreams, ideals, and values of every society. Accordingly, "southern mythology" must be seen as differing from

[2] For a view of myth in its larger American context see Nicholas Cords and Patrick Gerster (eds.), *Myth and the American Experience,* 2 vols. (New York and Beverly Hills, 1973).

[3] Thomas A. Bailey, "The Mythmakers of American History," *The Journal of American History,* 55 (June 1968), p. 5.

[4] Henry Nash Smith, *Virgin Land: The American West as Symbol and Myth* (New York, 1950), p. v.

[5] Mark Schorer, "The Necessity of Myth," in Henry A. Murray (ed.), *Myth and Mythmaking* (New York, 1960), p. 355.

[6] Mircea Eliade, "Survivals and Camouflages of Myth," *Diogenes,* 41 (Spring 1963), p. 1.

its American equivalent only in degree not in kind, just as "American mythology" stands in relation to that of the world at large. Paul M. Gaston concurred with this judgment in his recent work, *The New South Creed: A Study in Southern Mythmaking:*

> What does distinguish the South, at least from other parts of the United States, is the degree to which myths have been spawned and the extent to which they have asserted their hegemony over the Southern mind.[7]

In this sense, at least, the American South has successfully transcended the strictures of regionalism.

Finally, the identification of myth as an important element in the historical process demonstrates anew that history is the dual product of documentation and imagination—both the record of the past *and* the dialogue among historians. The basic documents and the personal and professional prejudices of the historian (for Wendell H. Stephenson, "the fallacies of assumptions and methods") all find their way into the historical "record." The historian cannot dismiss the controlling images or myths of the society within which he writes. Because the serious historian must factor for all of these as he engages his discipline, this volume is as much a commentary on the writing of southern history—that is to say historiography—as it is on the viability of myth in the historical process. In these pages there is much support of the observation that "myth[s] have been used for centuries in writing history as well as making it."[8] The reader will find that "mythology" has provided, as well as suggests, new realms of scholarly speculation. More specifically, it becomes evident that such an approach applied to the South has come of age. It is an approach to southern history both relevant and exciting, deserving to *take its stand* beside the more traditional and validated perspectives long provided by historians of the marketplace, the political and diplomatic arenas, and the social record.

Some years ago Wilbur Cash wrote of the importance of the South's frontier experience: ". . . the history of the roll of frontier upon frontier— and on to the frontier beyond."[9] Given George B. Tindall's scholarly directive and the focus provided by the following selections, perhaps the South's enigmatic frontiers of the past—even that elusive central theme—can now find clearer explanation and synthesis in terms of her "new frontier of mythology."

[7] Paul M. Gaston, *The New South Creed: A Study in Southern Mythmaking* (New York, 1970), p. 8.

[8] Alfred Stern, "Fiction and Myth in History," *Diogenes,* 42 (Summer 1963), p. 98.

[9] Wilbur Cash, *The Mind of the South* (New York, 1941), p. 4.

1

Mythology: A New Frontier in Southern History

George B. Tindall

The "reality" of history, irrespective of time or place, remains an elusive commodity, especially as regards the American South. Indeed, as George B. Tindall, Professor of History at the University of North Carolina, Chapel Hill, argues in the selection which follows, the basic problem of distinguishing *objective reality* from *perceived reality* is ever present for the historian. Historical reality involves not only that which is demonstrably true but also that which one believes to be true. As such, the historian has a dual role: he remains at once a "custodian of the past and keeper of the public memory." The role of the historian involves both countering misguided scholarship and identifying the public dreams which do so much to orchestrate human behavior. Both of these facets of the historical enterprise inevitably lead the historian into the province of myth. Thus, in determining the dimensions of the southern experience, the historian must reckon not only with peculiar regional characteristics but also the myths which have conditioned them. As a significant unit of the region's experience, myth supplies an internal structure and a sustaining symmetry to our understanding of the South. Professor Tindall's exploration of this new frontier of mythology does much to establish the context—the perspective and technique—for this entire work.

From George Tindall, "Mythology: A New Frontier in Southern History," in Frank E. Vandiver (ed.), *The Idea of the South: Pursuit of a Central Theme,* pp. 1–15. Reprinted by permission of the author and the University of Chicago Press. Copyright © 1964 by William Rice University. All rights reserved. Published 1964. Composed and printed by the University of Chicago Press, Chicago, Illinois, U.S.A.

The idea of the South—or more appropriately, the ideas of the South—belong in large part to the order of social myth. There are few areas of the modern world that have bred a regional mythology so potent, so profuse and diverse, even so paradoxical, as the American South. But the various mythical images of the South that have so significantly affected American history have yet to be subjected to the kind of broad and imaginative historical analysis that has been applied to the idea of the American West, particularly in Henry Nash Smith's *Virgin Land: The American West as Symbol and Myth*. The idea of the South has yet to be fully examined in the context of mythology, as essentially a problem of intellectual history.

To place the ideas of the South in the context of mythology, of course, is not necessarily to pass judgment upon them as illusions. The game of debunking myths, Harry Levin has warned us, starts "in the denunciation of myth as falsehood from the vantage-point of a rival myth."[1] Mythology has other meanings, not all of them pejorative, and myths have a life of their own which to some degree renders irrelevant the question of their correlation to empirical fact. Setting aside for the moment the multiple connotations of the term, we may say that social myths in general, including those of the South, are simply mental pictures that portray the pattern of what a people think they are (or ought to be) or what somebody else thinks they are. They tend to develop abstract ideas in more or less concrete and dramatic terms. In the words of Henry Nash Smith, they fuse "concept and emotion into an image."[2]

They may serve a variety of functions. "A myth," Mark Schorer has observed, "is a large, controlling image that gives philosophical meaning to the facts of ordinary life; that is, which has organizing value for experience."[3] It may offer useful generalizations by which data may be tested. But being also "charged with values, aspirations, ideals and meanings,"[4] myths may become the ground for belief, for either loyalty and defense on the one hand or hostility and opposition on the other. In such circumstances a myth itself becomes one of the realities of history, significantly influencing the course of human action, for good or ill. There is, of course, always a danger of illusion, a danger that in ordering one's vision of reality, the myth may predetermine the categories of perception, rendering one blind to things that do not fit into the mental image.

[1] Harry Levin, "Some Meanings of Myth," in Henry A. Murray (ed.), *Myth and Mythmakers* (New York, 1960), p. 106.

[2] Henry Nash Smith, *Virgin Land: The American West as Symbol and Myth* (Vintage ed., New York, 1957), p. v.

[3] Mark Schorer, "The Necessity for Myth," in Murray (ed.), *Myth and Mythmakers*, p. 355.

[4] C. Vann Woodward, "The Antislavery Myth," *American Scholar*, XXXI (Spring, 1962), 325.

Since the Southern mind is reputed to be peculiarly resistant to pure abstraction and more receptive to the concrete and dramatic image, it may be unusually susceptible to mythology. Perhaps for the same reason our subject can best be approached through reference to the contrasting experiences of two Southerners—one recent, the other about forty-five years ago.

The first is the experience of a contemporary Louisiana writer, John T. Westbrook.

> During the thirties and early forties [Westbrook has written] when I was an English instructor at the University of Missouri, I was often mildly irritated by the average northerner's Jeeter-Lester-and-potlikker idea of the South. Even today the northern visitor inertia-headedly maintains his misconception: he hankers to see eroded hills and rednecks, scrub cotton and sharecropper shacks.

> It little profits me to drive him through Baton Rouge, show him the oil-ethyl-rubber-aluminum-chemical miles of industry along the Mississippi River, and say, "This . . . is the fastest-growing city of over 100,-000 in America. We can amply substantiate our claim that we are atomic target number one, that in the next war the Russians will obliterate us first. . . ."

> Our northerner is suspicious of all this crass evidence presented to his senses. It bewilders and befuddles him. He is too deeply steeped in William Faulkner and Robert Penn Warren. The fumes of progress are in his nose and the bright steel of industry towers before his eyes, but his heart is away in Yoknapatawpha County with razorback hogs and night riders. On this trip to the South he wants, above all else, to sniff the effluvium of backwoods-and-sand-hill subhumanity and to see at least one barn burn at midnight. So he looks at me with crafty misgiving, as if to say, "Well, you *do* drive a Cadillac, talk rather glibly about Kierkegaard and Sartre . . . but, after all, you *are* only fooling, aren't you? You do, don't you, sometimes, go out secretly by owl-light to drink swamp water and feed on sowbelly and collard greens?"[5]

The other story was the experience of a Southern historian, Frank L. Owsley, who traveled during World War I from Chicago via Cincinnati to Montgomery with a group of young ladies on the way to visit their menfolk at an army camp. He wrote later that, "despite everything which had ever been said to the contrary," the young ladies had a romantic conception of the "Sunny South" and looked forward to the journey with considerable ex-

John T. Westbrook, "Twilight of Southern Regionalism," *Southwest Review,* XLII (Summer, 1957), 231.

citement. "They expected to enter a pleasant land of white columned mansions, green pastures, expansive cotton and tobacco fields where negroes sang spirituals all the day through." Except in the bluegrass basins of central Kentucky and Tennessee, what they actually found "were gutted hillsides; scrub oak and pine; bramble and blackberry thickets, bottom lands once fertile now senile and exhausted, with spindling tobacco, corn, or cotton stalks . . . ; unpainted houses which were hardly more than shacks or here and there the crumbling ruins of old mansions covered with briars, the homes of snakes and lizards."[6] The disappointment of Dr. Owsley's ladies was, no doubt, even greater than that of Mr. Westbrook's friend in Baton Rouge.

There is a striking contrast between these two episodes, both in the picture of Southern reality and in the differing popular images that they present. The fact that they are four decades apart helps to account for the discrepancies, but what is not apparent at first is the common ancestry of the two images. They are not very distant cousins, collateral descendants from the standard image of the Old South, the plantation myth. The version of Owsley's lady friends is closer to the original primogenitor, which despite its advancing age and debility, still lives amid a flourishing progeny of legendary Southern gentility. According to Francis Pendleton Gaines, author of *The Southern Plantation,* the pattern appeared full-blown at least as early as 1832 in John Pendleton Kennedy's romance, *Swallow Barn.*[7] It has had a long career in story and novel and song, in the drama and motion picture. The corrosions of age seem to have ended its Hollywood career, although the old films still turn up on the late late. It may still be found in the tourist bait of shapely beauties in hoop skirts posed against the backdrop of white columns at Natchez, Orton, or a hundred other places.

These pictures are enough to trigger in the mind the whole euphoric pattern of kindly old marster with his mint julep; happy darkies singing in fields perpetually white to the harvest or, as the case may be, sadly recalling the long lost days of old; coquettish belles wooed by slender gallants in gray underneath the moonlight and magnolias. It is a pattern that yields all too easily to caricature and ridicule, for in its more sophisticated versions the figure of the planter carries a heavy freight of the aristocratic virtues: courtliness, grace, hospitality, honor, *noblesse oblige,* as well as many no less charming aristocratic vices: a lordly indifference to the balance sheet, hot temper, profanity, overindulgence, a certain stubborn obstinacy. The old-time Negro, when not a figure of comedy, is the very embodiment of

---

[6] Frank L. Owsley, "The Old South and the New," *American Review,* VI (February, 1936), 475.

[7] Francis Pendleton Gaines, *The Southern Plantation: A Study in the Development and Accuracy of a Tradition* (New York, 1925), p. 23.

loyalty. And the Southern belle: "Beautiful, graceful, accomplished in social charm, bewitching in coquetry, yet strangely steadfast in soul," Gaines has written, "she is perhaps the most winsome figure in the whole field of our fancy."[8] "The plantation romance," Gaines says, "remains our chief social idyl of the past; of an Arcadian scheme of existence, less material, less hurried, less prosaically equalitarian, less futile, richer in picturesqueness, festivity, in realized pleasure that recked not of hope or fear or unrejoicing labor."[9]

But there is still more to the traditional pattern. Somewhere off in the piney woods and erosion-gutted clay hills, away from the white columns and gentility, there existed Po' White Trash: the crackers; hillbillies; sandhillers; rag, tag, and bobtail; squatters; "po' buckra" to the Negroes; the Ransy Sniffle of A. B. Longstreet's *Georgia Scenes* and his literary descendants like Jeeter Lester and Ab Snopes, abandoned to poverty and degeneracy—the victims, it was later discovered, of hookworm, malaria, and pellagra. Somewhere in the pattern the respectable small farmer was lost from sight. He seemed to be neither romantic nor outrageous enough to fit in. His neglect provides the classic example in Southern history of the blind spots engendered by the power of mythology. It was not until the 1930's that Frank L. Owsley and his students at Vanderbilt rediscovered the Southern yeoman farmer as the characteristic, or at least the most numerous, ante bellum white Southerner.[10] More about the yeoman presently; neglected in the plantation myth, he was in the foreground of another.

In contrast to the legitimate heirs of the plantation myth, the image of John T. Westbrook's Yankee visitor in Baton Rouge seems to be descended from what might be called the illegitimate line of the plantation myth, out of abolition. It is one of the ironies of our history that, as Gaines put it, the "two opposing sides of the fiercest controversy that ever shook national thought agreed concerning certain picturesque elements of plantation life and joined hands to set the conception unforgettably in public consciousness."[11] The abolitionists found it difficult, or even undesirable, to escape the standard image. It was pretty fully developed even in *Uncle Tom's Cabin*. Harriet Beecher Stowe made her villain a Yankee overseer, and has been accused by at least one latter-day abolitionist of implanting deeply in the American mind the stereotype of the faithful darkey. For others the plantation myth simply appeared in reverse, as a pattern of corrupt opulence resting upon human exploitation. Gentle old marster became the ar-

[8] *Ibid.*, p. 16.
[9] *Ibid.*, p. 4.
[10] Frank L. Owsley, *Plain Folk of the Old South* (Baton Rouge, 1949).
[11] Gaines, *The Southern Plantation*, p. 30.

rogant, haughty, imperious potentate, the very embodiment of sin, the central target of the antislavery attack. He maintained a seraglio in the slave quarters; he bred Negroes like cattle and sold them down the river to certain death in the sugar mills, separating families if that served his purpose, while Southern women suffered in silence the guilty knowledge of their men's infidelity. The happy darkies in this picture became white men in black skins, an oppressed people longing for freedom, the victims of countless atrocities so ghastly as to be unbelievable except for undeniable evidence, forever seeking an opportunity to follow the North Star to freedom. The masses of the white folks were simply poor whites, relegated to ignorance and degeneracy by the slavocracy.

Both lines of the plantation myth have been remarkably prolific, but the more adaptable one has been that of the abolitionists. It has repeatedly readjusted to new conditions while the more legitimate line has courted extinction, running out finally into the decadence perpetrated by Tennessee Williams. Meanwhile, the abolitionist image of brutality persisted through and beyond Reconstruction in the Republican outrage mills and bloody shirt political campaigns. For several decades it was more than overbalanced by the Southern image of Reconstruction horrors, disarmed by prophets of a New South created in the image of the North, and almost completely submerged under the popularity of plantation romances in the generation before Owsley's trainload of ladies ventured into their "Sunny South" of the teens. At about that time, however, the undercurrents began to emerge once again into the mainstream of American thought. In the clever decade of the twenties a kind of neoabolitionist myth of the Savage South was compounded. It seemed that the benighted South, after a period of relative neglect, suddenly became an object of concern to every publicist in the country. One Southern abomination after another was ground through their mills: child labor, peonage, lynching, hookworm, pellagra, the Scopes trial, the Fundamentalist crusade against Al Smith. The guiding genius was Henry L. Mencken, the hatchet man from Baltimore who developed the game of South-baiting into a national pastime, a fine art at which he had no peer. In 1917, when he started constructing his image of "Baptist and Methodist barbarism" below the Potomac, he began with the sterility of Southern literature and went on from there. With characteristic glee he anointed one J. Gordon Coogler of South Carolina "the last bard of Dixie" and quoted his immortal couplet:

> Alas, for the South! Her books have grown fewer—
> She never was much given to literature.

"Down there," Mencken wrote, "a poet is now almost as rare as an oboe-player, a dry-point etcher or a metaphysician." As for "critics, musical composers, painters, sculptors, architects . . . there is not even a bad one between the Potomac mud-flats and the Gulf. Nor an historian. Nor a sociologist. Nor a philosopher. Nor a theologian. Nor a scientist. In all these fields the south is an awe-inspiring blank. . . ."[12] It was as complete a vacuity as the interstellar spaces, the "Sahara of the Bozart," "The Bible Belt." He summed it all up in one basic catalogue of Southern grotesqueries: "Fundamentalism, Ku Kluxry, revivals, lynchings, hog wallow politics— these are the things that always occur to a northerner when he thinks of the south."[13] The South, in short, had fallen prey to its poor whites, who would soon achieve apotheosis in the Snopes family.

It did not end with the twenties. The image was reinforced by a variety of episodes: the Scottsboro trials, chain gang exposés, Bilbo and Rankin, Senate filibusters, labor wars; much later by Central High and Orval Faubus, Emmett Till and Autherine Lucy and James Meredith, bus boycotts and Freedom Riders; and not least of all by the lush growth of literature that covered Mencken's Sahara, with Caldwell's *Tobacco Road* and Faulkner's *Sanctuary* and various other products of what Ellen Glasgow labeled the Southern Gothic and a less elegant Mississippi editor called the "privy school" of literature. In the words of Faulkner's character, Gavin Stevens, the North suffered from a curious "gullibility: a volitionless, almost helpless capacity and eagerness to believe anything about the South not even provided it be derogatory but merely bizarre enough and strange enough."[14] And Faulkner, to be sure, did not altogether neglect that market. Not surprisingly, he was taken in some quarters for a realist, and the image of Southern savagery long obscured the critics' recognition of his manifold merits.

The family line of the plantation myth can be traced only so far in the legendary gentility and savagery of the South. Other family lines seem to be entirely independent—if sometimes on friendly terms. In an excellent study, "The New South Creed, 1865–1900," soon to be published, Paul M. Gaston has traced the evolution of the creed into a genuine myth. In the aftermath of the Civil War, apostles of a "New South," led by Henry W. Grady, preached with almost evangelical fervor the gospel of industry. Their dream, Gaston writes, "was essentially a promise of American life for the South. It proffered all the glitter and glory and freedom from guilt that inhered in the American ideal."[15] From advocacy, from this vision of

---

[12] Henry L. Mencken, "The Sahara of the Bozart," in *Prejudices: Second Series* (New York, 1920), pp. 136, 137, 139.

[13] Henry L. Mencken, "The South Rebels Again," in Robert McHugh (ed.), *The Bathtub Hoax and Other Blasts & Bravos from the Chicago Tribune* (New York, 1958), p. 249. From a column in the Chicago *Tribune*, December 7, 1924.

[14] William Faulkner, *Intruder in the Dust* (New York, 1948), p. 153.

[15] Paul Morton Gaston, "The New South Creed, 1865–1900" (Ph.D. dissertation, Department of History, University of North Carolina, 1961), p. 193.

the future, the prophets soon advanced to the belief that "their promised land [was] at hand, no longer merely a gleaming goal." "By the twentieth century . . . there was established for many in the South a pattern of belief within which they could see themselves and their section as rich, success-oriented, and just . . . opulence and power were at hand . . . the Negro lived in the best of all possible worlds."[16]

As the twentieth century advanced, and wealth did in fact increase, the creed of the New South took on an additional burden of crusades for good roads and education, blending them into what Francis B. Simkins has called the "trinity of Southern progress": industrial growth, good roads, and schools. When the American Historical Association went to Durham in 1929 for its annual meeting, Robert D. W. Connor of the University of North Carolina presented the picture of a rehabilitated South that had "shaken itself free from its heritage of war and Reconstruction. Its self-confidence restored, its political stability assured, its prosperity regained, its social problems on the way to solution. . . ."[17] Two months before Connor spoke, the New York Stock Exchange had broken badly, and in the aftermath the image he described was seriously blurred, but before the end of the thirties it was being brought back into focus by renewed industrial expansion that received increased momentum from World War II and postwar prosperity.

Two new and disparate images emerged in the depression years, both with the altogether novel feature of academic trappings and affiliations. One was the burgeoning school of sociological regionalism led by Howard W. Odum and Rupert B. Vance at the University of North Carolina. It was neither altogether the image of the Savage South nor that of industrial progress, although both entered into the compound. It was rather a concept of the "Problem South," which Franklin D. Roosevelt labeled "the Nation's Economic Problem No. 1," a region with indisputable shortcomings but with potentialities that needed constructive attention and the application of rational social planning. Through the disciples of Odum as well as the agencies of the New Deal, the vision issued in a flood of social science monographs and programs for reform and development. To one undergraduate in Chapel Hill at the time, it seemed in retrospect that "we had more of an attitude of service to the South as the South than was true later. . . ."[18]

The regionalists were challenged by the Vanderbilt Agrarians, who de-

[16] *Ibid.,* pp. 195, 216.

[17] Robert D. W. Connor, "The Rehabilitation of a Rural Commonwealth," *American Historical Review,* XXXVI (October, 1930), 62.

[18] Alexander Heard, quoted in Wilma Dykeman and James Stokely, *Seeds of Southern Change: The Life of Will Alexander* (Chicago, 1962), p. 303.

veloped a myth of the traditional South. Their manifesto, *I'll Take My Stand,* by Twelve Southerners, appeared by fortuitous circumstance in 1930 when industrial capitalism seemed on the verge of collapse. In reaction against both the progressive New South and Mencken's image of savagery they championed, in Donald Davidson's words, a "traditional society . . . that is stable, religious, more rural than urban, and politically conservative," in which human needs were supplied by "Family, bloodkinship, clanship, folkways, custom, community. . . ."[19] The ideal of the traditional virtues took on the texture of myth in their image of the agrarian South. Of course, in the end, their agrarianism proved less important as a social-economic force than as a context for creative literature. The central figures in the movement were the Fugitive poets John Crowe Ransom, Donald Davidson, Allen Tate, and Robert Penn Warren. But, as Professor Louis Rubin has emphasized, "Through their vision of an agrarian community, the authors of *I'll Take My Stand* presented a critique of the modern world. In contrast to the hurried, nervous life of cities, the image of the agrarian South was of a life in which human beings existed serenely and harmoniously." Their critique of the modern frenzy "has since been echoed by commentator after commentator."[20]

While it never became altogether clear whether the Agrarians were celebrating the aristocratic graces or following the old Jeffersonian dictum that "Those who labor in the earth are the chosen people of God . . . ," most of them seemed to come down eventually on the side of the farmer rather than the planter. Frank L. Owsley, who rediscovered the ante bellum yeoman farmer, was one of them. Insofar as they extolled the yeoman farmer, the Agrarians laid hold upon an image older than any of the others—the Jeffersonian South. David M. Potter, a Southerner in exile at Stanford University, has remarked how difficult it is for many people to realize that the benighted South "was, until recently, regarded by many liberals as the birthplace and the natural bulwark of the Jeffersonian ideal. . . ."[21] The theme has long had an appeal for historians as well as others, Frederick Jackson Turner developed it for the West and William E. Dodd for the South. According to Dodd the democratic, equalitarian South of the Jeffersonian image was the norm; the plantation slavocracy was the great aberration. Dodd's theme has been reflected in the writing of other his-

---

[19] Donald Davidson, "Why the Modern South Has a Great Literature," *Vanderbilt Studies in the Humanities,* I (1951), 12.

[20] Louis D. Rubin, Jr., "Introduction to the Torchbook Edition," in Twelve Southerners, *I'll Take My Stand* (Torchbook ed.; New York, 1962), pp. xiv, xvii. See also Herman Clarence Nixon, "A Thirty Years' Personal View," *Mississippi Quarterly,* XIII (Spring, 1960), 79, for parallels in recent social criticism.

[21] David M. Potter, "The Enigma of the South," *Yale Review,* LI (Autumn, 1961), 143.

torians, largely in terms of a region subjected to economic colonialism by an imperial Northeast: Charles A. Beard, for example, who saw the sectional conflict as a struggle between agrarianism and industrialism; Howard K. Beale, who interpreted Reconstruction in similar terms; C. Vann Woodward, defender of Populism; Arthur S. Link, who first rediscovered the Southern progressives; and Walter Prescott Webb, who found the nation divided between an exploited South and West on the one hand, and a predatory Northeast on the other. Jefferson, like the South, it sometimes seems, can mean all things to all men, and the Jefferson image of agrarian democracy has been a favorite recourse of Southern liberals, just as his state-rights doctrines have nourished conservatism.

In stark contrast to radical agrarianism there stands the concept of monolithic conservatism in Southern politics. It seems to be a proposition generally taken for granted now that the South is, by definition, conservative—and always has been. Yet the South in the late nineteenth century produced some of the most radical Populists and in the twentieth was a bulwark of Wilsonian progressivism and Roosevelt's New Deal, at least up to a point. A good case has been made out by Arthur S. Link that Southern agrarian radicals pushed Wilson further into progressivism than he intended to go.[22] During the twenties Southern minority leadership in Congress kept up such a running battle against the conservative tax policies of Andrew Mellon that, believe it or not, there was real fear among some Northern businessmen during the 1932 campaign that Franklin D. Roosevelt might be succeeded by that radical Southern income-taxer, John Nance Garner![23] The conservative image of course has considerable validity, but it obscures understanding of such phenomena as Albert Gore, Russell Long, Lister Hill, John Sparkman, Olin D. Johnston, William Fulbright, the Yarboroughs of Texas, or the late Estes Kefauver. In the 1960 campaign the conservative image seriously victimized Lyndon B. Johnson, who started in politics as a vigorous New Dealer and later maneuvered through the Senate the first civil rights legislation since Reconstruction.

The infinite variety of Southern mythology could be catalogued and analyzed endlessly. A suggestive list would include the Proslavery South; the Confederate South; the Demagogic South; the State Rights South; the Fighting South; the Lazy South; the Folklore South; the South of jazz and the blues; the Booster South; the Rapacious South running away with Northern industries; the Liberal South of the interracial movement; the White Supremacy South of racial segregation, which seems to be for some

---

[22] Arthur S. Link, "The South and the 'New Freedom': An Interpretation," *American Scholar*, XX (Summer, 1951), 314–24.

[23] A. G. Hopkins to Sam Rayburn, July 29, 1932; Rayburn to J. Andrew West, October 26, 1932, in Sam Rayburn Library, Bonham, Texas.

the all-encompassing "Southern way of life"; the Anglo-Saxon (or was it the Scotch-Irish?) South, the most American of all regions because of its native population; or the Internationalist South, a mainstay of the Wilson, Roosevelt, and Truman foreign policies.

The South, then, has been the seedbed for a proliferation of paradoxical myths, all of which have some basis in empirical fact and all of which doubtlessly have, or have had, their true believers. The result has been, in David Potter's words, that the South has become an enigma, "a kind of Sphinx on the American land."[24] What is really the answer to the riddle, what is at bottom the foundation of Southern distinctiveness has never been established with finality, but the quest for a central theme of Southern history has repeatedly engaged the region's historians. Like Frederick Jackson Turner, who extracted the essential West in his frontier thesis, Southern historians have sought to distill the quintessence of the South into some kind of central theme.

In a recent survey of these efforts David L. Smiley of Wake Forest College has concluded that they turn upon two basic lines of thought: "the causal effects of environment, and the development of certain acquired characteristics of the people called Southern."[25] The distinctive climate and weather of the South, it has been argued, slowed the pace of life, tempered the speech of the South, dictated the system of staple crops and Negro slavery—in short, predetermined the plantation economy. The more persuasive suggestions have resulted from concentration upon human factors and causation. The best known is that set forth by U. B. Phillips. The quintessence of Southernism, he wrote in 1928, was "a common resolve indomitably maintained" that the South "shall be and remain a white man's country." Whether "expressed with the frenzy of a demagogue or maintained with a patrician's quietude," this was "the cardinal test of a Southerner and the central theme of Southern history."[26] Other historians have pointed to the rural nature of Southern society as the basic conditioning factor, to the prevalence of the country gentleman ideal imported from England, to the experience of the South as a conscious minority unified by criticism and attack from outside, to the fundamental piety of the Bible Belt, and to various other factors. It has even been suggested by one writer that a chart of the mule population would determine the boundaries of the South.

More recently, two historians have attempted new explanations. In his

[24] Potter, "The Enigma of the South," p. 142.

[25] David L. Smiley, "The Quest for the Central Theme in Southern History," paper read before the Southern Historical Association, Miami Beach, Florida, November 8, 1962, p. 2.

[26] Ulrich B. Phillips, "The Central Theme of Southern History," in E. Merton Coulter (ed.), *The Course of the South to Secession* (New York, 1939), p. 152.

search for a Southern identity, C. Vann Woodward advances several crucial factors: the experience of poverty in a land of plenty; failure and defeat
in a land that glorifies success; sin and guilt amid the legend of American
innocence; and a sense of place and belonging among a people given to
abstraction.[27] David M. Potter, probing the enigma of the South, has found
the key to the riddle in the prevalence of a folk society. "This folk culture,
we know, was far from being ideal or utopian," he writes, "and was in fact
full of inequality and wrong, but if the nostalgia persists was it because
even the inequality and wrong were parts of a life that still had a relatedness and meaning which our more bountiful life in the mass culture seems
to lack?"[28]

It is significant that both explanations are expressed largely in the past
tense, Potter's explicitly in terms of nostalgia. They recognize, by implication at least, still another image—that of the Dynamic or the Changing
South. The image may be rather nebulous and the ultimate ends unclear,
but the fact of change is written inescapably across the Southern scene. The
consciousness of change has been present so long as to become in itself
one of the abiding facts of Southern life. Surely, it was a part of the inspiration for the symposium that resulted in this volume. As far back as the
twenties it was the consciousness of change that quickened the imaginations
of a cultivated and sensitive minority, giving us the Southern renaissance
in literature. The peculiar historical consciousness of the Southern writer,
Allen Tate has suggested, "made possible the curious burst of intelligence
that we get at a crossing of the ways, not unlike, on an infinitesmal scale,
the outburst of poetic genius at the end of the sixteenth century when commercial England had already begun to crush feudal England."[29] Trace it
through modern Southern writing, and at the center—in Ellen Glasgow, in
Faulkner, Wolfe, Caldwell, the Fugitive-Agrarian poets, and all the others
—there is the consciousness of change, of suspension between two worlds, a
double focus looking both backward and forward.

The Southerner of the present generation has seen the old landmarks
crumble with great rapidity: the one-crop agriculture and the very pre-
dominance of agriculture itself, the one-party system, the white primary,
the poll tax, racial segregation, the poor white (at least in his classic connotations), the provincial isolation—virtually all the foundations of the
established order. Yet, sometimes, the old traditions endure in surprising
new forms. Southern folkways have been carried even into the factory,

---

[27] C. Vann Woodward, "The Search for a Southern Identity," in *The Burden of Southern History* (Baton Rouge, 1960), pp. 3–25.

[28] Potter, "The Enigma of the South," p. 151.

[29] Allen Tate, "The New Provincialism," *Virginia Quarterly Review*, XXI (Spring, 1945), 272.

and the Bible Belt has revealed resources undreamed of in Mencken's philosophy—but who, in the twenties, could have anticipated Martin Luther King?

One wonders what new images, what new myths, might be nurtured by the emerging South. Some, like Harry Ashmore, have merely written *An Epitaph for Dixie*. It is the conclusion of two Southern sociologists, John M. Maclachlan and Joe S. Floyd, Jr., that present trends "might well hasten the day when the South, once perhaps the most distinctively 'different' American region, will have become . . . virtually indistinguishable from the other urban-industrial areas of the nation."[30] U. B. Phillips long ago suggested that the disappearance of race as a major issue would end Southern distinctiveness. One may wonder if Southern distinctiveness might even be preserved in new conditions entirely antithetic to his image. Charles L. Black, Jr., another *émigré* Southerner (at Yale Law School) has confessed to a fantastic dream that Southern whites and Negroes, bound in a special bond of common tragedy, may come to recognize their kinship. There is not the slightest warrant for it, he admits, in history, sociology, or common sense. But if it should come to pass, he suggests, "The South, which has always felt itself reserved for a high destiny, would have found it, and would have come to flower at last. And the fragrance of it would spread, beyond calculation, over the world."[31]

Despite the consciousness of change, perhaps even more because of it, Southerners still feel a persistent pull toward identification with their native region as a ground for belief and loyalty. Is there not yet something more than nostalgia to the idea of the South? Is there not some living heritage with which the modern Southerner can identify? Is there not, in short, a viable myth of the South? The quest for myth has been a powerful factor in recent Southern literature, and the suspicion is strong that it will irresistibly affect any historian's quest for the central theme of Southern history. It has all too clearly happened before—in the climatic theory, for example, which operated through its geographical determinism to justify the social order of the plantation, or the Phillips thesis of white supremacy, which has become almost a touchstone of the historian's attitude toward the whole contemporary issue of race. "To elaborate a central theme," David L. Smiley has asserted, is "but to reduce a multi-faceted story to a single aspect, and its result . . . but to find new footnotes to confirm revealed truths and prescribed views."[32] The trouble is that the quest for the central

[30] John M. Maclachlan and Joe S. Floyd, Jr., *This Changing South* (Gainesville, Fla., 1956), p. 151.

[31] Charles L. Black, Jr., "Paths to Desegregation," *New Republic*, CXXXVII (October 21, 1957), 15.

[32] Smiley, "The Quest for the Central Theme in Southern History," p. 1.

theme, like Turner's frontier thesis, becomes absorbed willy-nilly into the process of myth making.

To pursue the Turner analogy a little further, the conviction grows that the frontier thesis, with all its elaborations and critiques, has been exhausted (and in part exploded) as a source of new historical insight. It is no derogation of insights already gained to suggest that the same thing has happened to the quest for the central theme, and that the historian, *as historian,* may be better able to illuminate our understanding of the South now by turning to a new focus upon the regional mythology.

To undertake the analysis of mythology will no longer require him to venture into uncharted wilderness. A substantial conceptual framework of mythology has already been developed by anthropologists, philosophers, psychologists, theologians, and literary critics. The historian, while his field has always been closely related to mythology, has come only lately to the critique of it. But there now exists a considerable body of historical literature on the American national mythology and the related subject of the national character, and Smith's stimulating *Virgin Land* suggests the trails that may be followed into the idea of the South.

Several trails, in fact, have already been blazed. Nearly forty years ago, Francis Pendleton Gaines successfully traced the rise and progress of the plantation myth, and two recent authors have belatedly taken to the same trail. Howard R. Floan has considerably increased our knowledge of the abolitionist version in his study of Northern writers, *The South in Northern Eyes,* while William R. Taylor has approached the subject from an entirely new perspective in his *Cavalier and Yankee.* Shields McIlwaine has traced the literary image of the poor white, while Stanley Elkins' *Slavery* has broken sharply from established concepts on both sides of that controversial question.[33] One foray into the New South has been made in Paul Gaston's "The New South Creed, 1865–1900." Yet many important areas —the Confederate and Reconstruction myths, for example—still remain almost untouched.

Some of the basic questions that need to be answered have been attacked in these studies; some have not. It is significant that students of literature have led the way and have pointed up the value of even third-rate creative literature in the critique of myth. The historian, however, should be able to contribute other perspectives. With his peculiar time perspective he can seek to unravel the tangled genealogy of myth that runs back from the modern Changing South to Jefferson's yeoman and Kennedy's plantation.

---

[33] Howard R. Floan, *The South in Northern Eyes, 1831–1860* (Austin, 1958); William R. Taylor, *Cavalier and Yankee: The Old South and American National Character* (New York, 1961); Shields McIlwaine, *The Southern Poor White from Lubberland to Tobacco Road* (Norman, Okla., 1939); Stanley M. Elkins, *Slavery: A Problem in American Institutional and Intellectual Life* (Chicago, 1959).

Along the way he should investigate the possibility that some obscure dialectic may be at work in the pairing of obverse images: the two versions of the plantation, New South and Old, Cavalier and Yankee, genteel and savage, regionalist and agrarian, nativist and internationalist.

What, the historian may ask, have been the historical origins and functions of the myths? The plantation myth, according to Gaines and Floan, was born in the controversy and emotion of the struggle over slavery. It had polemical uses for both sides. Taylor, on the other hand, finds it origin in the psychological need, both North and South, to find a corrective for the grasping, materialistic, rootless society symbolized by the image of the Yankee. Vann Woodward and Gaston have noted its later psychological uses in bolstering the morale of the New South. The image of the Savage South has obvious polemical uses, but has it not others? Has it not served the function of national catharsis? Has it not created for many Americans a convenient scapegoat upon which the sins of all may be symbolically laid and thereby expiated—a most convenient escape from problem solving?[34] To what extent, indeed, has the mythology of the South in general welled up from the subconscious depths? Taylor, especially, has emphasized this question, but the skeptical historian will also be concerned with the degree to which it has been the product or the device of deliberate manipulation by propagandists and vested interests seeking identification with the "real" South.

Certainly any effort to delineate the unique character of a people must take into account its mythology. "Poets," James G. Randall suggested, "have done better in expressing this oneness of the South than historians in explaining it."[35] Can it be that the historians have been looking in the wrong places, that they have failed to seek the key to the enigma where the poets have so readily found it—in the mythology that has had so much to do with shaping character, unifying society, developing a sense of community, of common ideals and shared goals, making the region conscious of its distinctiveness?[36] Perhaps by turning to different and untrodden paths we shall encounter the central theme of Southern history at last on the new frontier of mythology.

---

[34] "In a sense, the southern writer has been a scapegoat for his fellow Americans, for in taking his guilt upon himself and dramatizing it he has borne the sins of us all." C. Hugh Holman, "The Southerner as American Writer," in Charles Grier Sellers, Jr. (ed.), *The Southerner as American* (Chapel Hill, 1960), p. 199.

[35] James G. Randall, *The Civil War and Reconstruction* (Boston, 1937), pp. 3–4.

[36] Josiah Royce's definition of a "province" is pertinent here: ". . . any one part of a national domain which is geographically and socially sufficiently unified to have a true consciousness of its own ideals and customs and to possess a sense of its distinction from other parts of the country." Quoted in Frederick Jackson Turner, *The Significance of Sections in American History* (New York, 1932), p. 45.

2

The Colonial Search for a Southern Eden

Louis B. Wright

It is commonly accepted among historians that America has been, to a large degree, an extension of the European imagination—"the dream of Europe." Perhaps less tenable, but nevertheless widely accepted, is the belief that the English were more motivated by imaginative, edenic, even utopian strains of thought than other Europeans. In this article, Louis B. Wright, recently retired Director of the Folger Shakespeare Library in Washington, D.C., and currently History Consultant to the National Geographic Society, focuses on the edenic impulse prompting colonial settlement to the south of Virginia. As settlement proceeded, Mr. Wright argues, and although imaginative visions would at times be altered greatly by economic realities, a highly favorable and temperate climate together with the development of lucrative overseas trade worked to sustain lingering dreams of prosperity. It would seem that The South was fast becoming a state of mind. Indeed, as myth and reality repeatedly intersected in these formative years, many southerners learned that the latter could be as elusive and uncontrollable as the former. Viewed within a wider historical context, however, this utopian thrust carried with it even greater implications for the future. Born of such an impulse, and despite the fiction and delusion often involved, the southern colonies were thus intellectually conditioned to becoming a land at ease with myth and legend. Professor Wright's article supports the premise that within the matrix of myth is to be discovered the soil in which southern history found its roots.

From "Eden and Utopia South of Virginia" in *The Colonial Search for a Southern Eden,* by Louis B. Wright. University, Alabama: University of Alabama Press, 1953. Reprinted by permission of the author.

The notion that the earthly paradise, similar to if not the veritable site of the Scriptural Eden, might be found in some southern region of the New World was widely held in the seventeenth and early eighteenth centuries. Explorers from Virginia expected to find the Great South Sea somewhere to the southwest and they believed its shores would be a land like Eden. In the summer of 1650, Edward Bland, an English merchant resident in Virginia, and Abraham Wood, a militia captain and Indian trader, led an expedition from the site of Petersburg to a point in southwest Virginia where they discovered a river which they believed ran west into the South Sea.[1] The next year Bland printed in London *The Discovery of New Britain* (1651), which carried a preface extolling the land and urging all who desired "the advancement of God's glory by the conversion of the Indians [and] the augmentation of the English commonwealth in extending its liberties" to consider "the present benefit and future profits" of settling the new territory lying between thirty-five and thirty-seven degrees of north latitude.

This geographical position carried a mystical significance. Bland's book reprinted a passage attributed to Sir Walter Raleigh's *Marrow of History,* pointing out that God had placed Eden on the thirty-fifth parallel of north latitude.[2] This location guaranteed an ideal climate of perpetual spring and summer, a garden shaded by palm trees, described by Raleigh as the greatest blessing and wonder of nature. Other earthly paradises, the passage implied, would be found along the thirty-fifth parallel, presumably also shaded by palm trees and producing dates, raisins, spices, and everything else which Adam had had for his comfort. This location would put paradise along a line connecting Newbern and Fayetteville, North Carolina, with Chattanooga and Memphis, Tennessee.

When Lieutenant Governor Alexander Spotswood of Virginia in 1716 led an exploring expedition across the Blue Ridge Mountains, he discovered a river which we now call the Shenandoah but which Spotswood and his company named the Euphrates, after one of the four rivers of Eden, because the country looked to them like paradise. The explanation of why this spot appeared so rosy at that time may be found, however, in an account of the expedition, which must have been one of the most convivial on record. On the very crest of the ridge, the explorers stopped to drink the health of King George I, and the opportunity seemed appropriate to celebrate still further. "We had a good dinner," reported John Fontaine, chronicler of the expedition, "and after it we got the men together, and

---

[1] A part of this first appeared in Louis B. Wright, "The Westward Advance of the Atlantic Frontier," *The Huntington Library Quarterly,* XI (1948), 261–275.

[2] *The First Explorations of the Trans-Allegheny Region by the Virginians, 1650–1674,* ed. Clarence W. Alvord and Lee Bidgood (Cleveland, Ohio, 1912), pp. 112–113.

loaded all their arms, and we drank the King's health in champagne, and fired a volley; the Princess' health in burgundy, and fired a volley; and all the rest of the royal family in claret, and fired a volley. We drank the Governor's health and fired another volley: We had several sorts of liquor, viz., Virginia red wine and white wine, Irish usquebaugh, brandy, shrub, two sorts of rum, champagne, canary, cherry punch, water, cider, etc."[3] After these potations, the driest river bed in Arizona, much less the Valley of Virginia, would have seemed a land flowing with milk and honey.

When William Byrd II of Westover, Virginia, set out to promote the sale of a large tract of land which he had acquired on the Dan River near the border between North Carolina and Virginia, he called his property the Land of Eden and supplied notes to a German-Swiss land agent named Jenner who published in Switzerland in 1737 an alluring promotional tract under the title of *Neu-gefundenes Eden* [New Found Eden]. The description of Byrd's property was intended to leave no doubt in the reader's mind that here indeed was the earthly paradise.

Because promoters had lately been recommending South Carolina and Georgia to hopeful Swiss emigrants as lands of fertility and felicity, Byrd's agent goes to some pains to prove that this particular Eden far surpasses any other. "I am pleased to have the opportunity to make it known to my fellow countrymen, the Swiss," Jenner remarks with an air of objectivity, "that they [may] turn their thoughts to this beautiful, healthful and fertile land, and renounce miserable and unhealthful South Carolina, since [there] they will find after all nothing but poverty, sickness, and early death. . . ." South Carolina, Jenner argues, is trying to create a fortress on its southern border, or Georgia, and wants settlers in that unwholesome spot. And he cites what he says is an English proverb, "Whoever desires to die soon, just go to Carolina."[4]

The exact reverse is Byrd's Land of Eden. There the climate is perfect, the air is pure, the water is as sweet as milk, and the sun shines every day of the year. When it rains, it rains gently at night sufficient to keep the heavenly place well-watered. In this mild and beneficent land, disease is practically unknown and Europeans who come ailing soon find themselves restored to health, and "what is much more miraculous, the old people receive quite new strength, feel as if they were wholly born anew, that is, much stronger, much more light-footed, and in every way much more comfortable than before. . . ."[5]

---

[3] *Memoirs of a Huguenot Family,* ed. Ann Maury (New York, 1872), pp. 288–289.

[4] Richmond C. Beatty and William J. Mulloy (eds.), *William Byrd's Natural History of Virginia or The Newly Discovered Eden* (Richmond, Va., 1940), pp. 11, 14.

[5] *Ibid.,* pp. 2–3.

The products of this Eden, we will not be surprised to learn, are practically all those which a settler—or the British Board of Trade—might desire. At last, in the Dan River bottoms, if one believes this tract, the production of silk and wine is assured, along with other good things. "One could make silk also very easily," the author asserts, "because the land is full of mulberry trees, and requires little exertion. People have already tried this, and obtained very beautiful silk. The English, however, do not want to go to any trouble in this. Cotton grows in sufficiency in this land. One can merely pick it and spin it, and make all kinds of materials from it for use. It is also a very good ware in trade." Flax, hemp, indigo, grains, fruits, and herbs of all descriptions flourish. Grapes grow in great abundance and have already proved their utility and "therefore nothing is lacking but good grape people."[6] Especially valuable is the sugar maple tree: "This is the most useful tree in the whole world, because one makes wine, spirits, vinegar, honey, and sugar from it, which comes from its juice."[7] Verily nothing was lacking in Eden but a happy people to consume its products. Unfortunately the ship loaded with the Swiss emigrants who heeded the siren words of the promoter wrecked off the coast of North Carolina and only a handful survived to reach the promised land. For all the fine promises, William Byrd never succeeded in turning the rich bottom lands along the Dan River into the paradise his agent pictured. To this day the land is reasonably fertile but its products have always been such prosaic things as corn, cotton, and tobacco.

Notwithstanding William Byrd's low opinion of South Carolina, as indicated in the *New Found Eden,* and an equally low opinion of North Carolina, which he had expressed in *The History of the Dividing Line,* the Carolinas proved highly profitable to the empire and won the approval of merchants, bankers, and politicians in London. Although their products were not precisely the ones which the mercantilists had originally intended, they fulfilled perfectly the current idea of the proper relation between colony and mother country. Even that irascible and hard-to-please agent of the Crown, Edward Randolph, surveyor-general of His Majesty's Customs for North America, had only words of praise in a report which he made to the Board of Trade in London on March 16, 1699. "The great improvement made in this Province is wholly owing to the industry and labour of the Inhabitants," he wrote. "They have applied themselves to make such commodities as might increase the revenue of the Crown, as Cotton, Wool, Ginger, Indigo, etc. But finding them not to answer the end, they are set upon making Pitch, Tar, and Turpentine, and planting of rice, and can

[6] *Ibid.,* p. 33.
[7] *Ibid.,* p. 35.

send over great quantityes yearly, if they had encouragement from England,
. . ."[8]

The Carolinas, Randolph reported, are a much better source for naval stores than New England: "My Lords, I did formerly present Your Lordships with proposals for supplying England with Pitch and Tar, Masts and all our Naval Stores from New England. . . . But since my arrival here I find I am come into the only place for such commodities upon the Continent of America."[9] By this statement he meant the *best* place, not literally the only place. The value of the tar, pitch, masts, and other supplies helped to bring prosperity to the Carolinas and security to the Royal Navy.

In other ways the Carolinas, especially South Carolina, pleased the mercantilists. A constant stream of raw materials poured out of Charleston and into English channels of industry and commerce. For instance, South Carolina developed a great trade in deerskins needed by the leathermakers and glovers. Furs from the backcountry also added to the revenue. Unlike the Chesapeake Bay colonies, which depended upon tobacco for their money crop, the Southeast developed a diverse commerce centered in Charleston, and of this commerce, the deerskin and fur trade contributed much to colonial and imperial prosperity.

So much attention has been lavished on the fur trade of other regions that we forget the importance of the South in this connection. Louisiana is still the largest fur-producing region in North America. Throughout the eighteenth century Charleston, South Carolina, was the great skin and fur market. Some of the toughest characters in all North America brought their pack trains of deerskins and furs to Charleston each spring. The tinkle of the packhorse bells and the clatter of hoofs on the cobble stones of the Battery brought Charlestonians to their windows to view picturesque traders, some well-known and famous as Indian fighters.

The caravans often brought long strings of Indian captives to be sold as slaves to Barbádos and other islands of the West Indies. We must also remember this dark chapter in the history of commerce. Charleston was an important slaving port. Captured Indians by the hundreds were sold to ship captains headed for the West Indies, and Negroes by the thousands were brought into Charleston from Africa. Indian slaves were not dependable in the Carolinas, for they might escape to the forests and make their way back to their tribes, but African Negroes had no such hope. They proved useful laborers in the pine forests and hot fields of the coastal plain. The traffic in slaves and the commodities which they produced made rich

[8] Alexander S. Salley, Jr. (ed.), *Narratives of Early Carolina, 1650–1708* (New York, 1911), p. 207.

[9] *Ibid.,* p. 208.

the merchants and shipowners of London and Bristol as well as their agents in Charleston.

South Carolina gave promise late in the seventeenth century of becoming the dream colony of the English mercantilists. Some of the inhabitants wrote to London in the year 1691 that "We are encouraged with severall new rich Comodityes as Silck, Cotton, Rice and Indigo, which are naturally produced here."[10] Silk remained a delusion, but rice, indigo, and eventually cotton became indeed "rich commodities." The first of these to be grown extensively was rice, which flourished in the alluvial swamp lands of the coastal region. Although colonists even in Virginia had experimented with rice, not until the last decade of the seventeenth century, in South Carolina, was it grown extensively. The legend that a shipmaster from Madagascar, accidentally touching at Charleston in 1696, left a half-bushel of rice seed from which grew the Carolina rice industry, is apparently only a half-truth,[11] but from that date until the mid-nineteenth century rice was an increasingly important article of commerce with England.

To an extraordinary woman, Eliza Lucas, South Carolina owed the development of the production of indigo, a vegetable dye much in demand in the eighteenth century when clothing of this hue was especially fashionable. In the year 1739, Eliza Lucas, then just sixteen, found herself established as manager of a plantation on the west side of the Ashley River above Charleston. Her father, Lieutenant Colonel George Lucas, was stationed at Antigua in the West Indies, but since his wife was sickly and could not endure that climate, he moved his family to South Carolina and put this remarkable girl in charge of the family plantation. In a letter to her father written in July 1739, she reported that she was trying "to bring the Indigo, Ginger, Cotton, and Lucern and Casada [cassava] to perfection and had greater hopes from the Indigo (if I could have the seed earlier next year from the West Indies) than of ye rest of ye things I had try'd."[12] After many discouragements, not only in raising the plants, but in producing the dye, Eliza achieved success. By 1747–48, the production was such that the port of Charleston exported 138,334 pounds of the dyestuff. When the British government offered a bounty in 1748 for the production of the dye in the British-American colonies, some growers found it so profitable that they doubled their capital every three or four years.[13]

The production of indigo within the empire was important, for the

[10] Lewis C. Gray and Esther K. Thompson, *History of Agriculture in the Southern United States* (Washington, D. C., 1933), I, 278; quoted from the *Calendar of State Papers, America and West Indies, 1677–1680*, p. 59.

[11] *Ibid.*, I, 278–279.

[12] *Ibid.*, I, 290.

[13] *Ibid.*, I, 292.

source of most of the dye would otherwise have been the French West Indies. Since England was at war with France through a good part of the eighteenth century, it was imperative that she not buy this useful commodity from the enemy. The power of fashion was such, however, that the clothiers and dyers would have obtained the dye even if they had been obliged to deal in the enemy's black market. The solution of course was to stimulate production in the tropical and semi-tropical areas of the British dominions, an operation which proved highly successful.

The production of cotton, another article which England had bought outside the empire, was less successful than indigo and rice, but some cotton was produced in the various Southern colonies and in the West Indies in the period before the Revolution. Few of us stop to realize the importance of cotton in the social progress of mankind. The importation into England of cheap cotton textiles from India, brought about by the expansion of the East India Company's activities in the seventeenth century, for the first time made it possible for Englishmen of average means to be reasonably clean. Up to that time linen was the only available fabric for undergarments, and linen, then as now, was expensive.[14]

The East India Company brought in chintzes, muslins, calicoes, and other fabrics. The word calico comes from the name of an Indian town, Calicut. Though the importation of cotton from India gave English merchants an article of trade much in demand on the continent of Europe, the East India Company had to pay out cash for its textiles. If raw cotton could be produced within the empire and woven at home, this would be an advantage to both the industry and commerce of Great Britain.

Although efforts continued throughout the colonial period to stimulate the production of raw cotton, only small amounts reached the markets. In the year 1768, Virginia led the South by exporting 43,350 pounds of ginned cotton. In the same year South Carolina exported only 3,000 pounds, and Georgia, only 300 pounds.[15] During most of the period, planters lacked confidence in the stability of cotton prices—an old complaint—and they found other crops more profitable. The separation of the lint from the seed was also a troublesome problem. Although roller gins were known and used in the colonial period, not until Eli Whitney invented the saw gin in the last decade of the eighteenth century was this problem solved.

By the end of the century South Carolina and Georgia were producing several million pounds of cotton. Although the colonies were now politically free of Great Britain, trade retained many of its old characteristics. The South continued to supply raw materials for English industry; and of

---

[14] James A. Williamson, *The Ocean in English History* (Oxford, 1941), p. 107.
[15] Gray & Thompson, *History of Agriculture,* I, 184. See also *Ibid.,* II, 680 ff.

these raw materials, cotton rapidly increased in importance. By the mid-nineteenth century, cotton spinning and weaving had become one of Great Britain's most valuable industries, and raw cotton from the plantations of the Southern states was an essential of international trade. By a curious irony of history, cotton textiles of English manufacture in the nineteenth century ruined the native weaving industry of India, which had first supplied cottons to Britain. And by another reversal of the process, the cheap labor in the Indian cotton mills in the twentieth century ruined the English textile industry by destroying its Asiatic market for cotton goods.

Paralleling the British emphasis on trade in the eighteenth century was a growing spirit of humanitarianism. As in the United States in the twentieth century, the brotherhood of man and the acquisition of material property were somehow equated. As humanitarians and mercantilists, often one and the same, viewed the southern American colonies, they warmed with enthusiasm over the prospect of discovering there at last the perfect paradise where all men could be happy and prosperous as they produced the commodities which served the best interests of the British Empire. Occasionally the humanitarians contemplated the institution of slavery, which seemed to be necessary for prosperity, and found it disturbing; but usually they salved their consciences by thinking of the boon of Christianity which slavery had brought to the heathen whom they imported from Africa. George Whitefield, the evangelist, for example, wept over man's sins and distress, but he recommended slavery for Georgia and helped pay the expenses of Bethesda, his orphan home, from the profits of a South Carolina plantation worked with slaves.

As the humanitarian planners contemplated the opportunities in the South, they had visions of new Edens in which the poor and oppressed of England would find a refuge; there the erstwhile indigents would work out their salvation and keep a steady stream of profitable raw materials pouring into the home ports. Some of the planners had read More's *Utopia,* Bacon's essay "Of Plantations," James Harrington's *The Commonwealth of Oceana* (1656), or some other treatise on ideal commonwealths. The spirit of social experiment was in the air. Furthermore the atmosphere was also heavily charged with the excitement of speculation. During 1719 and the early part of 1720, men and women rushed to buy stock in the South Sea Company which doubled, trebled, quadrupled and further multiplied in value as they watched it. Before the bubble burst in August 1720, other speculations promised similar incredible profits. It was an age of "projectors," or promoters, some of whom picked the region embracing this very spot as the scene of their activities. No scheme seemed impossible, not even Swift's satirical project to extract sunbeams from cucumbers.

For reasons not difficult to comprehend, the hope of finding a fruitful land in the South appealed strongly to Scots. No country could have been more unlike the hills of Scotland than the coastal plains and river bottoms of the Carolinas and Georgia. Perhaps that was its greatest attraction. During the eighteenth century Scots were among the most important immigrant groups received in the Southern colonies. Because we usually think of the Scots as a practical and thrifty people, convinced that destiny has already settled the affairs of man in accordance with the theology of John Calvin, it may be a surprise to find that some of the most fantastic of the Utopian projects were dreamed up by Scots.

One of the better known and most colorful schemes was hatched in the mind of a Scottish baronet, Sir Robert Montgomery of Skelmorly, who in 1717 published *A Discourse Concerning the design'd Establishment Of a New Colony To The South of Carolina, In The Most delightful Country of the Universe*. This was a plan to establish a colony in the country embraced between the mouths of the Savannah and Altamaha rivers and extending westward to the Great South Sea [the Pacific Ocean]. That included most of the present state of Alabama, not to mention the states westward to the California coast.

Sir Robert described this country, which he named Azilia, as "our future Eden," and he further declared that English writers "universally agree that Carolina, and especially in its Southern Bounds, is the most amiable Country in the Universe: that Nature has not bless'd the World with any Tract, which can be preferable to it, that Paradise, with all her Virgin Beauties, may be modestly suppos'd at most but equal to its Native Excellencies."[16] This territory which exceeded Paradise itself in excellence was claimed by South Carolina, but the Lords Proprietors were more than glad to encourage Scottish settlers who would serve as a protection against the Spaniards in Florida and the French in Louisiana. Accordingly they granted permission to Sir Robert and his colleagues to settle Azilia.

In a literary genre characterized by optimism, Sir Robert Montgomery's *Discourse* is surely one of the most hopeful ever printed. Azilia, as he describes it, "lies in the same Latitude with Palestine Herself, That promis'd Canaan, which was pointed out by God's own Choice, to bless the Labours of a favourite People. It abounds with Rivers, Woods, and Meadows. Its gentle Hills are full of Mines, Lead, Copper, Iron, and even some of Silver. 'Tis beautified with odiferous Plants, green all the Year. . . . The Air is healthy, and the Soil in general fruitful, and of infinite Variety; Vines, naturally flourishing upon the Hills, bear Grapes in most luxuriant Plenty. They have every Growth which we possess in England, and almost every Thing that England wants besides. The Orange and the

---

[16] J. Max Patrick (ed.), *Azilia: A Discourse by Sir Robert Montgomery, 1717, Projecting a Settlement in the Colony Later Known as Georgia,* Emory University Publications: Sources and Reprints, Series IV (Atlanta, 1948), p. 18.

Limon thrive in the same common Orchard with the Apple, and the Pear-Tree, Plumbs, Peaches, Apricots, and Nectarins bear from Stones in three years growing. The Planters raise large Orchards of these Fruits to feed their Hogs with."[17] To Scots and Englishmen, who knew oranges from Seville and lemons from Portugal merely as symbols of luxury, this country, in the same latitude as Palestine, must have appeared indeed as a new Canaan.

To help him in the colonization of Azilia, Montgomery had as associates Aaron Hill, a theatrical poet who claimed to have an invention for making potash, and Amos Kettleby, merchant and politician of London, whom the South Carolina Assembly had dismissed in the previous year from his post as colonial agent. Montgomery was to have the title of Margrave, with a great palace at the exact center of the district where he would reside. There he would live in splendor and rule over a feudal principality peopled with a hierarchy of gentry, tenants, and slaves. Aaron Hill and Amos Kettleby appear to have been more concerned with the financial returns from the venture than with the glories of title.

The chapter in Montgomery's tract headed "Of some Designs in View for making Profit" assures the reader that at long last imperial and mercantilist ambitions are about to be realized in Azilia. "Our Prospects in this Point are more extensive than we think it needful to discover," Montgomery remarks with an air of mystery. "It were a shame shou'd we confine the Fruitfulness of such a rich and lovely Country to some single Product, which Example first makes common, and the being common robs of Benefit. Thus Sugar in Barbadoes, Rice in Carolina, and Tobacco in Virginia take up all the Labours of their People, overstock the Markets, stifle the Demand, and make their Industry their Ruin, . . ." Azilia, however, will not be a one-crop country. Instead it will produce the very commodities which England still has had to buy from foreigners. Montgomery makes this explicit: "Coffee, Tea, Figs, Raisins, Currants, Almonds, Olives, Silk, Wine, Cochineal, and a great Variety of still more rich Commodities which we are forc'd to buy at mighty Rates from Countries lying in the very Latitude of our Plantations: All these we certainly shall Propagate, . . . mean while we shall confine our first Endeavours to such easy Benefits as will (without the smallest waiting for the Growth of Plants) be offer'd to our Industry from the spontaneous Wealth which overruns the Country."[18] With Aaron Hill's alleged invention in mind, Montgomery promises that potash will be a source of immediate profit.

The happy Margravate of Azilia, alas, was doomed to be a delusion. To transport colonists, to clear land, to build a palace, and even to make

---

[17] *Ibid.*, p. 18.
[18] *Ibid.*, p. 23.

potash required capital. There were also political complications. Discouraged at frustrations and delays, Sir Robert Montgomery sold his interest late in 1718 to Aaron Hill the poet. But after the failure of the South Sea Company in 1720, not even Aaron Hill's literary style was sufficiently purple to lure investors in Azilia, and the scheme collapsed. Yet such was the hopefulness of the projectors that one of them, possibly Hill, published two further pamphlets late in 1720, one of which was entitled *A Description of the Golden Islands, with an Account of the Undertaking Now on Foot for Making a Settlement There*. This tract outlined a plan for making a paradise of the sea islands along the coast of Georgia and producing there not only silk and almonds, but "many more Fruits and Drugs, growing in Persia, in India about Lahore, in China, and in Japan."[19] But the public had its fingers too thoroughly burned on the South Sea Company stock to take an interest in the Golden Islands. The Azilian project is worth detailed consideration, however, because it epitomizes the search for Eden which had obsessed British thinking since the beginning of the colonial effort and which was to continue to the end.

Another Scottish baronet, Sir Alexander Cuming of Coulter, even more erratic than Sir Robert Montgomery, conceived a project to settle three hundred thousand Jews on the Cherokee tribal lands in the backcountry of South Carolina. This proposal for a Zion on the Carolina frontier had as its object the relief of oppressed Jewish families in Europe by taking them out of crowded ghettos and establishing them on the land where they could turn their talents and industry to farming and the production of commodities useful to the British Empire. If the government would underwrite the enterprise, Sir Alexander promised, it would presently be able to retire a large portion of the national debt from the profits.

Sir Alexander attributed his zeal for colonial affairs to a vision of his wife's which suggested that he make a journey to the backcountry of South Carolina. Considering the Scot's peculiarities, we cannot escape the suspicion that his wife's vision was a clever ruse to procure a little peace at home. But whatever the motive, Sir Alexander set out in 1729 on a self-appointed mission to Carolina and the Cherokees. Surely the Scottish baronet had read books similar to those which had sent Cervantes' good knight of La Mancha on his adventures, for his travels read like a chapter from *Don Quixote*. Leaving Charleston on March 13, 1730, Sir Alexander travelled during the following month nearly a thousand miles through the Cherokee tribes. Armed to the teeth and boasting of the power and brilliance of his King, George II, the baronet astonished his Indian hearers and persuaded them that he was a great chief representing a king whose power reached even to the hills of South Carolina. At a tribal council he

---

[19] *Ibid.*, p. 12.

persuaded the chiefs to kneel and swear allegiance to King George—or so he thought—and he had himself acclaimed the King's viceroy. So persuasive was Sir Alexander's eloquence that he induced six Cherokees, a minor chief and five warriors, to set out with him for London and the King's court. Near Charleston they picked up another stray Indian. When they all reached England, the chief was a king and the other Indians were described as generals or chiefs. On June 18, 1730, King George received the Scot and his Indian protegés. During the next three months the Cherokee "king" and his fellow "chiefs" were the sensation of London. They were entertained, feted, and taught English vices. On September 28, the play of *Orinoco* was performed in their honor at Lincoln's Inn Fields, and so great was the public excitement over the Indians that the theatre's box office receipts trebled that night. When they returned to their tribesmen, the Indians' report of the glories of the English nation probably helped to keep the Cherokees loyal to England in the succeeding wars with France.[20]

Fantastic as were Sir Alexander Cuming's schemes for Cherokee-Jewish Utopias in the foothills of Carolina, the publicity which they received helped to focus further interest on the Southern colonies. The settlement of Georgia itself was a manifestation of the freshly aroused humanitarian, mercantilist, and imperialistic interest in expansion south of the Carolina settlements.

During the summer of 1730, about the time the Cherokees were exciting the London populace, General James Oglethorpe and some of his friends were petitioning the King to make them a grant of land south of the Carolina border "for settling poor persons of London."[21] The plan, as every school child knows, was prompted by a desire on the part of this philanthropic group to provide relief for imprisoned debtors. It received favorable consideration from the government for other reasons. The need for a bulwark against Spain and France from the South and southwest was greater than ever. And once more the merchants and bankers of London were dreaming of a source for those raw materials which they still found it necessary to buy from their enemies. Moved by so many worthy reasons, the King granted a charter to Oglethorpe and his fellow trustees on June 9, 1732. This time a Utopian scheme was to succeed, but not precisely as Oglethorpe or the government planned it. For few debtors ever came to Georgia and once more the vision of exotic produce was a mirage. Nevertheless Georgia did become a useful colony and an element in the imperial organization.

[20] Verner W. Crane, *The Southern Frontier, 1670–1732* (Durham, N. C., 1928), p. 280.

[21] E. Merton Coulter, *Georgia: A Short History* (Chapel Hill, N. C., 1947), pp. 17–18.

The Trustees tried earnestly to make Georgia the combination of Eden and Utopia which they had envisioned. They opened the country to oppressed folk not only of England but of the Continent as well. They passed regulations aimed at keeping the commonwealth pure by excluding rum and forbidding slavery. And they were determined to produce silk, wine, olives, and other good things which had always eluded Englishmen. A poet writing in the *South Carolina Gazette* in 1733 pictured the new colony as a garden of Hesperides. Its silks would clothe England's beauties; its wine would flow unstinted, "refreshing Labour and dispelling Woe"; and its orchards and groves would be fruitful with dates, lemons, oranges, citrons, limes, almonds, tea and coffee.[22] The trustees included some hardheaded businessmen who knew such beneficence would not be spontaneous, even in Paradise, in the rational eighteenth century. They therefore encouraged Swiss and other Continental silkworkers to come to Georgia; they ordered every recipient of a grant of land to plant mulberry trees; and they encouraged experimentation with other exotic commodities. But it was all to no avail. Georgia followed South Carolina in depending upon rice, the skin and fur trade, and upon naval stores for the basis of its economy.

The search for an exotic Eden did not end with the settlement of Georgia. The ink on the Treaty of Paris was hardly dry in 1763 before Archibald Menzies of Megerny Castle, Perthshire, devised a plan to people Florida with Armenians, Greeks, and Minorcans, who would be expert in growing olives, grapes, and silk worms. Nothing came of his proposal but four years later a brother Scot, Dr. Andrew Turnbull, and two English associates, Sir William Duncan and Sir Richard Temple, formed a partnership to settle other Greeks, Italians, and Minorcans in Florida. They succeeded actually in establishing a group at New Smyrna on the coast below St. Augustine, but quarreling and fighting among the settlers quickly ruined the enterprises in which the promoters had pinned such hope. When a Scot takes leave of practical matters and begins to spin ingenious plans, the extent of his fantasy is illimitable

The faith in a Southern Utopia persisted and manifested itself in numerous projects throughout the colonial period and afterward. Time will not permit even the mention of various schemes to create a paradise in the lands south of Virginia. Perhaps the most visionary of all was a project of a sentimental and mystical German from Saxony, one Christian Gottlieb Priber, who devised a plan for a Utopia among the Cherokees on the headwaters of the Tennessee River. A precursor of Rousseau, Priber's state represented a fusion of ideas from Plato's *Republic,* current doctrines of humanitarianism, and concepts of the noble savage which

---

[22] *Ibid.*

had cropped up from time to time. His efforts to found a communistic state among the Cherokees and to teach them to resist the inroads of the whites and the knavery of traders aroused the antagonism of Georgians who succeeded in arresting Priber in 1743. He was kept a political prisoner and died at Frederica on St. Simon's Island a few years later. Among his manuscripts was one describing his projected Utopian state as the "Kingdom of Paradise." In the opinion of his captors it was "extremely wicked" because "he enumerates many whimsical privileges and natural rights, as he calls them, which his citizens are to be entitled to, particularly dissolving marriages and allowing community of women, and all kinds of licentiousness."[23] His greatest sin, however, lay in his success in winning the friendship of the Indians and developing an organization which threatened the expansion of the British.

The British Empire profited immensely from the Southern colonies, but the mercantilists never succeeded in making these colonies the source of all the exotic commodities they yearned to produce within the empire. The economic planners, then as now, never grasped all of the factors involved in their schemes. For example, they never realized that silk production required both skilled and cheap labor, which the colonies always lacked, a lack which indeed has always been a serious problem in the New World.

The dream of making the South the source of many of the luxuries which mankind requires has never died. In modern times we have seen a certain realization of these hopes in the expansion of the textile industry. If we do not produce worm silk in the South, we at least have manu-factories of rayon, nylon, and other chemical substitutes. A Japanese economist was in my office recently lamenting the shift in fashion and production, which had ruined the silk industry of Japan.

Not far from where Swiss and Italian colonists in the eighteenth century sought to establish new industries on the upper Savannah River the United States government is today building a great plant to transform hydrogen into energy. The end product of that effort is yet unknown. Some believe that ultimately the release of energy from such an abundant source will solve most of the problems of mankind. Others, more gloomy, see in it the destruction of civilization. But we are witnessing one more effort to establish Utopia, even at the risk of universal destruction.

[23] Verner W. Crane, "A Lost Utopia of the First American Frontier," *Sewanee Review*, XXVII (1919), pp. 48–61.

3

The Southern Ethic in a Puritan World

C. Vann Woodward

Of those forces said to have been instrumental in forging the American character, "Puritanism" and its concomitant the Protestant Ethic are generally granted singular importance. Though subject to considerable myth in its own right, not all have come to grant Puritanism such exalted status. Arguments in favor of seeing the distinctiveness of a southern culture quite at odds with "Puritan" theory and practice have long prevailed on both sides of the Mason-Dixon line. While speaking of the entire range of the southern experience, C. Vann Woodward, Sterling Professor of History at Yale, here attempts to analyze the Puritan ethic and its southern counterpart, and to judge their relationship. By isolating the leisure-laziness myth, a basic ingredient of the "southern ethic," Professor Woodward attempts not its destruction but rather a serious critique. While essentially a review article examining the impact of recent historical scholarship as it relates to this theme, it remains as well a status report on a staple of southern mythology: leisure as a mythical element which continues to pervade the "real life" of the South. Finally, the article suggests that the southern inclination toward a leisured and mannered society had sufficient grounding in the colonial era to allow southerners largely to escape the extremes of the Puritan ethic.

Myths that support the notion of a distinctive Southern culture tend to be Janus-faced, presenting both an attractive and an unattractive countenance. The side they present depends on which way they are turned and

From C. Vann Woodward, "The Southern Ethic in a Puritan World," *William and Mary Quarterly*, 25 (1968). Reprinted by permission of the author and publisher.

who is manipulating them. The reverse side of Chivalry is Arrogance, and the other side of Paternalism is Racism. The Plantation myth is similarly coupled with the Poor White myth, the myth of Honor with that of Violence. Graciousness, Harmony, and Hospitality also have their less appealing faces. And for Leisure there is its long-standing counterpart, Laziness—together with the synonyms, idleness, indolence, slothfulness, languor, lethargy, and dissipation.

Early and late Southerners and their friends and critics have worried the Leisure-Laziness myth. It began with Captain John Smith's jeremiad against "idleness and sloth" at Jamestown and continued with Robert Beverley's disquisition on industrious beavers and William Byrd's lamentations on the slothful Carolinians of "Lubberland." An impressive literature on the subject has proliferated over the centuries. Leisure, the brighter side of the coin, has been repeatedly praised as an ideal, a redeeming quality of the Southern way that sets it off against the ant-like busyness and grubby materialism of the Northern way, another adornment of the Cavalier to shame the Yankee. Laziness, the darker face of the legend, has been deplored, denied, lamented, and endlessly explained. The explanations include climate, geography, slavery, and the staple crop economy, not to mention pellagra and a formidable list of parasites. No matter which face of the myth is favored and which explanation is stressed, agreement is general that this is a fundamental aspect of Southern distinctiveness.

As much as they deplored laziness, even exponents of the New South and the Northern way of bustle and enterprise often retained a fondness for the reverse side of the stereotype and clung to leisureliness as an essential mark of regional identity. Although Walter Hines Page scorned many characteristics of the old regime and urged a program of industrialization for the South, he cherished "the inestimable boon of leisure," hoped that "in the march of industrialism these qualities of fellowship and leisure may be retained in the mass of people," and thought that "no man who knows the gentleness and dignity and the leisure of the old Southern life would like to see these qualities blunted by too rude a growth of sheer industrialism."[1]

At the opposite pole from Page on the matter of industrialization for the South, John Crowe Ransom, arch-champion of agrarianism and "the old-time life," also fixed upon leisure as the essence of the Southern Ethic. Whatever the shortcomings of the Old South, "the fault of being intemperately addicted to work and to gross material prosperity" was hardly among them, he says. "The South never conceded that the whole

---

[1] Walter Hines Page, *The Rebuilding of Old Commonwealths* (New York, 1902), 111, 114, 141.

duty of man was to increase material production, or that the index to the degree of his culture was the volume of his material production." The arts of the South were "arts of living and not arts of escape." All classes participated in these arts and their participation created the solid sense of community in the South. "It is my thesis," he writes, "that all were committed to a form of leisure, and that their labor itself was leisurely."[2]

Between Page and Ransom, though much closer in ideology to the former than the latter, W. J. Cash was more ambivalent than either about leisure. Conceding that the South's "ancient leisureliness—the assumption that the first end of life is living itself . . . is surely one of its greatest virtues," he thought that "all the elaborately built-up pattern of leisure and hedonistic *drift;* all the slow, cool, gracious and graceful gesturing of movement . . . was plainly marked out for abandonment as incompatible with success" and the ethic of the new industrial order. This was not to be written off as pure loss. The lot of the poor white had been a "void of pointless leisure," and for that matter, "in every rank men lolled much on their verandas or under their oaks, sat much on fences, dreaming." Leisure easily degenerated into laziness. Both leisure and laziness perpetuated frontier conditions and neither produced cities or a real sense of community. Cash leaned to the Northern view that culture and community are largely developed in towns, "and usually in great towns."[3]

When one gets down to modern economists and the theory of under-developed countries and regions like the South, ambivalence about leisure and laziness tends to disappear. The two become almost indistinguishable and equally reprehensible. In the opinion of one Southern economist, leisure becomes "a cover-up for lack of enterprise and even sheer laziness among Southerners." For the mass of them, in fact, "leisure was probably from early days a virtue by necessity rather than by choice. If they were small landowners they lacked sufficient resources to keep them busy more than half of the year. If they were slaves or sharecroppers the near impossibility of advancing themselves by their own efforts bred inefficiency, lassitude, and improvidence." The phenomenon of television aerials over rural slums "may clearly make (through its positive effect on incentives) its own substantial contribution to regional economic progress." But the tradition of leisure has been a major cause of underdevelopment.[4]

[2] Twelve Southerners, *I'll Take My Stand: The South and the Agrarian Tradition* (New York, 1930), 12–14.
[3] W. J. Cash, *The Mind of the South* (New York, 1941), 384, 150, 50, 95.
[4] William H. Nicholls, *Southern Tradition and Regional Progress* (Chapel Hill, 1960), 34–39.

I

New light on this ancient dispute comes from a number of sources—
new works on moral, intellectual, economic, and slavery history—and a
reconsideration of the debate would seem to be in order. One of these
new sources is a work by David Bertelson, whose preference between the
Janus faces is clearly announced by the title of his book, *The Lazy South*.
The informality of the title might suggest to some that this is another
light-hearted and genial essay on regional foibles. Nothing could be
further from the author's intentions. He is fully conscious of the "strong
volitional and moral connotations" of the word "laziness" and never
flinches in his employment of it. This presumes to be the history of a
failure, the moral failure of a whole society.

Mr. Bertelson is not one to borrow support casually from conventional
assumptions and traditional explanations. Much has been written of
geographical determinants of Southern history. "But geography did not
create the South," he writes. Pennsylvania, with its waterways and its soil,
was as easily adaptable to a tobacco staple culture as Virginia. Nor will
he seek an out in economic determinism: rather he asks what determined
the economy. He scarcely pauses over the old climatic and ethnic chestnuts.
As for the uses of the Peculiar Institution, he is simply not in the market.
"Negro servitude did not make the southern colonies different from New
England and Pennsylvania. They were different first. That is why slavery
became so widespread there. The presence of a small number of slaves
in the northern colonies did not change the essential conditions of life
in these either. That is why the number remained so small." He has little
space for the familiar biological determinants—pellagra, malaria, hookworm, and the rest. They were the accompaniments of poverty and laziness,
not their causes. Laziness afflicted the affluent as often as the parasites
afflicted the indigent.[5]

What then does account for this distinctive trait of the South? "The
difference lay not in the land but in the people," we are told, "and that
difference was ultimately due to the different attitudes and assumptions
which they brought with them and their descendants perpetuated." The
attitudes and assumptions derive ultimately from values, in other words
morals, ethics. "To get at what lies behind poverty, slavery, staple crops,
and stressing personal enjoyment one must consider historically the
meaning of work in the South." It all boils down to an analysis of the
Southern Ethic—though that is not a term the author uses.[6]

Virginia existed first in the minds of Englishmen as an answer to the

[5] David Bertelson, *The Lazy South* (New York, 1967), 244, 104.
[6] *Ibid.*, 244, viii.

problem of idleness in England. The cure for idleness, it was thought, lay in the allurements of material gain in the New World which would induce men to work without the necessity of violating their freedom. Spokesmen of Virginia were sometimes vague about personal responsibility to society and a sense of community. Puritans, on the other hand, "thought of themselves as small societies before they established communities."[7] Authoritarians failed in Virginia, and no prophet of a godly community prevailed, no Chesapeake Zion appeared. The same was true of Maryland, the Carolinas, and after abortive experiments, Georgia.

Without coercion and community, Southern colonists established societies based on the exploitation of natural resources. The motive force was individual aggrandizement, we are told, not social purpose or community aims. They established plantations, not cities, and cultivated staples, not trade. The result was dispersion, fragmentation, and chaotic self-aggrandizement. The meaning of work in the Southern colonies thus came to have no social dimension or content. Work there *was,* hard work, but it produced idleness with plenty and was intermittent according to seasonal necessities.

"The problem then is," it seems to Mr. Bertelson, "to explain why most men in the southern colonies *seemed* to lead idle lives while in actuality they were often very busy. The answer lies in the fact that they were not busy all of the time." When crops were laid by they tended to go fishing. Max Weber, to whom the author attributes the conception of his study, associated with "the spirit of capitalism" a pattern of industry and diligence that was not based on economic considerations. This pattern is found to be conspicuously absent in the South, along with "the intellectual climate to favor diligence." As a figure of contrast the author pictures "young Benjamin Franklin trudging the streets of Philadelphia in the early morning and his remark that he took care not only to be industrious but to appear industrious." It is conceded that the South was "not without examples of industrious people like Franklin, but . . . most of them were recently arrived foreign Protestants." Your genuine Southerner did not even bother to *appear* industrious.[8]

Yet we are told that the Southerners were deeply troubled with guilt about laziness and took extreme measures to overcome an oppressive sense of purposelessness with sheer "busyness." Thus William Byrd, for all his pre-dawn vigils with Hebrew, Greek, and Latin, was desperately driven by the specter of laziness and futility. Even that model of methodical industriousness Thomas Jefferson, in advising his daughter about work

---

[7] *Ibid.,* 40–41.
[8] *Ibid.,* 75–77.

habits, "was advocating simply keeping busy rather than purposefulness." Anyway, Jefferson and James Madison "expressed very little of the South" in the way, presumably, that Cotton Mather expressed New England and Benjamin Franklin, New England and Pennsylvania. As for George Washington, he proves to have had very rational and Yankeefied notions about work (though the evidence offered is not very persuasive), notions shared by Patrick Henry and Richard Henry Lee. Apart from these unrepresentative deviants, the pattern of Virginia prevailed among Southerners generally. James Winthrop, a Massachusetts Federalist, is quoted as distinguishing sharply between the "idle and dissolute inhabitants of the South" and "the sober and active people of the North."[9]

The trouble with the South, one of the many troubles perceived, was its total inability to conceptualize social unity in terms other than personal relationships, to achieve any real sense of community, or to define industry in social terms. The plantation as community is written off as "imaginary." Southerners, it seems, proved unable to derive social unity "from a community of belief in God and love for one another as it had been for early Puritans."[10] Their efforts to define community in terms of home, personal affections, and local loyalties, the very essence of patriarchal community in the South, are summarily dismissed as futile. Southerners are also said to have been incapable of any real sense of loyalty. Unlike charity, loyalty does not appear to begin at home.[11] "While many Southerners doubtless had great affection for family and friends," he concedes, "and for the localities in which they lived, this did not involve any larger social unity nor any sense of loyalty to the South as a whole—but rather a pervasive particularism."[12]

Personalism and persistent local attachments have been offered by David M. Potter as evidence of the survival of an authentic folk culture in the South long after it had disappeared in urban culture elsewhere.[13] While Mr. Bertelson concedes that "at times in the past or in certain

----

[9] *Ibid.*, 166, 161.

[10] *Ibid.*, 65.

[11] In a strongly contrasting analysis of the roots of loyalty, David M. Potter writes, "The strength of the whole is not enhanced by destroying the parts, but is made up of the sum of the parts. The only citizens who are capable of strong national loyalty are those who are capable of strong group loyalty, and such people are likely to express this capacity in their devotion to their religion, their community, and their families, as well as in their love of country." "The Historian's Use of Nationalism and Vice Versa," *American Historical Review,* LXVII (1961–1962), 932.

[12] Bertelson, *The Lazy South,* 210.

[13] David M. Potter, "The Enigma of the South," *Yale Review,* LI (1961–1962), 150–151.

limited areas of the South people's lives did attain relatedness and meaning," in the region as a whole disruptive economic forces, pursuit of gain, and chaotic mobility have made impossible "the kind of stability which one usually associates with folk culture." Far from constituting evidence of a sense of community, "courtesy, hospitality, graciousness—is simply a series of devices for minimizing friction only to create the appearance of intimacy or affection."[14] If these particular myths *are* indeed Janus-faced, one face would seem to be effectively veiled from the author's vision.

The emphasis throughout is on the want of any meaningful sense of community in the South. The essence of community is tacitly assumed to be urban, something associated with cities—preferably built on a hill or in a wilderness. "Both the Quakers and to an even greater degree the Puritans in New England founded societies based on communities of consent and common goals. Imbued with a sense of community and social purposefulness, these people were truly able to build cities in the wilderness."[15] It is perhaps inevitable and even appropriate that the myths of an urban society should attach symbolic significance to cities, and it is understandable that these symbols should retain their appeal long after the metropolis has become something less than the ideal embodiment of community, has become in fact the symbol of anti-community. What is surprising is the total unconsciousness of the mythic quality of these symbols and the faith that they embody.

Harry Levin has commented on the "mythoclastic rigors" of the early Christians. "Myths were pagan," he writes, "and therefore false in the light of true belief—albeit that true belief might today be considered merely another variety of mythopoeic faith. Here is where the game of debunking starts in the denunciation of myth as falsehood from the vantage point of a rival myth."[16]

Mr. Bertelson erects at least one guard against the charge of drawing a geographical line between virtue and vice. He concedes that "Northern society only imperfectly exemplified a sense of community," and that personal aggrandizement, anarchic individualism, and maybe Old Adam himself have been known to break out at times above the Potomac. "The South," he nevertheless maintains, "represents the logical extreme of this tendency. To the degree that America has meant economic opportunity without social obligations or limitations, Southerners are Americans and Americans are Southerners."[17] Some comfort is gratefully derived

[14] Bertelson, *The Lazy South*, 242–243.
[15] *Ibid.*, 244.
[16] Harry Levin, "Some Meanings of Myth," *Daedalus*, LXXXVIII (1959), 225.
[17] Bertelson, *The Lazy South*, 245.

from this remarkable concession, even if it is the comfort the poor white derives in Southern myth as repository of the less fortunate traits: at least he belongs.

II

It is, however, just on this score of Southern distinctiveness that a vulnerable spot occurs in the thesis. In a recent analysis of what he calls "the Puritan Ethic," Edmund S. Morgan addresses himself to many of the traditional values that Mr. Bertelson denies the South.[18] Yet in Mr. Morgan's analysis these were "the values that all Americans held," even though the claim upon them varied in authenticity, and adherence to them differed in consistency and tenacity. And in spite of the name assigned to the ethic, he disavows any proprietary regional exclusiveness about it and holds that "it prevailed widely among Americans of different times and places," and that "most Americans made adherence to the Puritan ethic an article of faith."[19] Indeed, leaders of North and South found "room for agreement in the shared values of the Puritan Ethic" until the break over slavery. Thomas Jefferson was "devoted to the values of the Puritan Ethic," and Mr. Morgan quotes the identical letters containing Jefferson's advice to his daughter that Mr. Bertelson presents as evidence of the Southern syndrome about idleness and remarks that they "sound as though they were written by Cotton Mather."[20] In a mood of generosity he makes honorary Puritans of numerous Southerners: Richard Henry Lee of Virginia was "a New Englander manqué," Henry Laurens of South Carolina had characteristics that made him "sound like a Puritan," Hugh Williamson of North Carolina was forever "drawing upon another precept of the Puritan Ethic," and the thousands of Southerners who poured into Kentucky and Tennessee in the 1780's "carried the values of the Puritan Ethic with them," whence they presumably suffused the Cotton Belt.[21]

These references are undoubtedly of generous intent, and there are rules about looking a gift horse in the mouth. Mr. Morgan is careful to say that " 'The Puritan Ethic' is used here simply as an appropriate shorthand term" to designate widely held American ideas and attitudes. And perhaps he is right that "it matters little by what name we call them or where they came from."[22] What's in a name? Yet there is *something* about

[18] Edmund S. Morgan, "The Puritan Ethic and the American Revolution," *William and Mary Quarterly*, 3d Ser., XXIV (1967), 3–43.

[19] *Ibid.*, 7, 23, 24, 33, 42.

[20] *Ibid.*, 7, 24, 42.

[21] *Ibid.*, 21–22, 28–29, 38.

[22] *Ibid.*, 6.

the name that does raise questions. One cannot help wondering at times how some of those Southern mavericks, sinners that they were, might have reacted to being branded with the Puritan iron. It might have brought out the recalcitrance, or laziness, or orneriness in them—or whatever it was that was Southern and not Puritan. There are in fact, as will later appear, certain limits to the indiscriminate applicability of the Puritan Ethic down South.

By whatever name, however, Mr. Morgan's insights provide needed help in understanding the polemical uses of regional myth and the study of regional character. And he does have a point that in sectional disputes, each side often tended to appeal to the same values. He notes that in the sectional conflict between East and West that followed the Revolution and was accompanied by talk of secession of the lower Mississippi and Ohio Valley, "each side tended to see the other as deficient in the same virtues": "To westerners the eastern-dominated governments seemed to be in the grip of speculators and merchants determined to satisfy their own avarice by sacrificing the interests of the industrious farmers of the West. To easterners, or at least to some easterners, the West seemed to be filled up with shiftless adventurers, as lazy and lawless and unconcerned with the values of the Puritan Ethic as were the native Indians." In this confrontation of East and West the tendency of each to accuse the other of deficiencies in the same virtues and delinquencies in the same code, Mr. Morgan holds that "the role of the Puritan Ethic in the situation was characteristic."[23]

This sectional encounter of the 1780's recalls another one a century later when the Populists were the spokesmen of Southern (and Western) grievances against the East. The Populist Ethic—perhaps I had better say myth—the Populist Myth had much in common with this Puritan Ethic. According to Populist doctrine, labor was the source of all values, and work to be productive had to have social meaning. Productive labor was the index to the health of a society. Populists swore by producer values. Farmers and laborers were "producers." Merchants were the favored symbol of non-productive labor. They were "middle men" who merely moved things around. With them were classified bankers and "monopolists" and "speculators." Their work was not socially useful and served only selfish ends. They exploited the industrious farmers and laborers of the South and West. They deprived men of the just fruits of their labors and removed one of the main motives of industry and frugality. Their gains were ill-gotten, and they could be justly deprived of such gains by the state for the welfare of the community, for their profits were not the fruit of virtuous industry and frugality.

Populists were by and large an inner-directed lot, geared to austerity by

[23] *Ibid.*, 20.

necessity, suspicious of affluence, and fearful of prosperity. They were the children of a life-long depression. They looked with baleful eye upon the city as productive of idleness, luxury, extravagance, and avarice. If the city was an appropriate symbol of community for the Puritan Myth, it was just as naturally a symbol of anti-community for the Populist Myth. Cities were full of non-producers—merchants, bankers, usurers, monopolists. Merchants and cities were concentrated in the East and particularly in New England. A great deal of Populist animus therefore had a regional target.

The Populists believed they had a direct line of inspiration and continuity from the American Revolution, that Thomas Jefferson was its true spokesman, and that their creed of agrarian radicalism was authentically blessed. They harked back continually to the Revolutionary period for fundamental principles and lamented with traditional jeremiads the expiring of republican virtue. It was their historic mission, they believed, to restore virtue and ideals and drive out those who had fouled the temple.[24]

True to tradition, spokesmen of the urban East in the 1890's replied in kind. They pronounced the Populists deficient in virtue and wholly given over to shiftlessness, laziness, and greed. It was the Populists who had defected from the code, not the Eastern capitalist. It was their own deficiencies and lapses from virtue and not exploitation by the East or hostile policies of the government that had brought the farmers to their unhappy plight. Populist resort to government aid and monetary manipulation for relief instead of reliance on frugality and the sweat of their brows was further evidence of shiftlessness and moral delinquency.

Sectional confrontation between the South and other parts of the country in the 1960's has hinged more on moral than on economic issues, but these encounters nevertheless have called forth many familiar recriminations and echoes of the traditional rhetoric of sectional polemics, including those of the 1860's, and their deep moral cleavages. Once again, each side has tended to view the other as deficient in similar virtues while proclaiming its own undeviating adherence. It is, however, perhaps the first instance in the annals of sectional recrimination (not even excepting the 1860's) in which one region has been seriously denied any allegiance to a common ethic, in which historic violations have been treated not as defections but as the promptings of an alien code. For in this instance the delinquencies have been attributed not to some institutional peculiarity that could be eradicated at a cost, nor to some impersonal force of nature or economics for which allowance might be made, but to indigenous,

[24] For examples from Populist literature see Norman Pollack, ed., *The Populist Mind* (Indianapolis, 1967), 51, 66–69, 211–221, 501–519, and *passim*.

ineradicable attitudes of a whole people "which they brought with them and their descendants perpetuated." This introduces a modern use for an ancient concept resembling the tragic flaw that cursed families in Greek tragedy, something inexorable and fatefully ineluctable.

III

Nothing in this vein of critical evaluation, however, is intended as endorsement of the concept of an undifferentiated national ethic, whether it is called Puritan, Protestant, or by any other name. To be sure, there do exist deep ethical commitments that override barriers of section, class, religion, or race. Otherwise there is no accounting for such limited success as the country has enjoyed in achieving national unity. Mr. Morgan and other historians have served their calling well in bringing these commitments to light. But there still remain sectional differences to be accounted for, and the distinctiveness of the South in this respect is especially unavoidable. The evidence of this distinctiveness, however unsatisfactory the explanations for it may be, is too massive to deny. Where there is so much smoke—whether the superficial stereotypes of the Leisure-Laziness sort, or the bulky literature of lamentation, denial, or celebration that runs back to the seventeenth century, or the analytical monographs of the present day—there must be fire. It remains to find a satisfactory explanation for this aspect of Southern distinctiveness.

Before exploring some explanatory approaches to this problem it would be well to start with an underpinning of agreement, if possible. First there is the question of the foundations of settlement and what the settlers brought with them. Perhaps we could do no better for this purpose than to quote the views of Perry Miller. He pointed out that "however much Virginia and New England differed in ecclesiastical politics, they were both recruited from the same type of Englishmen, pious, hard-working, middle-class, accepting literally and solemnly the tenets of Puritanism—original sin, predestination, and election—who could conceive of the society they were erecting in America only within a religious framework." It is true, he went on to say, that even before Massachusetts was settled, "Virginia had already gone through the cycle of exploration, religious dedication, disillusionment, and then reconciliation to a world in which making a living was the ultimate reality." But even after "the glorious mission of Virginia came down to growing a weed," and even though there were never any Winthrop-type "saints" hanging around Jamestown, the religious underpinnings remained.[25]

---

[25] Perry Miller, *Errand into the Wilderness* (Cambridge, Mass., 1956), 108, 138, 139.

In her exhaustive study of Puritanism in the Southern colonies, Babette M. Levy avoids estimates of percentage, but her investigation suggests that a majority of the original settlers were Puritans or Calvinists of some persuasion. Of Virginia she writes that "their presence was felt throughout the colony," and that it was felt extensively in the other Southern colonies as well.[26] Southern colonies sustained two further infusions of Puritans, the Huguenots in the seventeenth century and the Scotch-Irish in the eighteenth. They were assimilated in the evolving Southern Ethic, but not without leaving their mark. Then there were the Methodists. Quoting John Wesley to the effect that "the Methodists in every place grow diligent and frugal," Max Weber comments that "the idea of duty in one's calling prowls about in our lives like the ghost of dead religious beliefs."[27] Even after the Enlightenment and the cotton gin those ghosts continued to prowl under the magnolias and, perhaps more wanly, even in the Spanish-moss and cabbage-palm latitudes. Doubtless they were less at home under the palm than under the pine, but their presence was felt nonetheless.

Yet it is Weber who points out "the difference between the Puritan North, where, on account of the ascetic compulsion to save, capital in search of investment was always available" and "the condition in the South," where such compulsions were inoperative and such capital was not forthcoming.[28] He goes further to compare religio-cultural contrasts in England with those in America. "Through the whole of English society in the time since the seventeenth century," he writes, "goes the conflict between the squirearchy . . . and the Puritan circles of widely varying social influence. . . . Similarly, the early history of the North American Colonies is dominated by the sharp contrast of the adventurers, who wanted to set up plantations with the labour of indentured servants, and live as feudal lords, and the specifically middle-class outlook of the Puritans."[29] Weber was conscious of the paradox that the New England colonies, founded in the interest of religion, became a seedbed of the capitalist spirit, while the Southern colonies, developed in the interest of business, generated a climate uncongenial to that spirit.

This is not the place to enter the "scholarly meleé"[30] over the validity of Max Weber's thesis regarding the influence of the Protestant Ethic in the

[26] Babette M. Levy, "Early Puritanism in the Southern and Island Colonies," in American Antiquarian Society, *Proceedings,* LXX (1960), Pt. i, 60–348, esp. 86, 119, 308.

[27] Max Weber, *The Protestant Ethic and the Spirit of Capitalism,* trans. Talcott Parsons (London, 1930), 175, 182.

[28] *Ibid.,* 278n. But see Gabriel Kolko, "Max Weber on America: Theory and Evidence," *History and Theory,* I (1960–1961), 243–260.

[29] Weber, *The Protestant Ethic,* trans. Parsons, 173–174.

[30] For examples see Robert W. Green, ed., *Protestantism and Capitalism: The Weber Thesis and Its Critics* (Boston, 1959), *passim.*

development of modern capitalism. But here is Weber's delineation of the Puritan Ethic based on his gloss of Richard Baxter's *Saints' Everlasting Rest* (London, 1650) and *Christian Directory* (London, 1673), which he describes as "the most complete compendium of Puritan ethics":

> Not leisure and enjoyment, but only activity serves to increase the glory of God, according to the definite manifestations of His will.
>
> Waste of time is thus the first and in principle the deadliest of sins. The span of human life is infinitely short and precious to make sure of one's own election. Loss of time through sociability, idle talk, luxury, even more sleep than is necessary for health, six to at most eight hours, is worthy of absolute moral condemnation. It does not yet hold, with Franklin, that time is money, but the proposition is true in a certain spiritual sense. It is infinitely valuable because every hour lost is lost to labour for the glory of God. Thus inactive contemplation is also value-less, or even directly reprehensible if it is at the expense of one's daily work.[31]

With regard to "the Puritan aversion to sport," unless it "served a rational purpose" or was "necessary for physical efficiency," Weber observes that "impulsive enjoyment of life, which leads away both from work in a calling and from religion, was as such the enemy of rational asceticism, whether in the form of seigneurial sports, or the enjoyment of the dance-hall or the public-house of the common man."[32]

The precise relation of Puritan asceticism to the "spirit of capitalism" is disputed, but in his characterization of the latter, Weber's friend Ernst Troeltsch makes apparent the affinity between the two:

> For this spirit displays an untiring activity, a boundlessness of grasp, quite contrary to the natural impulse to enjoyment and ease, and con-tentment with the mere necessaries of existence; it makes work and gain an end in themselves, and makes men the slaves of work for work's sake; it brings the whole of life and action within the sphere of an absolutely rationalised and systematic calculation, combines all means to its end, uses every minute to the full, employs every kind of force, and in the alliance with scientific technology and the calculus which unites all these things together, gives to life a clear calculability and abstract exactness.[33]

---

[31] Weber, *The Protestant Ethic,* trans. Parsons, 157–158.

[32] *Ibid.,* 167–168.

[33] Ernst Troeltsch, *Protestantism and Progress, A Historical Study of the Relation of Protestantism to the Modern World,* trans. W. Montgomery (Boston, 1958), 133–134.

Commenting upon the influence of the Puritan Ethic on "the development of a capitalistic way of life," Weber adds that "this asceticism turned with all its force against one thing: the spontaneous enjoyment of life and all it had to offer."[34]

With all deference to Weber's reputation, this would seem to be an excessively harsh characterization of the Puritan Ethic. He does remind us that "Puritanism included a world of contradictions."[35] Surely the code must have been honored in the breach as well as in the observance, and even Puritans in good standing must have had occasional moments of "the spontaneous enjoyment of life." One would hope so, and one is comforted by assurances of modern authorities on the subject that they in fact occasionally did. If not, then it is obvious that "a capitalistic way of life," even with a couple of industrial revolutions thrown in for good measure, came at much too high a cost.

The views of Max Weber, nevertheless, still carry weight.[36] And if his delineation of the Puritan Ethic bears any resemblance to the real thing, then it is abundantly clear that no appreciable number of Southerners came up to scratch. There are to be found, of course, authentic instances of Puritan-like behavior in various periods down South. And no doubt a genuine deviant occasionally appeared, some "New Englander manqué," just as a Southerner manqué might, more rarely, turn up in the valleys of Vermont or even on State Street. By and large, however, the great majority of Southerners, including those concerned about their "election," shamelessly and notoriously stole time for sociability and idle talk, and the few who could afford it stole time, and sometimes more than time, for luxury. It is likely that a statistically significant number of them of a given Sunday morning stole more than their allotted eight hours of sleep. It is extremely unlikely that a sports event—horse race, fox hunt, cock fight, or gander pulling anywhere from the Tidewater to the Delta—was typically preceded by a prayerful debate over whether it "served a rational purpose" or was "necessary for physical efficiency." It was more likely to be contaminated with "the spontaneous expression of undisciplined impulses." Such "inactive contemplation" as went on below the Potomac does not appear to have altered the mainstream of western civilization, but the temptation to indulge the impulse would rarely have struck the inactive contemplator as morally reprehensible.

A regional propensity for living it up had tangible manifestations of more practical consequence than habits of sociability, sleeping, and sports.

---

[34] Weber, *The Protestant Ethic*, trans. Parsons, 166.

[35] *Ibid.*, 169.

[36] For a spirited and persuasive defense of Weber from a recent critic, see Edmund S. Morgan's review of Kurt Samuelsson, *Religion and Economic Action* (New York, 1961), in *Wm. and Mary Qtly.*, 3d Ser., XX (1963), 135–140.

Modern economists have often sought to explain why a region of such abundant natural and human resources as the South should have remained economically underdeveloped in a nation of highly developed regional economies—some with poorer natural resources—and suffered the attendant penalties of strikingly lower levels of per capita wealth and income. The Southern scene as of 1930 could be described as "an almost classic picture of an underdeveloped society."[37] Many explanations are offered and no one alone is adequate, but of prime importance in modern theory on the subject is the factor of capital formation. Apart from sheer productivity, the ability to produce more than enough to support the population, the key variable in the rate of capital growth is the willingness to save, or the other side of the coin, the propensity to consume. "Any difference among regions," one economist writes, "in their tendency to consume rather than to save will probably be reflected in their respective rates of capital formation."[38]

Economic and social historians have long remarked on distinctive spending habits, not to say extravagance, of Southerners—the Populist Myth to the contrary notwithstanding. Most often such habits have been attributed to antebellum planters and their tastes for fast horses, fine furniture, and expensive houses. The flaunting of wealth in an aristocratic society was, according to Weber, a weapon in the struggle for power. These generalizations of historians about extravagance in the South have been based on more or less well-founded impressions and random samples. The only comprehensive statistical study of regional spending habits of which I am aware is one made by several agencies of the federal government covering the years 1935 and 1936 and embracing thousands of families analyzed by population segments and income groups. The limited samples studied indicate that "people in the South did spend, in given income classes, a larger amount for consumption than did residents of other regions"; that in small-city samples low-income groups saved less in the South than in other parts of the country; that at higher income levels in this urban sector "southerners showed a tendency towards higher levels of consumption and less saving"; and that among high farm-income groups in the South "the proportion spent for consumption was significantly higher than that for the same farm income levels elsewhere."[39]

Thus the differences between the Puritan North and the Southern

---

[37] Douglas F. Dowd, "A Comparative Analysis of Economic Development in the American West and South," *Journal of Economic History,* XVI (1956), 563, and *passim.*

[38] W. H. Baughn, "Capital Formation and Entrepreneurship in the South," *Southern Economic Journal,* XVI (1949–1950), 162.

[39] *Ibid.,* 165–166. Since no allowance was made in these computations for the lower living costs in the South, according to Mr. Baughn, they tend to understate the extent of Southern spending.

colonies over "the ascetic compulsion to save" that Weber saw operating to influence the availability of capital for investment in the 1600's appeared to be still operative in the 1930's. If the ascetic compulsion is rightly attributed to the Puritan Ethic, then the absence or remission of that compulsion might be another indication of a distinctive Southern Ethic.

IV

The real question then is not whether Southerners fell under the discipline of the Puritan Ethic, but rather—given their heritage and the extent of their exposure—how it was they managed to escape it, in so far as they did. To attribute their deliverance to attitudes they brought with them to America seems rather unhelpful in view of the fact that they brought so many of the same attitudes the New Englanders brought and that these were reinforced by massive transfusions of Puritan blood in later years. Their escape would seem to be more plausibly derived from something that happened to them after they arrived. An acceptable explanation would probably turn out to be plural rather than singular, complex rather than simple, and rather more "environmental" than ideological. To explore and test all the reasonably eligible hypotheses would be the work of elaborate researches and much *active* contemplation. Here it is only possible to suggest a few hypotheses that would appear worth such attention.

Slavery would not come first in any chronological ordering of causal determinants of Southern attitudes toward work, but it hardly seems wise to brush it off entirely into the category of consequences. Granting that some distinctive Southern attitudes on work appeared before slavery attained very much importance in the economy, and conceding that these attitudes played a certain part in the spread of the institution, it would be willful blindness to deny the influence it had, once entrenched, in the evolution of the Southern Ethic. The causes of slavery are another subject—a very large one. But once the system became rooted in the land in the seventeenth century, its influence was all-pervasive, and the impact it had on the status of important categories of necessary work and on white and black attitudes toward them was profound and lasting. For not only were these types of work associated firmly with a degraded status, but also fatefully linked with a despised race that continued to perform the same types of work, with no appreciable improvement in racial status, long after slavery disappeared. The testimony of white Southerners themselves, ranging in authority and prestige from Thomas Jefferson to Hinton Rowan Helper, is impressive on the effect that slavery had upon the honor and esteem accorded work in the South. Statistical analysis of the comparative figures on employment might be effectively used in testing these impressions.

Regional variations in the nature of work might also deserve attention as determinants of the Southern Ethic. Much of the work required of men in all parts of early America was crude and hard, and little of it anywhere could honestly be characterized as stimulating, creative, or inherently enjoyable. Those who wrote of its joys and rewards probably had a larger share of work that could be so characterized than those who failed to record their impressions. Perhaps it was somewhat easier to surround the labors of shop, countinghouse, and trade with the aura of honor and glamor. That type of work was in short supply in the South.

The agrarian myth of yeoman farmers as "the chosen people of God" certainly did bestow honor and a literary aura of dignity, even glamor, upon a way of making a living, but not necessarily on work itself. No other class of Americans was so persistently and assiduously flattered. The qualities for which the hero of the myth was admired, however, were his independence, his republican virtues, his purifying communion with nature. It was the political and public qualities of the yeomanry that Jefferson had in mind when he wrote that "the small land holders are the most precious part of the state." Work itself was not the essential thing, and certainly not the religion-driven, compulsive, ascetic work of the Puritan Ethic. In fact, neither the hired man nor the slave who did the same work (and probably more of it) shared the dignity and honor conferred by the myth on the yeoman, while the employer or owner of such labor might do little work by himself and yet enjoy the blessings of the myth. In its full flower in the late eighteenth century the agrarian myth, in fact, stressed escape from the bustle of the world and celebrated pastoral contentment and ease, the blandishments and pleasures of the simple life—the very "impulsive enjoyment of life" held up by Puritan divines as "the deadliest of sins." Never did the agrarian myth regard yeomen as "slaves of work for work's sake." The myth of the happy yeoman was much more congenial to the Southern Ethic than it was to the Puritan Ethic.[40]

As for the black slaves, their very existence did violence to the Puritan Ethic. No one could have a "calling"—in Weber's sense of the term—to be a slave. Since slaves were denied the fruits of their labor, they were deprived of the basic motive for industry and frugality. Circumstance made laziness the virtue and frugality the vice of slaves. Work was a necessary evil to be avoided as ingeniously as possible. Such work as was required of slaves—as well as of those who did work slaves typically performed—was rather difficult to associate with the glory of God or many of the finer aspirations of man. Could such work have been endowed with the mystique of a "calling" or a conviction of divine purpose, it might have

[40] Henry Nash Smith, *Virgin Land: The American West as Symbol and Myth* (New York, 1957), 138–150.

rested more lightly on the shoulders of those of whom it was required and on the conscience of those who required it. That seems to have been the way it worked with onerous non-slave work elsewhere. There appears, however, to have been less stomach for such theological exercises—indeed more need for stomach—in the South than in some other parts. Few sermons to slaves indulged in them. Work therefore lacked the sort of sanctification it might have derived from this source. The attitude of the slave toward work, like many of his attitudes and ways, found secure lodgement in the Southern Ethic.

Turning from the slave to the slave holder and the plantation system for a look at their influence on the evolution of the Southern Ethic, we move into more troubled waters. Genuine and important differences of opinion about the fundamental nature of the slave economy exist among experts in the field. Members of one school, the most distinguished of whom was Lewis C. Gray, think of the slave holder as a "planter-capitalist." According to Gray, the plantation system was a "capitalist type of agricultural organization in which a considerable number of unfree laborers were employed under a unified direction and control in the production of a staple crop."[41] The crop was produced for a remote market in response to standard laws of supply and demand by the use of capital sometimes obtained from banks or factors that was invested in land and in slaves. The whole operation was "rational," in the peculiar way economists use that remarkable word—that is, it operated single-mindedly to maximize profits on investment. A contrasting view was that of Ulrich B. Phillips, who believed that the plantation system was not nearly that simple, that it was a complicated "way of life," a social as well as an economic system. It contained numerous "irrational" elements, goals unrelated or antithetical to the profit motive. It was something of an anachronism, a pre-capitalist economy existing in a capitalist world.[42]

It makes a great deal of difference for the implications of the plantation system in accounting for the distinctiveness of the Southern Ethic as to which of these schools is "sound on the goose." For if Gray and his school are right, then there is relatively little to be learned from the political economy of slavery about the distinctiveness of the South from the rest of a uniformly capitalist America. If Phillips is on the right track, however, there might be a great deal to learn. It may be a long time before a consensus on the slave economy is reached among scholars, and certainly no attempt is made to settle the dispute here.

It is instructive to note, however, a convergence between the old-school

[41] Lewis C. Gray, *History of Agriculture in the Southern United States to 1860*, I (Washington, 1933), 302.

[42] Ulrich B. Phillips, *American Negro Slavery: A Survey of the Supply, Employment and Control of Negro Labor as Determined by the Plantation Régime* (Baton Rouge, 1966), *passim*.

views of Phillips and a new-school view developed by the investigations of Eugene D. Genovese.[43] In the findings of the latter, the plantation economy was shot through with "irrationality" (in the market-place sense) and given to wild deviations from the capitalistic norm. "The planters were not mere capitalists," he writes. "They were pre-capitalist, quasi-aristocratic landowners who had to adjust their economy and ways of thinking to a capitalist world market. Their society, in its spirit and fundamental direction, represented the antithesis of capitalism, however many compromises it had to make." He elaborates on the antithesis as follows:

The planters commanded Southern politics and set the tone of social life. Theirs was an aristocratic, antibourgeois spirit with values and mores emphasizing family and status, a strong code of honor, and aspirations to luxury, ease, and accomplishment. In the planters' community, paternalism provided the standard of human relationships, and politics and statecraft were the duties and responsibilities of gentlemen. The gentleman lived for politics, not, like the bourgeois politician, off politics.

The planter typically recoiled at the notions that profit should be the goal of life; that the approach to production and exchange should be internally rational and uncomplicated by social values; that thrift and hard work should be the great virtues; and that the test of the wholesomeness of a community should be the vigor with which its citizens expand the economy. The planter was no less acquisitive than the bourgeois, but an acquisitive spirit is compatible with values antithetical to capitalism. The aristocratic spirit of the planters absorbed acquisitiveness and directed it into channels that were socially desirable to a slave society: the accumulation of slaves and land and the achievement of military and political honors. Whereas in the North people followed the lure of business and money for their own sake, in the South specific forms of property carried the badges of honor, prestige, and power.[44]

He goes on to observe that "at their best, Southern ideals constituted a rejection of the crass, vulgar, inhumane elements of capitalist society. The slaveholders simply could not accept the idea that the cash nexus offered a permissible basis for human relations." The planters reinforced their paternalism toward their slaves by a semipaternalism toward their neighbors and "grew into the closest thing to feudal lords imaginable in a nineteenth-century bourgeois republic."[45]

[43] See for example Genovese's "Foreword" to the 1966 edition of Phillips, *American Negro Slavery* cited above.

[44] Eugene D. Genovese, *The Political Economy of Slavery: Studies in the Economy and Society of the Slave South* (New York, 1965), 23, 28.

[45] *Ibid.,* 30, 31.

Mr. Genovese has greatly complicated and enhanced the fascination of the game of ethic identification. One shrinks at the prospect of encouraging studies of "feudal" and "aristocratic" themes in Southern history, and even more at anticipated glances from colleagues in European history. It would be well to emphasize the prefix *quasi* that Mr. Genovese judiciously attaches to these terms. With these precautions (and misgivings) and with no disposition to prejudge the outcome of the revived and flourishing controversy over the political economy of American slavery, one might at least say that this interpretation of the slave South contains a number of suggestive hypotheses relating to the distinctiveness of the Southern Ethic.

On the themes of pre-capitalist economies the work of Max Weber again becomes relevant. He strongly emphasized the "irrational" characteristics of slave economies, particularly in master-slave relationships, consumer behavior, and politics. At the risk of reviving the Waverly-novel approach, the following characterization of the aristocratic ethic by Weber is offered as summarized by his biographer:

> In feudal ideology the most important relations in life are pervaded by personalized ties, in contrast to all factual and impersonal relationships. . . . From this standpoint luxury is not a superfluous frill but a means of self-assertion and a weapon in the struggle for power. This antiutilitarian attitude toward consumption was of a piece with the equally antiutilitarian orientation toward one's life. Aristocratic strata specifically rejected any idea of a 'mission in life,' any suggestion that a man should have a purpose or seek to realize an ideal; the value of aristocratic existence was self-contained. . . . Aristocrats deliberately cultivated a nonchalance that stemmed from the conventions of chivalry, pride of status, and a sense of honor.[46]

Social role-playing is a broad mark for satire, but all societies engage in it consciously or unconsciously. The sharpest ridicule is reserved for the unfortunate society that is caught at the height of collective posturing, brought low with humiliating exposure of its pretenses, and forced to acknowledge them—or live with them. The Old South has had its share of exposure along this particular line, and more at this juncture has rather low priority among the pressing tasks of historiography. More needful are analytical appraisals of the social content of the patriarchal, paternalistic, and aristocratic values and the remarkable qualities of leadership they developed. A comparative approach could be helpful, but the traditional moralistic comparison with the contemporary society to the north might profitably be ex-

---

[46] Reinhard Bendix, *Max Weber: An Intellectual Portrait* (New York, 1962), 364–365.

changed for comparisons with English and Latin slave societies to the south
that shared more of the South's traditions, institutions, and values.

An abhorrence of slavery and an identification with abolitionists on the
part of both liberal and radical historians have skewed and clouded their
interpretation of the Old South. In a critique of Marxian and liberal historiography of slavery, Mr. Genovese holds that the main problem "arises
from the duality inherent in a class approach to morality" and contends
that both liberals and Marxists have made the mistake of judging the ruling
class of Southern planters "by the standards of bourgeois society or by the
standards of a projected socialist society." With reference to rulers of the
Old Regime, he continues:

> These men were class conscious, socially responsible, and personally
> honorable; they selflessly fulfilled their duties and did what their class
> and society required of them. It is rather hard to assert that class respon-
> sibility is the highest test of morality and then to condemn as immoral
> those who behave responsibly toward their class instead of someone
> else's. There is no reason, unless we count as reason the indignation
> flowing from a passionate hatred for oppression, to withhold from such
> people full respect and even admiration; nor is there any reason to per-
> mit such respect and admiration to prevent their being treated harshly if
> the liberation of oppressed peoples demands it. The issue transcends con-
> siderations of abstract justice or a desire to be fair to one's enemies; it
> involves political judgment. If we blind ourselves to everything noble,
> virtuous, honorable, decent, and selfless in a ruling class, how do we ac-
> count for its hegemony? . . . Such hegemony could never be maintained
> without some leaders whose individual qualities are intrinsically ad-
> mirable.[47]

Also needed are discerning assessments of the skill, conviction, and zest
which other players brought to the colorful variety of roles assigned them
by the Old Regime. That of "Sambo" has been subjected to appreciative
analysis of late, with commendable efforts to illuminate the personality and
values of his descendants. The roles of his master and mistress, Lord and
Lady Bountiful, as well as those of the lesser gentry, the squirearchy, the
yeomanry, and the poor whites deserve comparable study. It is possible that
a majority of the players identified completely with their roles as "real life"
—as completely perhaps as the saints, prophets, and come-outers in other
quarters found identity in their roles. At least the cast for the Old South

[47] Eugene D. Genovese, "Marxian Interpretations of the Slave South," in Barton
J. Bernstein, ed., *Toward a New Past: Dissenting Essays in American History* (New
York, 1968), 114.

drama, slaves included, often acted as if they did, and sometimes they put on rather magnificent performances. Study of the institutional setting in which they performed—the patriarchal tradition, the caste system, the martial spirit, the racial etiquette, the familial charisma—all deserve attention from the historian of the Southern Ethic.

V

After the curtain fell on the Old South in 1865, the same cast of characters had to be taught strange roles and learn new lines. For a people who had been schooled so long in the traditional roles, and especially for those who played them for "real life," this was not an easy assignment. The social dislocations and traumas of Reconstruction and the period that followed can be seen as drastic experiments from two sides: the conservative side trying to preserve the Southern Ethic, and the radical side trying to destroy it. As we shall see, neither of these experiments was destined wholly to succeed.

To convert the ex-slaves miraculously into "slaves of work for work's sake" in the classic model of Weber's "spirit of capitalism" was clearly beyond the reasonable expectations of either side. Given the freedman's age-long indoctrination in a work ethic appropriate to his enslavement, and given the necessity of his now doing the same kinds of work without the old compulsions, the question was whether he could be induced to do any work beyond what would provide him a bare subsistence, if that. Planter conservatives were convinced that the only answer was force in some guise, and in lieu of bondage they put forward schemes of apprenticeship and vagrancy laws embodied in "Black Codes." In effect they offered the old allegiance of paternalistic responsibility for abject dependents while tacitly retaining the sanction of the whip.

Ruling these schemes illegal and a travesty on freedom, Northern agencies, including the Freedmen's Bureau, missionaries, and private speculators, confidently maintained that "normal" economic incentives were the solution: wages, profits, and assurance of the fruits of one's labor. Northern agencies and employers launched their program with a campaign of indoctrination laced with the rhetoric of diligence, frugality, and the sanctity of contracts—staples of the Puritan Ethic. Needless to say, the Puritan Ethic had acquired its own Janus face over the centuries, and it was the face of Yankee acquisitiveness that was presented to the South. Along with this went the promise of free land held out to the freedmen by Congress and the Freedmen's Bureau. But that promise ran afoul of two conflicting principles of their own: the sanctity of property and the doctrine of equal rewards for equal labor. The first blocked the confiscation of planters' property to provide the free land, and the second inhibited the granting of special privilege unearned by honest labor. The North reneged on the promise of free land,

and the freedmen sulked. The "normal" incentives were not operating. Northern business joined Southern planters in demanding that the Freedmen's Bureau get the Negro back to the cotton fields. When General O. O. Howard, head of the bureau, received "authentic complaints of idleness for which no remedy seemed to exist," he ordered enforcement and extension of state vagrancy laws. His assistants withheld relief, compelled freedmen to accept labor contracts, and enforced their harsh terms with penalties of forfeited wages and withheld rations. Gradually the North withdrew and left the freedmen to make what terms they could with planters.[48]

In the meantime the campaign to convert Southern white men went forward briskly and at first hopefully. "It is intended," declared Thaddeus Stevens, "to revolutionize their principles and feelings," to "work a radical reorganization in Southern institutions, habits, and manners."[49] The difficulties of the undertaking were acknowledged. "The conversion of the Southern whites to the ways and ideas of what is called the industrial stage in social progress," wrote Edwin L. Godkin, was a "formidable task." He believed that "the South, in the structure of its society, in its manners and social traditions, differs nearly as much from the North as Ireland does, or Hungary, or Turkey."[50] But the revolutionizing process would go forward, promised Horatio Seymour, "until their ideas of business, industry, money making, spindles and looms were in accord with those of Massachusetts."[51] The Southern whites, like the Negroes, were subjected to indoctrination in diligence, austerity, frugality, and the gospel of work. They were advised to put behind them the "irrationality" of the Old Order, outmoded notions of honor, chivalry, paternalism, pride of status, and noblesse oblige, together with all associated habits of indolence, extravagance, idle sports, and postures of leisure and enjoyment. In the name of "rationality" they were adjured to get in there like proper Americans and maximize profits.

The verbal response from the South, after a refractory interlude and apart from a continued undertone of muttered dissent, must have been gratifying. The antebellum business community, long inhibited by ties to the Old Order, burst into effusions of assent and hosannas of delivery. "We have sowed towns and cities in the place of theories and put business above politics," announced Henry W. Grady to the cheering members of the New

[48] Willie Lee Rose, *Rehearsal for Reconstruction: The Port Royal Experiment* (Indianapolis, 1964), 212–216, 308–310; George R. Bentley, *A History of the Freedmen's Bureau* (Philadelphia, 1955), 79–86; for a revisionary estimate of the bureau see a forthcoming work of William McFeely, *Yankee Stepfather: General O. O. Howard and the Freedmen's Bureau* (New Haven, 1968).

[49] Quoted in Howard K. Beale, *The Critical Year: A Study of Andrew Johnson and Reconstruction* (New York, 1930), 149.

[50] *Nation,* XXXI (1880), 126.

[51] *Herald* (New York), Oct. 31, 1866.

England Society of New York. "We have fallen in love with work."[52] And Richard H. Edmunds of the *Manufacturers' Record,* invoking the spirit of Franklin, announced, "The South has learned that 'time is money.' "[53] A Richmond editor rejoiced that "the almighty dollar is fast becoming a power here, and he who commands the most money holds the strongest hand. We no longer condemn the filthy lucre."[54] The range of New South rhetoric left unsounded no maxim of the self-made man, no crassness of the booster, no vulgarity of the shopkeeper, no philistinism of the profit maximizer. For egregious accommodation and willing compliance the capitulation was to all appearances complete.

But appearances were deceptive, and the North was in some measure taken in by them. The New South orators and businessmen-politicians who took over the old planter states gained consent to speak for the region only on their promise that Southerners could have their cake and eat it too. That was one of the meanings of the Compromise of 1877. The South could retain its old ways, the semblance or outer shell at any rate, and at the same time have an "industrial revolution"—of a sort, and at a price. White supremacy was assured anyway, but home rule and states' rights meant further that the South was left to make its own arrangements regarding the plantation system, the accommodation of the freedman and his work ethic, and his status as well as that of white labor in the new economy and polity. The price of the "industrial revolution" and the reason for the distorted and truncated shape it took was an agreement that the North furnish the bulk of investment capital and entrepreneurship, while the New South managers smoothed the way by a "cooperative spirit" that assured generous tax exemptions, franchises, land grants, and most important of all an abundant supply of cheap, docile, and unorganized labor.

The South got its railroads and mines, its Birmingham heavy industry and its Piedmont factories. That is, they were located in the South. But they were largely owned elsewhere and they were operated in the interest of their owners. They were of one general type: low-wage, low value-creating industries that processed roughly the region's agricultural and mineral products but left the more profitable functions of finishing, transporting, distributing, and financing to the imperial Northeast. The South remained essentially a raw-material economy organized and run as a colonial dependency. On the agricultural side a sort of plantation system survived along with the one-crop staple culture, but the absentee owners dropped the wage contracts, substituted debt slavery for chattel slavery, and organized the

[52] Raymond B. Nixon, *Henry W. Grady: Spokesman of the New South* (New York, 1943), 345.

[53] *Manufacturers' Record* (Baltimore), Nov. 3, 1888.

[54] *Whig and Advertiser* (Richmond), Apr. 4, 1876.

labor force, now more white than black, as share croppers or tenants bound by an iron crop lien into virtual peonage. The cropper-tenants rarely handled any money, subsisted on fatback, cornbread, and molasses, and constituted a mass market for Southern manufacturers of chewing tobacco, moonshine whiskey, and very little else. They were in fact a non-market.

The New South neither preserved the Southern Ethic intact nor abandoned the allegiance entirely. It substituted a compromise that retained a semblance at the expense of the essence. The substitute was more defiantly proclaimed, articulately defended, and punctiliously observed than the genuine article had been. The cult of the Lost Cause covered the compromise with a mantle of romantic dignity and heroism. Surviving heroes in gray became Tennysonian knights. The Plantation Legend took on a splendor that shamed antebellum efforts. There was a place in the new cast —with important exceptions to be noted—for all players of the old roles as well as for newcomers with only imaginary identification with them, and there was a gratuitous upgrading of status all around. Great energy went into the performance. Spectators were impressed with the graciousness and hospitality, the leisurely elegance and quaint courtliness at upper levels, and with a pervasive kindliness, a familial warmth, and a deferential courtesy that prevailed generally.

There were even those who affected the patriarchal and paternalistic roles. Right here, however, came the sad falling off, the point at which the sacrificed essence—aristocratic obligations of noblesse oblige, responsibilities of leadership, solicitude for dependents and subordinates, and an anti-bourgeois disdain for the main chance and the fast buck—gave way to the bourgeois surrogate. For the children of the new patriarchs and the dependents of the new paternalists were the mass of forlorn croppers and tenants, black and white, in their miserable rural slums, undefended victims of ruinous interest rates, mined-out soil, outmoded techniques, debt slavery, and peonage—these and the first-generation industrial proletariat, white and black, in their urban or company-town slums, victims of the lowest wages, longest hours, and deadliest working conditions in the country.

The oppressed were not so docile as to submit without show of resistance. As the nineties came on, Negroes and white labor under the leadership of desperate farmers combined in the Populist Revolt to mount the most serious indigenous political rebellion an established order ever faced in the South. In their panic over the rebellion, the New South leaders relinquished their last claim to responsibility derived from the Old Order. Abandoning their commitment to moderation in racial policy, they turned politics over to racists. In the name of white solidarity and one-party loyalty, they disfranchised the Negro and many lower-class whites and unleashed the fanatics and lynchers. In their banks and businesses, in their clubs and social life, as well as in their inner political councils, they moved over to make room for increasing delegations of Snopeses. In place of the old sense of community based on an ordered if flexible hierarchy, they substituted a mystique of kinship, or clanship, that extended the familial ambit spuriously to all whites—and to such Negroes as had mastered and sedulously practiced the Sambo role to perfection.

There have been lamentations for the passing of the Southern Ethic all down the years and periodic jeremiads for its demise. Referring to the Puritan Ethic, Edmund Morgan writes that "it has continued to be in the process of expiring," that it has "always been known by its epitaphs," and that "perhaps it is not quite dead yet."[55] The future of either of these two historic relics in an affluent, consumer-oriented society of the short work week, early retirement, and talk of a guaranteed income looks rather dubious, though in a giant supermarket world the ethic of the grasshopper would seem to have somewhat more relevance than that of the ant. And puritanical condemnations of leisure already seem a bit quaint. Whether the Southern Ethic is dead or not, the lamentations and jeremiads show no sign of languishing. In fact, the works of William Faulkner constitute the most impressive contribution to that branch of literature yet. If epitaphs are indeed a sign of life in this paradoxical field of ethical history, then the lamentations here, too, may be premature.

[55] Morgan, "The Puritan Ethic," 42–43.

4

The First South

John Richard Alden

A definite consensus persists among students of the southern past
that the distinct regional identification, so long a hallmark of southernism, was first articulated and defined via the sectional contro-
versies of the pre–Civil War decades. Such consensus has concluded
that The South did not function as a consistent regional entity, nor
did it have a particularly graphic perception of itself as distinct
from the North, at least not until the decade of the 1820s. John
Richard Alden, Professor of History at Duke University, Durham,
North Carolina, challenges this standard interpretation, taking
notable exception to these "classic" explanations of southern regional consciousness. Lying beyond the historical horizon of the
familiar Old South, Alden contends, lies an earlier South—a First
South if you will. Though geographically distinct from its later
counterpart, the First South was of kindred spirit in terms of climate, people, economy, and social order. In short, the land to the
south of the Susquehanna "behaved as a section before 1789."
Focusing on the Revolutionary War period, Professor Alden notes
that perceptions of a constitutional, economic, and racial nature
were already surfacing which foreshadowed an eventual southern
Confederacy. It would be for later generations to reinforce and
firmly establish these sectional feelings.

We Americans who are not too familiar with our history harbor a haunting
memory of an Old South—an Old South of broad plantations; of their
gracious masters and charming mistresses; of humble, cheerful, and loyal

From John R. Alden, *The First South*. Baton Rouge, Louisiana State University
Press, 1961. Reprinted by permission of the publisher.

slaves who rose occasionally in ferocious revolt; of poor whites fearing naught but the wrath of Heaven; of cotton, magnolias, and Spanish moss—an Old South menaced and at last overwhelmed and demolished by Northern masses and machinery. We see through a glass doubtfully, and it is surely true that every general idea we have of that Old South is subject to exception and fuller description. The thousands of earnest historians who have delved into its remains must and do tell us that it was not as we are accustomed to think it was. Herein it is not intended to try to correct and clarify your vision, erroneous as it may be, of that familiar Old South, but to limn as truthfully as talents and energies will permit an even older South, which shall be named for convenience the First South.

This First South existed during the years 1775–1789. It appeared with the American nation; it was christened as early as 1778; and it clashed ever more sharply with a First North during and immediately after the War of Independence. This First South did not hasten under the Federal Roof with swift and certain steps, but haltingly and uncertainly. Many of her people feared that the Federal cover would offer greater protection north of the Susquehanna than it would south of that river. It should not be said that their alarm was without cause, that they saw troubles which the future did not bring. They feared lest they become a minority in an American union dominated by a Northern majority, lest they suffer in consequence. Whatever may be the merits of measures since imposed upon the South by the North—and the West—it will not be denied that the South has felt the power of external American forces, especially since the middle of the nineteenth century.

Now this First South, the Revolutionary South, the South of Patrick Henry, Light-Horse Harry Lee, and John Rutledge, was not the Old South of John C. Calhoun nor that of Jefferson Davis. In essence, nevertheless, they were the same, for they were alike in land, climate, people, economy, and social order. Even with respect to political structure and relations with the North, they were not so different as historians have commonly conceived. The Old South sought to leave the Union and to form a new nation; the First South—and for similar reasons—was not at all sure in the years 1787–1789 that it was wise to become part of that Union. Indeed, surprising as it may be, there were those in South Carolina, especially William Henry Drayton, who feared that South Carolina might suffer from the tyranny of Congress by giving consent to the Articles of Confederation. To be sure, the doubts of the First South were set aside, and it ultimately endorsed the Constitution of 1787, while the doubts of the Old South regarding the Union became so great that it denounced and sought to leave the Union. Here we have, however, an important difference in degree, not opposites absolutely.

There may be captious scholars—are not scholars by definition captious?

—who will go so far as to deny that there was a South in the Revolutionary time.[1] One may be tempted to find importance in the fact that the First South and the Old South were geographically not the same. Obviously enough, the First South was definitely limited by the Mississippi, while the Old South stretched westward into the empire of Texas; the First South was principally on the Atlantic seaboard, while the Old South contained both that seaboard and the lower half of the valley of the Mississippi. No matter, for the limits of a section, unless they be remarkably narrow, do not determine whether or not it exists.

More seriously, it may be asserted that the First South cannot have been because it lacked unity. It has been well said by Carl Bridenbaugh that there were actually three or four societies in the states from Maryland to Georgia at the beginning of the Revolution: an aristocratic order on the shores of the Chesapeake; another in the Carolina Low Country; a frontier society in the Old West; and possibly a fourth society not easily described in central North Carolina. But if there were three, or even four, societies below the Mason-Dixon line, it must be remembered that these were not three or four permanent societies completely distinct from each other. Those of the Chesapeake and the Low Country actually had much in common, including well-established American aristocracies and very large bodies of Negro slaves; and that of the Old West was actually only a passing phenomenon, since it would vanish with the frontier. Nor did central North Carolina possess one which could easily and positively be distinguished from those of the Chesapeake and the Low Country. The social differences to be discerned in the First South were hardly more impressive than were those in the Old South, the existence of which is not frequently or forcefully denied. The First South was not monolithic; neither was the Old South. Again, during the period 1775–1789, as afterward, heat, geography, racial and national composition, economic pursuits, social order, and even political structure, were ties of unity rather than sources of discord below the Susquehanna. That such was so is proven by events, for the First South frequently behaved as a section before 1789. It may be added that it was increasingly taken for granted by political men of the Revolutionary generation that the South was a distinct area with special and common interests that could not be ignored in the affairs of the nation.

All of which is not to say that there was such a region generally or even frequently referred to in 1775 or 1789 as the South. That name was used on a few interesting occasions, but the region was usually described between those years as the "Southern states." It follows, then, that there was

[1] The writer indicated briefly in his *The South in the Revolution, 1763–1789* (Baton Rouge, 1957) that there was such a South. So far as he is aware, none of the reviewers of that volume expressed dissent.

a South even before the name came into common use, a fact which hardly surprises, since the infant should precede the christening. Before the War of Independence the colonies were often divided by observers into "Eastern" and "Southern," the term "Eastern" covering New England, the word "Southern" including all the colonies from New York to Georgia. Sometimes "Northern" was used as a synonym for "Eastern." Thus in 1767, when advising General Thomas Gage to establish a military base at or near Manhattan, General Guy Carleton pointed out that such a fortified place would not only provide security for military stores but would also "separate the Northern from the Southern colonies." The division between "Eastern" and "Southern" endured through the early years of the war, a usage which has confused some historians, who have occasionally and forgivably assumed that no one could think of Pennsylvania or New Jersey as Southern. It is nevertheless true that a quarrel between men of the Delaware valley and New England troops in 1776 was referred to as one between Southerners and Easterners. Even at that time, however, the word Southern was acquiring a more restrictive meaning, the phrase "Middle states" being used more and more to describe New York, New Jersey, Pennsylvania, and Delaware. These "Middle states" with the "Eastern states" were increasingly put together as the "Northern states," another usage which long endured.

Quickly shorn of the Middle states, the Southern states became a South and a section. The limits of that section were, of course, only gradually established in the minds of men; indeed, they cannot now be firmly laid down between it and the Middle states. There was disagreement about its northern boundaries at the time, although no one doubted that the Carolinas and Georgia were part of it.

Strange to say, none other than George Washington, until the adoption of the Constitution, was reluctant to include Virginia within the First South. In 1787 and again in 1788 he refers in his correspondence to the Carolinas and Georgia as the "Southern states." In 1786 he invited Don Diego de Gardoqui, the official emissary of Spain to the United States, to pay a visit to Mount Vernon "if you should ever feel an inclination to make an excursion into the middle states." It is apparent that Washington, a stout nationalist even before the close of the War of Independence, wished to minimize the South and its special interests. But he was forced to recognize that they existed, and he too began to refer to the region between Pennsylvania and the Floridas as the "Southern states." Not until his first term as president did he fully realize the vitality of a Southern section that included Virginia. Becoming genuinely and even gravely alarmed, he urged his countrymen, in his Farewell Address, to soften their sectional antagonisms.

Except for Washington, I have found no Revolutionary worthy who would have drawn a line between Virginia and the South. And I have discovered only one other Founding Father who did not include Maryland in the "Southern states." That person was William Henry Drayton of South Carolina, who declared most emphatically in the winter of 1777–1778 that Virginia, the Carolinas, and Georgia formed "the body of the southern interest." Almost invariably, men in public life perplexed by North-South contests said or assumed that Maryland belonged to the Southern connection. Frequently politicians referred to difficulties between the eight Northern states and the five Southern ones. Others indicated that the North and the South were set apart by the Susquehanna River. The prevailing view was put flatly in 1787 by Charles Pinckney of South Carolina, who declared, "When I say Southern, I mean Maryland, and the states to the southward of her."

However Maryland may be classified—Southern, border, or Northern—in the nineteenth and twentieth centuries, it is appropriate to place her with the South in the Revolutionary time. It is true that central Maryland and western Maryland, even then, were countries of farms rather than plantations; of corn, wheat, and livestock instead of tobacco; of yeoman farmers rather than white masters and black slaves. But it should be remembered that only eastern Maryland, a plantation region, was then fully settled. It is also true that Maryland was slightly more commercial and a trifle more urban than Virginia. Nevertheless, in the days of the Revolution, the two states above and below the Potomac were fundamentally identical both economically and socially. Maryland at that time belonged with Virginia, and both with the South.

It was assumed soon after the close of the War of Independence that the northern limits of the South were on the Ohio as well as the Mason-Dixon line. Before the end of that conflict Virginia abandoned her claim to the Old Northwest; and Southerners generally sanctioned the Northwest Ordinance, which effectively placed the region between the Ohio, the Mississippi, and the Great Lakes outside the South. There was, however, agreement among politicians Northern and Southern, that the new settlements of Kentucky and Tennessee were Southern. As parts of Virginia and North Carolina until after the adoption of the Constitution, it could hardly be doubted at the time that they were parts of the South. Nor should we doubt it, even though we may not share the alarm then felt by leaders of New England because they saw the occupation of Kentucky and Tennessee as evidence that the South was expanding at the cost of the North. The Revolutionary South included the settlements of Boonesborough and Nashville as well as Annapolis and Savannah.

Proportionally to the remainder of the Union, the Revolutionary South was the largest South, both in size and in people. In fact, the Southern population in the first Federal census of 1790 was only a trifle smaller than that of the rest of the nation, there being then counted about 1,900,000 persons below the Mason-Dixon line, slightly more than 2,000,000 above it. At that time Virginia was by far the most populous state, and North Carolina ranked fourth, behind Massachusetts and Pennsylvania. Had not Maine been a part of Massachusetts, North Carolina would have been the third state in numbers. Moreover, there were Southerners who believed that population was increasing more rapidly in the South than elsewhere. These facts had influence upon the decision of the Southern states to ratify the Constitution, for it could be asserted with some show of reason that the South would soon surpass the remainder of the Union in numbers. It was not fully realized, perhaps, that the three-fifths provision of the Constitution respecting the slaves would place the South in a minority position in the national House of Representatives, even in the composition of the first Congress based on the census. Besides, as it turned out, the appearance of more rapid growth in the Southern population was illusory—the gap between North and South soon widened rather than diminished, as the census of 1800 indicated.

Hitherto it has been asserted rather than shown that there was a Revolutionary South. Nor will all the proof that such was the case be marshalled in detail at this point. Much of the best sort of proof, consisting of sectional quarrels, will be offered later. Nevertheless, it may be well to bring forth at this point certain fundamental reasons why the First South was crudely a unit with interests and views opposed to those of the rest of the Union.

Nature herself certainly set apart the South, giving to the South tropical summers, long growing seasons, and mild winters. Nature also gave soils and waters suitable for growing vast quantities of tobacco and rice, products which could be consumed only in small part in the South, which were much desired by foreign peoples, especially Europeans. In the Chesapeake region tobacco growing long seemed to be the best road to wealth, although it obviously was a road marred by ruts and mudholes; in the Carolina Low Country after the middle of the eighteenth century rice growing, together with the production of indigo, offered a surer and smoother highway to affluence. In consequence, the South had become before the Revolution a country of general farming and also of highly specialized farming that sent forth exports in great quantity and value. Meanwhile, the people of the Northern colony-states, with their colder climates, continued to engage in general farming, fishing, and lumbering, but turned increasingly toward internal trade, shipbuilding, sea-borne commerce, and manufacturing. Thus the economic pursuits of South and North became not only different, but often seemingly opposed. Instances enough of clashes over economic issues in the Revolutionary time will be offered later.

The special farming of the South was also the chief cause for a profound racial divergence between the sections, since the raising of tobacco and rice led to the importation into the South of large numbers of Negroes. In the Northern states, except for Delaware, at the time of the Revolution, the Negroes formed only small minorities. Below the Mason-Dixon line it was otherwise, for in the South 35 of every 100 persons were Negroes. They made up a full 30 per cent of the populations of Maryland and North Carolina, 40 per cent of that of Virginia, and more than half of that of South Carolina. The Negroes, burgeoning in numbers because of the special farming of the South, in turn helped to perpetuate such farming. The Southerners could think of few occupations for them beyond toil in tobacco rows, care of rice plants, weeding of corn, and other field tasks. Moreover, the presence of the Negro, together with the Southern economy and climate, tended to discourage white immigration, a fact which was noted by and which alarmed some astute Southern observers even before 1775, a fact which census returns afterward made evident to all who would bother to read such reports.

Economic and racial divergences between South and North brought with them serious social variation. Negro slavery was quite fixed upon the South, while it had few and weak roots above the Susquehanna. Slavery and special farming widened social cleavage among the Southern whites, giving added strength to the principle of aristocracy below the Mason-Dixon line. At the day of the Revolution there were admittedly socially superior persons in the Northern colony-states, chiefly country magnates and wealthy merchants. They were fewer and less powerful in New England than they were in the Middle states; and they were more conspicuous and more influential on the Chesapeake and in the Carolina Low Country than they were on the Hudson or the Delaware. Even North Carolina had its Tidewater aristocracy. The tobacco and rice lords often could not see eye-to-eye with the dominant middle-class men of the North. John Adams did not feel unmixed respect and liking for the "nabobs" of South Carolina whom he met in Congress after 1774; nor did the aristocratic-minded Southern delegates feel unadulterated admiration for the Yankees with whom they considered men and measures in New York and Philadelphia.

There were indeed important differences between the Northerners and the Southern whites as a whole in the Revolutionary time, as Thomas Jefferson pointed out in a letter to the Marquis de Chastellux in 1785. He said:

In the North they are cool, sober, laborious, independent, jealous of their own liberties, and just to those of others, interested, chicaning, superstitious and hypocritical in their religion. In the South they are fiery, voluptuary, indolent, unsteady, zealous for their own liberties, but trampling on those of others, generous, candid, without attachment or pretentions to any religion but that of the heart.

"These characteristics," asserted the thoughtful Virginian, became "weaker and weaker by gradation from North to South and South to North, insomuch that an observing traveller, without the aid of the quadrant may always know his latitude by the character of the people among whom he finds himself. It is in Pennsylvania that the two characters seem to meet and blend and to form a people free from the extremes both of vice and virtue." We need not accept precisely the opinion of Jefferson regarding either Northerners or Southerners, and we may also doubt that the Golden Mean existed in Pennsylvania, but there is obvious merit in his analysis. Assuredly, it is significant that he saw contrasts, even mistakenly, and that he thought them important enough to relate to his French friend.

Since colonial federation, though occasionally talked about and even planned, never was undertaken, serious clash between North and South did not appear before 1775. There were many contests between colony and colony, but none in which the one region was challenged by the other. It is true that jealousies of a sectional nature arose because some Southern colonists fancied that their Northern brethren were too hasty and too forward in asserting American rights against Britain during the decade before Lexington and Concord. Conversely, Northern defenders of American rights sometimes felt that the Southerners moved too slowly and too uncertainly. When the program of general nonimportation of British goods was rather hastily abandoned in the Northern ports after the repeal of most of the Townshend duties in 1770, just as nonimportation was being effectively put into force in South Carolina, there was genuine resentment in Charleston.[2] But here we have passing irritations rather than enduring troubles. Actually the struggles of the Americans against Britain before 1775, and the War of Independence especially, served to bring the Americans together by supplying them with a common, dangerous, and detested enemy.

Indeed, let us not forget that there were many and powerful forces pushing the Americans together in both the colonial and Revolutionary epochs. Too much may be made of economic and social antagonisms between North and South; too little heed may be given to unifying vigors. It should be recalled that almost all the Americans, save the Negroes, had a common background in the British Isles and that part of the European continent west of the Elbe River; that nearly all of them spoke English—English with perhaps fewer differences between North and South than afterward; and that they shared the benefits and evils of an English cultural and political heritage. Moreover, the Americans had felt alike the influence of similar elements in their New World environment. At the opening of the Revolutionary time they were aware of their oneness, a fact indicated by their ever-increasing use of the term American as descriptive of all the inhabitants of the Thirteen Colonies—a usage which also became dominant in

---

[2] Yankee Josiah Quincy, Jr., found in Charleston in 1773, "a general doubt of the firmness and integrity of the Northern colonies."

Britain after 1763. The beginning of the Revolutionary contest with Britain near the end of the French and Indian War added, as has been suggested, a new dynamic toward unity, Britain the foe of America as a whole. Northerners and Southerners had a common political enemy before 1775; even more important, they were faced by a common military antagonist between 1775 and 1783; after the close of the War of Independence, they continued to share fears of British and European aggressions. Those who fear the same menaces, those who fight the same foes, tend to feel that they are one.

Above all, the War of Independence aroused an American emotion. Virginians served at Boston and Quebec, Carolinians at Brandywine and Germantown, Yankees at Trenton and Yorktown. The "hard core" of the Revolutionary forces was the Continental army; and "Continental" was, or rather soon became, a synonym for "American." Few of the men who served in it could afterward be easily convinced that they fought only for their home state, or for a South, or for a North.[3] For the Continental veteran, officer and man, and doubtless almost to a man, America was his country. None were more devoted to the nation than were Virginia soldiers George Washington, Light-Horse Harry Lee, Daniel Morgan, and John Marshall. If one had suggested to a Southern veteran that he had not found Connecticut or New Jersey troops remarkably congenial, he would almost surely have responded that such was sometimes the case, but that they had been, when all was said and done, true and worthy comrades in a great cause.[4] And that cause could hardly be the creation of a string of small independent countries along the Atlantic coast; or of two or three nations; or even of one confederacy so feeble at its heart that it would be absurd to describe it as an American union.

American nationalism during the Revolutionary era should not be considered minor, nor were the forces creating and supporting it meager or temporary. The same should be said for the divisive tendencies of sectionalism. In that era nationalism was to triumph.

The contest between South and North began even before the Declaration of Independence. In the first general American assembly—in the First Continental Congress in 1774—came the first quarrel. It was, as were most of such struggles before 1789, economic in nature. When that body con-

[3] A Virginia newspaper reported in June, 1780 that "Captain Lieutenant Richard Coleman of Spotsylvania county, fell in the defense of his country on the 29th day of May . . . in South Carolina."

[4] In early acquaintance Southerners often disliked New Englanders, whose worst qualities were only too evident, whose finer ones required time to discover. Even in the long run the Yankees were more likely to inspire respect rather than fondness in the Southerner. James Fallon of South Carolina offered an early impression of them in 1779: "The inhabitants hereabouts [Fishkill, N.Y.] are all Yankees. I mean not to reflect *nationally;* but their manners are, to me, abhorrent. I long to leave and get clear of their oddities. They are, for the most part, a *damned* generation."

sidered measures to compel Parliament and Crown to change their course to American wishes, it decided to use a weapon which had become familiar, a boycott of British goods. There was no sectional disagreement regarding the use of this boycott, even though the importation of Negro slaves was also forbidden. Nor was there any difficulty between North and South because the Congress decreed nonconsumption of British goods, this measure being calculated to prevent merchants from pulling profits out of scarcities. It was otherwise when the delegates decided to use the club of nonexportation to Britain and the British West Indies, in case of need, the date for cessation being set at September 10, 1775. The delegates from South Carolina, except for Christopher Gadsden, asked that rice and indigo be excepted from the embargo, and so raised a controversy.

In this clash varying economic interests were basic. On the surface, the South Carolina men in the Congress were asking a special favor for the Low Country; from their point of view they were merely requesting equal sacrifice from all sections. Because of British law and other circumstances rice and indigo markets in England and the British West Indies were very important to South Carolina. Were exportation of those products to those markets forbidden, the Low Country planters, almost utterly dependent upon sales of rice and dye stuffs, must suffer grievously. The Northern colonies would be able to sell outside Britain and the islands, as they had in the past; and even the Chesapeake colonies, their tobacco going largely to London, Bristol, and Liverpool because of Parliamentary law, could escape the worst effects of the self-inflicted punishment of embargo by turning to wheat-growing. Even so, the attitude of the South Carolina delegation was not generous, especially with respect to their fellow planters of the Chesapeake; and Gadsden was prepared to offer a total sacrifice. When Northerners in Congress cried favoritism, the dominant Carolinians withdrew their request for excepting indigo; and for the sake of creating a solid front against Britain, the free sending of South Carolina's rice to sea was permitted. Thus the quarrel was resolved by concession on the part of the others to the Low Country planters. It has been suggested that Gadsden's colleagues should not be judged too harshly; it is worthy of mention that the news of the arrangement did not create great joy in Charleston. Early in 1775 the South Carolina Provincial Congress, considering the situation, and perhaps feeling some pangs of conscience, defeated a motion to ban rice exportation by the narrow margin of 87 to 75.

Early in the Second Continental Congress another issue threatened sectional trouble, and was settled in such fashion that nationalism won a victory of vast consequences. When that body decided to form a Continental army, it was immediately faced by a momentous question: who should be its commander in chief? It is now well known that George Washington had many merits and that these were not entirely unfamiliar in Philadelphia.

However, New Englanders were inclined to favor the appointment of a Yankee, Israel Putnam or some other hero of the lands east of the Hudson. Aware that unity would be secured by choosing a Southerner and that Washington was otherwise suitable, John and Samuel Adams consented to the appointment of the Virginia colonel. The decision did allay sectional feeling at the time.[5] Far more important, the personal fortunes of Washington became entwined with those of a national army. He felt the adverse effects of particularism and sectionalism in the war effort as could no other person. It may even be said that Washington's fame came to depend in part upon the creation of a permanent American union. Were his military achievements to lead to the making of a number of small American nations, he could hardly be the mighty figure he became. Whether the commander in chief was fully conscious that his glory was inextricably linked with that of the United States is a question of no importance. Such was the fact; and there was no more sturdy, no more steady nationalist in the South than the great Virginian at the end of the war. As he said farewell to his army, he begged that his comrades give their support to a solid union; and he was to be more responsible than any other man for putting the Constitution into force. We are all accustomed to praising the man of Mount Vernon for his military merits, and there have been those who have contended—I think, without full cause—that his services as president were even more remarkable than those he offered in his campaigns and battles. Let it not be forgotten that he was also the man above all others responsible for the general adoption of the Constitution. Many a great American of his time and later ones was to be first a nationalist and later a regionalist, or a sectionalist and then a nationalist—the names of John C. Calhoun and Daniel Webster come to mind. Not so with Washington, who stoutly and firmly fought against sectional prejudice in the Continental army, in the struggle over the Constitution, and in the presidency. Even now we perhaps do not value

---

[5] Long afterward, the Reverend Jonathan Boucher, whose acquaintance with Washington was hardly intimate, said the Southern colonists feared in 1775 that they would be dominated by a Northern army after independence had been achieved and that Washington's acceptance of the supreme command was dictated, "more than anything else," by a desire to prevent such a horrid outcome. At the time, Governor Jonathan Trumbull of Connecticut expressed a hope that the selection of Washington would "cement the union between the Northern & Southern colonies— & remove any jealousies of a N England army (if they should prove successfull) being formidable to the other provinces." In the summer of 1776 General Persifor Frazer of Pennsylvania also commented from Fort Ticonderoga upon fear of New England. "No man was ever more disappointed in his expectations respecting New Englanders than I have been. They are a set of low, dirty, griping, cowardly, lying rascals. There are some few exceptions and very few.... You may inform all your acquaintance not to be afraid that they will ever conquer the other provinces (which you know was much talked of), 10,000 Pennsylvanians would I think be sufficient for ten times that number out of their own country. All the Southern troops live in great harmony."

fully his devotion to the nation. First in war, first in peace, first in the hearts of his countrymen, he was also first in his allegiance and contribution to American unity.

Although the appointment of Washington as commander in chief was a triumph for nationalism, sectionalism also had its victories during that part of the Revolutionary War which preceded the Declaration of Independence. It will be recalled that the movement toward complete separation from Britain during the first fifteen months of the Revolutionary War was accompanied by a movement toward an American union. Thus when Richard Henry Lee of Virginia introduced in Congress on June 7, 1776, his famous resolution declaring that "These United Colonies are and of right ought to be free and independent states," he also called for the making of an American federation. By most public men in Congress and out, independence and political union were considered as virtually inseparable. Indeed, there were Patriot leaders in the spring of 1776, including Patrick Henry, who asserted that the Americans should marry each other before they declared themselves divorced from the British. These claimed that independence would be easier to achieve if union were secured before issuing a formal announcement that America had left the empire. As early as the fall of 1775 the Revolutionary legislature of North Carolina indicated its disapproval of the famous plan of confederation submitted by Benjamin Franklin because it gave New England larger representation in the federal legislature than the North Carolina men were willing to concede to it. This was much to the satisfaction of Josiah Martin, the last royal governor of North Carolina, who claimed that Franklin's arrangements would enable the North "to give law" to the South and who gleefully asserted that the North would use its power, since there was in New England a "lust of domination."

Any argument which might serve to sow dissension among the Patriots was welcomed by Josiah Martin, and also by James Anderson, another supporter of the Crown, who sought to frighten the South to the advantage of Britain. In a pamphlet published at Edinburgh in 1776 Anderson predicted that an independent American union would be disastrous for the Southerners. They would form a minority in an American legislature, and their economic interests would be injured to the benefit of those of the Northerners. Time would bring so great exasperation at the South that the Southerners would seek to form a new nation. They would not be permitted to leave the union peacefully; and, fewer in numbers and enervated by heat, they would be defeated in war. Thereafter they would live in a state of inferiority and subjection to the North. It turned out that there was basic truth coupled with error in Anderson's calculations and predictions. And his reputation as a prophet must also suffer because he foresaw what he wished to foresee, that parting from England would not bring such sweet tomorrows to the Americans.

Josiah Martin and James Anderson, not friends to American freedom, told the Southerners they should not join an American union. Other men not hostile to independence said such a union could not be formed because of the contrarieties which existed in the Thirteen. In the middle of the 1780's it was frequently suggested by Americans not seeking to return to the British empire that two or even three confederacies would rise along the Atlantic coast. One of these would be Southern, including Maryland and the states to her southward. There might be two confederations north of the Mason-Dixon line, one in New England and another composed of the Middle states; or New England and the Middle states might form one union. As late as 1788 Patrick Henry was accused, and not entirely without reason, of seeking to create a Southern confederacy. There were even Southern public men of the Revolutionary period who believed, because of the power of local loyalties, that the Thirteen States must go their separate ways. So Thomas Burke of North Carolina asserted in 1778 that an American union was a "chimerical project." So William Blount of the same state in July, 1787, declared, "I still think we shall ultimately and not many years . . . be separated and distinct governments perfectly independent of each other." To be sure, both Burke and Blount afterward changed their minds.

Because of the difficulty of assessing the conflicting forces which supported state loyalties, regional confederacies, and general union, no one could assuredly predict during the twelve years after the Declaration of Independence what political form or forms the Americans would adopt. It may be guessed that personalities, and even chance, affected the outcome, despite the conviction of George Bancroft that the course of events was personally and intimately directed by the Deity.

It could be safely predicted, however, that troubles must arise between South and North in a union with a central government possessing substantial powers. Sectional conflicts continued throughout the war. When Washington's army was undergoing its ordeal at Valley Forge in the winter of 1777–1778, Virginians and South Carolinians were voicing alarm lest Congress under the Articles of Confederation possess too great authority, to the detriment of Southern interests. That body during the years 1781–1787 was often riven by strife between South and North. Southern fears of Northern domination appeared in the Philadelphia Convention of 1787, and were frequently and forcefully asserted in the contests over ratification of the Constitution which took place below the Mason-Dixon line. Those fears were often based in part upon acute reasoning; indeed, in view of later occurrences, few will say they were without some solid foundation.

5

The Mind of the South:
Of Time and Frontiers

Wilbur J. Cash

Of those myths peculiar to the pre–Civil War South, none has proved more enduring than the belief in a historically continuous southern aristocracy. According to the romantic myth of the Old South, country gentlemen of courtliness and stately hospitality presided over southern society during the antebellum period. The late Wilbur Cash, freelance writer and former Associate Editor of the Charlotte (North Carolina) *News,* seeks to counter this image by forwarding arguments against such a legendary sociology. In pursuing the social reality of the antebellum South, Mr. Cash notes that two critical factors were perpetually at odds with the idea of an all-pervasive cavalier society—the element of time and the ever present frontier environment. In addition, the proven incidence of social mobility among earlier southerners scarcely suggests the existence of a full-blown, closed aristocracy in the making. To the degree that subtle notions of class did begin to manifest themselves in the Old South, such social distinctions were linked, as is invariably the case in most Western societies, not to lineage but rather to property ownership. The southern "aristocracy" of the Old Regime was at best one of rank rather than caste—a creation of the mind of the South.

Though . . . nobody any longer holds to the Cavalier thesis in its overt form, it remains true that the popular mind still clings to it in essence. Explicit or implicit in most considerations of the land, and despite a gathering tendency on the part of the more advanced among the professional historians, and lately even on the part of popular writers, to cast doubt on it, the assumption persists that the great South of the first half of the nineteenth century—the South which fought the Civil War—was the home of a genuine and fully realized aristocracy, coextensive and identical with the ruling class, the planters; and sharply set apart from the common people, still pretty often lumped indiscriminately together as the poor whites, not only by economic condition but also by the far vaster gulf of a different blood and a different (and long and solidly established) heritage.

To suppose this, however, is to ignore the frontier and that *sine qua non* of aristocracy everywhere—the dimension of time. And to ignore the frontier and time in setting up a conception of the social state of the Old South is to abandon reality. For the history of this South throughout a very great part of the period from the opening of the nineteenth century to the Civil War (in the South beyond the Mississippi until long after that war) is mainly the history of the roll of frontier upon frontier—and on to the frontier beyond.

Prior to the close of the Revolutionary period the great South, as such, has little history. Two hundred years had run since John Smith had saved Jamestown, but the land which was to become the cotton kingdom was still more wilderness than not. In Virginia—in the Northern Neck, all along the tidewater, spreading inland along the banks of the James, the York, the Rappahannock, flinging thinly across the redlands to the valley of the Shenandoah, echoing remotely about the dangerous water of Albemarle—in South Carolina and Georgia—along a sliver of swamp country running from Charleston to Georgetown and Savannah—and in and around Hispano-Gallic New Orleans, there was something which could be called effective settlement and societal organization.

Here, indeed, there was a genuine, if small, aristocracy. Here was all that in aftertime was to give color to the legend of the Old South. Here were silver and carriages and courtliness and manner. Here were great houses—not as great as we are sometimes told, but still great houses: the Shirleys, the Westovers, the Stratfords. Here were the names that were some time to flash with swords and grow tall in thunder—the Lees, the Stuarts, and the Beauregards. Charleston, called the most brilliant of American cities by Crèvecoeur, played a miniature London, with overtones of La Rochelle, to a small squirarchy of the rice plantations. In Virginia great earls played at Lord Bountiful, dispensing stately hospitality to every passer-by—to the barge captain on his way down the river, to the slaver who had this morning put into the inlet with a cargo of likely Fulah boys, to the wandering Yankee peddling his platitudinous wooden nutmeg, and to other great earls, who came, with their ladies, in canopied boats or in coach and six with liveried outriders. New Orleans was a pageant of dandies and coxcombs, and all the swamplands could show a social life of a considerable pretension.

It is well, however, to remember a thing or two about even these Virginians. (For brevity's sake, I shall treat only of the typical case of the Virginians, and shall hereafter generally apply the term as embracing all these little clumps of colonial aristocracy in the lowlands.) It is well to remember not only that they were not generally Cavaliers in their origin but also that they did not spring up to be aristocrats in a day. The two hundred years since Jamestown must not be forgotten. It is necessary to conceive Virginia as beginning very much as New England began—as emerging by slow stages from a primitive backwoods community, made up primarily of farmers and laborers. Undoubtedly there was a sprinkling of gentlemen of a sort—minor squires, younger sons of minor squires, or adventurers who had got themselves a crest, a fine coat, and title to huge slices of the country. And probably some considerable part of the aristocrats at the end of the Revolution are to be explained as stemming from these bright-plumed birds. It is certain that the great body of them cannot be so explained.

The odds were heavy against such gentlemen—against any gentlemen at all, for that matter. The land had to be wrested from the forest and the intractable red man. It was a harsh and bloody task, wholly unsuited to the talents which won applause in the neighborhood of Rotten Row and Covent Garden, or even in Hants or the West Riding. Leadership, for the great part, passed inevitably to rough and ready hands. While milord tarried at dice or languidly directed his even more languid workmen, his horny-palmed neighbors increasingly wrung profits from the earth, got themselves into position to extend their holdings, to send to England for redemptioners and convict servants in order to extend them still further, rose steadily toward equality with him, attained it, passed him, were presently buying up his bankrupt remains.

The very redemptioners and convict servants were apt to fare better than the gentleman. These are the people, of course, who are commonly said to explain the poor whites of the Old South, and so of our own time. It is generally held of them that they were uniformly shiftless or criminal, and that these characters, being inherent in the germ plasm, were handed on to their progeny, with the result that the whole body of them continually sank lower and lower in the social scale. The notion has the support of practically all the standard histories of the United States, as for example those of John Bach McMaster and James Ford Rhodes. But, as Professor G. W. Dyer, of Vanderbilt University, has pointed out in his monograph, *Democracy in the South before the Civil War,* it has little support in the known facts.

In the first place, there is no convincing evidence that, as a body, they came of congenitally inferior stock. If some of the convicts were thieves or cutthroats or prostitutes, then some of them were also mere political prisoners, and so, ironically, may very well have represented as good blood as there was in Virginia. Perhaps the majority were simply debtors. As for the redemptioners, the greater number of them seem to have been mere children or adolescents, lured from home by professional crimps or outright kidnapped. It is likely enough, to be sure, that most of them were still to be classed as laborers or the children of laborers; but it is an open question whether this involves any actual inferiority, and certainly it involved no practical inferiority in this frontier society.

On the contrary. Most of them were freed while still in their twenties. Every freeman was entitled to a headright of fifty acres. Unclaimed lands remained plentiful in even the earliest-settled areas until long after the importation of bound servants had died out before slavery. And to cap it all, tobacco prices rose steadily. Thus, given precisely those qualities of physical energy and dogged application which, in the absence of degeneracy, are pre-eminently the heritage of the laborer, the former redemptioner (or convict, for that matter) was very likely to do what so many other men of his same general stamp were doing all about him: steadily to build up his capital and become a man of substance and respect. There is abundant evidence that the thing did so happen. Adam Thoroughgood, who got to be the greatest planter in Norfolk, entered the colony as an indentured servant. Dozens of others who began in the same status are known to have become justices of the peace, vestrymen, and officers of the militia—positions reserved, of course, for gentlemen. And more than one established instance bears out *Moll Flanders*.

In sum, it is clear that distinctions were immensely supple, and that the test of a gentleman in seventeenth-century Virginia was what the test of a gentleman is likely to be in any rough young society—the possession of a sufficient property.

Aristocracy in any real sense did not develop until after the passage of a hundred years—until after 1700. From the foundations carefully built up by his father and grandfather, a Carter, a Page, a Shirley began to tower decisively above the ruck of farmers, pyramided his holdings in land and slaves, squeezed out his smaller neighbors and relegated them to the remote Shenandoah, abandoned his story-and-a-half house for his new "hall," sent his sons to William and Mary and afterward to the English universities or the law schools in London. These sons brought back the manners of the Georges and more developed and subtle notions of class. And the sons of these in turn began to think of themselves as true aristocrats and to be accepted as such by those about them—to set themselves consciously to the elaboration and propagation of a tradition.

But even here the matter must not be conceived too rigidly, or as having taken place very extensively. The number of those who had moved the whole way into aristocracy even by the time of the Revolution was small.

Most of the Virginians who counted themselves gentlemen were still, in reality, hardly more than superior farmers. Many great property-holders were still almost, if not quite, illiterate. Life in the greater part of the country was still more crude than not. The frontier still lent its tang to the manners of even the most advanced, all the young men who were presently to rule the Republic having been more or less shaped by it. And, as the emergence of Jeffersonian democracy from exactly this milieu testifies, rank had not generally hardened into caste.

But this Virginia was not the great South. By paradox, it was not even all of Virginia. It was a narrow world, confined to the areas where tobacco, rice, and indigo could profitably be grown on a large scale—to a relatively negligible fraction, that is, of the Southern country. All the rest, at the close of the Revolution, was still in the frontier or semi-frontier stage. Here were no baronies, no plantations, and no manors. And here was no aristocracy nor any fully established distinction save that eternal one between man and man.

In the vast backcountry of the seaboard states, there lived unchanged the pioneer breed—the unsuccessful and the restless from the older regions; the homespun Scotch-Irish, dogged out of Pennsylvania and Maryland by poverty and the love of freedom; pious Moravian brothers, as poor as they were pious; stolid Lutheran peasants from northern Germany; ragged, throat-slitting Highlanders, lusting for elbow-room and still singing hotly of Bonnie Prince Charlie; all that generally unpretentious and often hard-bitten crew which, from about 1740, had been slowly filling up the region. Houses, almost without exception, were cabins of logs. Farms were clearings, on which was grown enough corn to meet the grower's needs, and perhaps a little tobacco which once a year was "rolled" down to a landing on a navigable stream. Roads and trade hardly yet existed. Life had but ceased to be a business of Indian fighting. It was still largely a matter of coon-hunting, of "painter" tales and hard drinking.

Westward, Boone had barely yesterday blazed his trail. Kentucky and Tennessee were just opening up. And southward of the Nashville basin, the great Mississippi Valley, all that country which was to be Alabama, Mississippi, western Georgia, and northern Louisiana, was still mainly a wasteland, given over to the noble savage and peripatetic traders with an itch for adventure and a taste for squaw seraglios.

Then the Yankee, Eli Whitney, interested himself in the problem of extracting the seed from a recalcitrant fiber, and cotton was on its way to be king. The despised backcountry was coming into its own—but slowly at first. Cotton would release the plantation from the narrow confines of the coastlands and the tobacco belt, and stamp it as the reigning pattern on all the country. Cotton would end stagnation, beat back the wilderness, mow the forest, pour black men and plows and mules along the Yazoo and the

Arkansas, spin out the railroad, freight the yellow waters of the Mississippi with panting stern-wheelers—in brief, create the great South. But not in a day. It was necessary to wait until the gin could be proved a success, until experience had shown that the uplands of Carolina and Georgia were pregnant with wealth, until the rumor was abroad in the world that the blacklands of the valley constituted a new El Dorado.

It was 1800 before the advance of the plantation was really under way, and even then the pace was not too swift. The physical difficulties to be overcome were enormous. And beyond the mountains the first American was still a dismaying problem. It was necessary to wait until Andrew Jackson and the men of Tennessee could finally crush him. 1810 came and went, the battle of New Orleans was fought and won, and it was actually 1820 before the plantation was fully on the march, striding over the hills of Carolina to Mississippi—1820 before the tide of immigration was in full sweep about the base of the Appalachians.

From 1820 to 1860 is but forty years—a little more than the span of a single generation. The whole period from the invention of the cotton gin to the outbreak of the Civil War is less than seventy years—the lifetime of a single man. Yet it was wholly within the longer of these periods, and mainly within the shorter, that the development and growth of the great South took place. Men who, as children, had heard the war-whoop of the Cherokee in the Carolina backwoods lived to hear the guns at Vicksburg. And thousands of other men who had looked upon Alabama when it was still a wilderness and upon Mississippi when it was still a stubborn jungle, lived to fight—and to fight well, too—in the ranks of the Confederate armies.

The inference is plain. It is impossible to conceive the great South as being, on the whole, more than a few steps removed from the frontier stage at the beginning of the Civil War. It is imperative, indeed, to conceive it as having remained more or less fully in the frontier stage for a great part—maybe the greater part—of its antebellum history. However rapidly the plantation might advance, however much the slave might smooth the way, it is obvious that the mere physical process of subduing the vast territory which was involved, the essential frontier process of wresting a stable foothold from a hostile environment, must have consumed most of the years down to 1840.

6

Democracy in the Old South

Fletcher M. Green

The view is held by many that the Old South was different. The Mason-Dixon Line is purported to have separated a northern from a southern "way of life," and as a corollary the South is supposed to have achieved a model social order. In the words of the native southerner Thomas Nelson Page, the antebellum South was a magic blend, "the joint product of chivalry and Christianity." Thus a pervasive and prevailing myth concerning the Old South is its alleged aristocratic and even semi-feudal character. This image of antebellum southern society has been strategically reinforced by such disparate groups as abolitionists, southern apologists, Hollywood (*Gone With the Wind*), and historians themselves. Fletcher M. Green, one of the elder statesmen among historians of the South and Kenan Professor of History at the University of North Carolina, here challenges this encrusted stereotype. According to Green, the South before the Civil War was not in any full sense an economic and social democracy; in this respect it scarcely differed from the North. He finds that the South of the Old Regime did, however, manifest important inclinations toward *political democracy*. In the end, the South was not simply the land of aristocratic privilege and *noblesse oblige*. A conspiratorial cadre of "planter aristocrats" did not control southern politics. Rather, the South was as much committed to democratic principles and practice as the country at large.

Fletcher M. Green, "Democracy in the Old South," *Journal of Southern History*, 12 (February 1946), 3–23. Copyright 1946 by the Southern Historical Association. Reprinted by permission of the Managing Editor.

The American dream of democracy and equality, based upon the philosophy of natural rights and popular sovereignty, found full, free, and adequate expression in such Revolutionary documents as the Declaration of Independence and the bills of rights of the state constitutions.[1] "We hold these truths to be self-evident, that all men are created equal, that they are endowed by their Creator with certain unalienable Rights, that among these are Life, Liberty and the pursuit of Happiness." "All power is vested in, and consequently derived from, the people; ... magistrates are their trustees and servants, and at all times amenable to them." "No man, or set of men, are entitled to exclusive or separate emoluments or privileges from the community but in consideration of publick services." These and similar expressions of democratic equalitarianism were familiar to the people in all the states of the American Union.

The mere declaration of these ideals did not insure their acceptance and enforcement; a vigorous and continuous defense of liberty is essential if it is to be preserved. Thomas Jefferson, spokesman for democracy, early observed that men were by their constitutions naturally divided into two classes: (1) those who fear and distrust the people and seek to draw all power into their own hands; and (2) those who have confidence in the people and consider the people the safest depository of public happiness and general well being. These two classes he called aristocrats and democrats. From the very beginning of American independence these two groups began a contest for control of the governments. This contest between the forces of aristocracy and democracy was one of the most important issues in the political development of the American nation during the first half century of its existence. In the northern states it was fought between the commercial-financial aristocracy and the working men, in the southern states between the aristocratic slaveholding planters and the yeoman farmers.

The first state constitutions were framed in an atmosphere of equality and the recognition of human rights, without hint of race or class distinctions, but they established property and freehold qualifications for voting and office holding, and a system of representation, that gave control of the state governments to the wealthy, conservative, aristocratic classes. The power and influence of the aristocracy were further enhanced by the victory of the conservative group that established the Federal Constitution. The Jeffersonian democrats, accepting, in theory at least, the doctrines of natural rights, popular sovereignty, government by compact and contract, and the perfectability of mankind, began a militant assault upon the strongholds of aristocracy. They demanded and obtained a bill of rights to the Federal Constitution, and an extended suffrage and a greater equality of representa-

[1] [Omitted.]

tion in the state governments. Under their attacks the powers of aristocracy were gradually whittled away. Finally, with the accession of Andrew Jackson to the presidency in 1829, it seemed that democracy would certainly triumph. Most American people agreed with Alexis de Tocqueville that the democratic revolution was an irresistible one, and that to attempt to check it "would be to resist the will of God."[2]

As democratic reform moved into high gear under Jackson its forces were divided by the emergence of the bitter sectional controversy over slavery. The northern abolitionists saw in the institution of slavery the absolute negation of liberty and equality and they began to weigh and to find wanting almost every feature of southern society. In particular they condemned the southern state governments, declaring that in them political democracy was being overthrown by a slaveholding aristocracy. This change, said they, was the result not of caprice or political accident but of deliberate design on the part of the aristocracy; and it was succeeding because *"the non-slave-holding people of the South lacked the enterprise, intelligence and daring to demand and extract their democratic rights."*[3] In other words, they held that the masses of free whites were incapable of understanding or maintaining their rights, and that the planter aristocracy was bitterly hostile to free institutions and the democratic theory of government universally.

By the time the sectional controversy reached the breaking point, the abolitionists had decided that the slaveholders had become a *"Dominant class,* having positive control of the . . . political power of those States. . . . the system of slavery concentrating, as it does all political influence in a few men who are virtually absolute in their respective States."[4] Contrasting the two sections, Richard Hildreth, the historian, declared: "The Northern States of the Union are unquestionable Democracies, and every day they are verging nearer and nearer towards the simple idea and theoretic perfection of that form of government. The Southern States of the Union, though certain democratic principles are to be found in their constitutions and their laws, are in no modern sense of the word entitled to the appellation of Democracies: They are Aristocracies; and aristocracies of the sternest and most odious kind."[5]

This interpretation of southern society and government was based upon

[2] Alexis de Tocqueville, *Democracy in America,* Translated by Henry Reeve, 2 vols. (Fourth edition, New York, 1845), I, 1–2, 5.

[3] Thomas S. Goodwin, *The Natural History of Secession; or, Despotism and Democracy at Necessary, Eternal, Exterminating War* (New York, 1865), 40–41.

[4] Elhanon W. Reynolds, *The True Story of the Barons of the South; or, The Rationale of the American Conflict* (Boston, 1862), 34–35.

[5] Richard Hildreth, *Despotism in America: An Inquiry into the Nature, Results, and Legal Basis of the Slave-Holding System of the United States* (Boston, 1854), 8.

moral hatred of Negro slavery, rather than a true knowledge of southern state governments or a philosophical or realistic understanding of democracy. Its appeal to the excited and hostile North was so powerful that most people accepted it as unquestionably accurate; and the general historians of the United States incorporated it into their writings. For instance, James Ford Rhodes says in his *History of the United States from the Compromise of 1850* that the "slaveholders, and the members of that society which clustered round them, took the offices. . . . The political system of the South was an oligarchy under the republican form." And Lord Acton, the British historian and publicist, wrote that "Secession was an aristocratic rebellion against a democratic government."[6]

The abolitionist promoters of the theory of the aristocratic nature of southern governments never attempted to define just what they meant by either aristocracy or democracy. Indeed democracy has always been difficult of definition. It is a relative term, and has had various meanings among different peoples and for the same people at different stages of their political development. In this paper it will be used in its general sense as a form of government in which the sovereign power is held by the people and exercised through a system of representation in which the representatives are chosen by a fairly large electorate. The electorate has not been a fixed one in the United States. In the early days of the American republic the suffrage was bestowed upon adult male property owners; in the second quarter of the nineteenth century it was extended to all adult white males; during Reconstruction the Negro was given the ballot; and in 1920 women were permitted to vote in all elections. Recently, Georgia has given the ballot to youths eighteen years of age. No one would say that the state governments were undemocratic in 1850 simply because women did not vote; but they were *more* democratic in 1920 because women did vote. The same may be said in regard to Negro suffrage. Furthermore, up to the Civil War the emphasis on democracy was placed on *political* equality; since that time greater emphasis has been placed on social and economic equality. Modern thought presupposes that institutions, in order to be understood, must be seen in relation to the conditions of time, place, and thought in which they appear. It is difficult to look at democracy in this way, for one is prone to judge democracy of the past by the criteria of today. Yet the degree of democracy prevailing under the constitutions and governments of the Old South must be judged by the democracy of that era, not of the present. George Sidney Camp was but speaking for his generation when he wrote in 1840 that democracy "is not of an agrarian character or spirit. Its immediate object is an equal division of political rights, not of property. . . . But

[6] See also, Hermann E. von Holst, *The Constitutional and Political History of the United States,* 8 vols. (Chicago, 1876–1892), I, 348–49.

republicanism does aim a death blow at all those laws and usages the object of which is . . . to give it a particular and exclusive direction as a means of political power."[7]

As noted above, the Revolutionary state constitutions utilized to a large degree the framework of colonial governments and constitutional practices of the colonial period which had recognized and established a governing class of the wealthy aristocracy. Only eight of the thirteen states made any change in suffrage requirements; and these changes did not abolish the principle that only property holders should vote, they merely reduced the amount of property required. Property and freehold qualifications for voting and office holding meant that the governing class in the southern states was in large measure a planter aristocracy. The system of representation also favored the planter group of the eastern section. Though democratic in form, these constitutions were certainly not democratic in fact. They did, however, lay the basis for the expansion of popular control, the chief element in a political democracy, to the majority of the people.

Hardly had the landed aristocracy established themselves in power when demands for revision and readjustment were heard in each of the states. Among the specific reforms called for were the disestablishment of the church and the abolition of religious qualifications for office holding; the abolition of the laws of entail and primogeniture; the broadening of the suffrage; the equalization of representation; and the reduction of property qualifications for office holding. All looked toward the curbing of the powers of the landed aristocracy. Piecemeal amendment and revision of the constitutions partially satisfied these demands.

In South Carolina the dissenting Presbyterians and Congregationalists, led by William Tennent, a Presbyterian minister, and Christopher Gadsden, prepared a memorial which was signed by thousands of people and presented a petition to the legislature in 1777 asking "free and equal privileges, both religious and civil" for all Protestants. Another group of reformers joined forces with the dissenters and demanded an elective upper house of the legislature rather than the appointive council. These changes were too democratic for the conservative and aristocratic element; but when the next elections showed a majority of the people favorable to the reform, and after the popular party had blocked an appropriation bill, the conservatives yielded. Even then Edward Rutledge and Arthur Middleton resigned the governorship rather than approve the changes. Maryland, too, modified her constitution in favor of Quakers, Mennonists, and other minor religious groups. Jefferson, Madison, and Richard Henry Lee succeeded in securing

[7] George Sidney Camp, *Democracy* (New York, 1841), 155. Harper and Brothers were so anxious to spread the influence of this first general analysis of the principles of democracy by a native American that they brought it out in their Family Library.

the disestablishment of the Episcopal Church in Virginia by legislative enactment.

South Carolina amended her constitution and joined Georgia and North Carolina in prohibiting entails and primogeniture. While no change was made in the Virginia constitution, the democratic element led by Jefferson forced measures through the legislature in 1786 abolishing entails and primogeniture. Jefferson believed that this legislation formed part of a system by which "every fibre would be eradicated of ancient or future aristocracy and a foundation laid for a government truly republican." The Virginia aristocracy never forgave him for this action.

The aristocracy made some slight concessions to the democrats in regard to suffrage and representation. South Carolina reduced the property requirements for voting from one hundred to fifty acres of land, and Georgia reduced it from ten pounds to the payment of all taxes levied by the state. Both states reduced considerably the property qualifications for office holding. And the up-country counties, inhabited largely by small farmers, were given a more nearly equal share of representation in the state legislatures. All efforts at change in these particulars failed in Maryland, Virginia, and North Carolina. In spite of the concessions granted, the conservative aristocracy was still in control of all five of the original southern states at the close of the eighteenth century.

The constitutions of the two new southern states added to the Union during this period of readjustment, Kentucky and Tennessee, show some influence of the frontier ideals of democracy. Kentucky gave the suffrage in 1792 to all free adult male citizens, but limited it to free white males in 1799. Representation was apportioned to free adult male inhabitants in 1792, and to qualified electors in 1799. No property or religious qualifications for office were prescribed, and the governor, after 1799, was to be elected by popular vote rather than indirectly by an electoral college as in 1792. Tennessee showed somewhat more aristocratic leanings in her constitution of 1796. Suffrage was limited to freemen possessed of a freehold; legislators and the governor were required to possess freeholds of two hundred and five hundred acres of land, respectively; representation was apportioned to the counties according to taxable inhabitants; and no person who denied the existence of God was eligible for any civil office. Though somewhat more democratic than the seaboard states, Tennessee nevertheless belongs with the group of older states controlled by the landed aristocracy. It should be pointed out, however, that in all these states there was much cheap land to be had; hence, it was no great burden to qualify for voting in any of these states.

The political revolution of 1800 which brought Jefferson and his party to power in most of the southern states, as well as in the federal government, led to the demand that the principles of the bills of rights be translated into realistic democracy rather than to stand as mere glittering generalities. In every state, democratic leaders condemned the discrimination made between those who had property and those who had none. They declared that where property had representation the people could not be free; and they were able to show that under the existing system of representation a minority of wealthy men of the east had absolute control of the state governments. They appealed to the philosophy of natural rights and demanded equality of political rights and privileges. This movement came largely from the small farmer or yeoman class concentrated in the newer counties of the up-country or the western parts of the states; hence it took on something of the nature of an intrastate sectional fight. It naturally involved social and economic issues as well as political rights.

The rapid settlement of the piedmont and mountain region of these states in the first quarter of the nineteenth century gave to the up-country a majority of the white population. These small farmers had somewhat different interests from the low-country planters. They desired internal improvements—roads, canals, and railroads—at state expense, in order that they might have an economic outlet for their farm produce, cattle, and domestic manufactures. A supporter of reform predicted that if the westerners were given their way roads and canals would be built, domestic manufactures would increase, wealth would multiply, and that the "Old Families . . . imbecile and incorrigible," would be replaced by a "happy, bold and intelligent middle class."[8] But the legislatures were controlled by the planter aristocracy of the east, who feared heavier taxation if the western farmers were given equal representation and resisted all change.

The yeoman farmers were joined by a small class of industrial laborers of the eastern cities. These people were smarting under the provisions of the constitutions that required a freehold for voting just as the yeoman farmers were smarting under the unequal system of representation. The laborers demanded manhood suffrage. The aristocratic planters feared to grant their demands lest the laborers join the small farmers in taxing the wealth of the east.

The democratic reformers demanded conventions fresh from the people with power to rewrite completely the constitutions. But since most of the constitutions left it to the legislature or made no provision for calling a constituent assembly, and since the aristocracy with their control over the legislatures could prevent a call through that body, the democrats were blocked at the very threshold of reform. The aristocratic minority fought doggedly to maintain its favored position, contesting every move of the democrats, and yielding only in the face of an open revolt. In Maryland they permitted a series of amendments between 1805 and 1810 that brought reorganiza-

---

[8] *Niles' Register* (Baltimore, 1811–1849), XXXVII (1829), 145.

tion of the judicial system so as to bring justice closer to the people and make the courts more expeditious and less expensive. Property qualifications for officers were swept away; the suffrage was extended to adult white males, the written ballot was required, and the plural vote was abolished; and some minor officials were made elective. In South Carolina representation was reapportioned in the house on the basis of white inhabitants and taxes combined. By this method the large slaveholding districts and parishes lost some of their representatives as allotted under the earlier constitutions. Suffrage was extended to include all white adult males who had resided in the state two years and were possessed of a freehold of fifty acres or a town lot, or who, if possessed of neither, had lived six months in the election district. This in reality meant white manhood suffrage. A series of amendments in Georgia between 1808 and 1824 made all officers from constable to governor, including judges of all the courts, elective by popular vote. These changes looked toward a greater participation in governmental affairs by the people and made the governments more responsive to the public will but, except in South Carolina, they did not appease the democratic reform spirit. The conservatives had prevented any change in North Carolina and Virginia.

Four new southern states, Louisiana, Mississippi, Alabama, and Missouri, were admitted to the Union during these years. Louisiana, admitted in 1812, fell to the control of the landed aristocracy. Only free white males were permitted to vote, and they were required to pay a state tax before qualifying. Members of the legislature and the governor were required to possess freeholds ranging in value from five hundred to five thousand dollars. Representation was apportioned according to qualified voters, or property holders. The governor and other officers were chosen by popular vote. Mississippi, too, was controlled by property holders. All officers were elected by popular vote; voting was limited to free white males who were enrolled in the militia or paid a tax; representation was based on white population; but members of the legislature and the governor were required to possess land ranging from fifty to six hundred acres, or real estate ranging in value from five hundred to two thousand dollars. Alabama greatly broadened the base of political power. Suffrage was granted to all adult white male citizens; no property qualifications were required for state officials who were elected by popular vote; and representation was according to white inhabitants. Both Mississippi and Alabama declared that freemen only were possessed of equal rights. Missouri required no property qualifications for voting or office holding, though members of the legislature must pay taxes. Only whites could vote, and representation was based on free white male inhabitants.

Thwarted by the aristocratic minority in calling legitimate conventions, the democratic majority in the old states now threatened to take the matter in their own hands and call extra-legal conventions. Mass meetings were held in Georgia, North Carolina, Virginia, and Maryland; polls were conducted in various counties, all of which voted overwhelmingly for calling conventions; grand jury presentments called attention to the need for reform and recommended direct action if the legislatures failed to act; the voters in many counties instructed their representatives in the legislature to support a bill calling a constitutional convention; and hundreds of petitions went to the legislatures demanding relief. Typical of the sentiment for calling extra-legal conventions is the statement of a North Carolinian that if the legislature failed "to comply with the wishes of a great majority of the State," then "A convention will be assembled in the west, and the constitution amended without the concurrence of the east; and this being the act of a majority, and the legal act, will consequently be obligatory on the whole State. The constitution *will be amended.*"[9]

A statewide reform convention assembled at Milledgeville, Georgia, on May 10, 1832, and issued a call for an election of delegates to a convention to meet at the capital in February, 1833, to alter, revise, or amend the constitution, or write a new one. It issued an address to the people in which it declared "that the people have an undoubted right, in their sovereign capacity, to alter or change their form of government, whenever in their opinion it becomes too obnoxious or oppressive to be borne. That crisis . . . has arrived, when the people should assert their rights, and boldly and fearlessly maintain them."[10] The legislature now capitulated and called a convention to meet at the same time and place as that called extra-legally. Comparable action took place in Maryland in 1836, but the legislature passed a series of amendments similar to those proposed by the reform convention and forestalled extra-legal action. In like manner the legislatures of Virginia and North Carolina capitulated to the reform party, and submitted the question of a "Convention or No Convention" to the voters. In both states the call was adopted by large majorities. Mississippi and Tennessee, too, at the demand of the people, called conventions to revise their constitutions. This was one of the most signal victories for majority or popular rule in American history. In these states the people without political voice had, by threat of appeal to numerical majority action, forced the landed aristocracy who possessed the legitimate and constitutional political power to submit the fundamental law to the scrutiny and revision of delegates elected from the people for that purpose alone.

Democracy had won a victory over aristocracy. The people had compelled the wealthy planter class in control of the legislatures to call conventions to revise the fundamental law of the states. Majority rule had

[9] Salisbury *Western Carolinian,* July 17, 1821.
[10] Milledgeville *Southern Recorder,* May 31, 1832.

exerted its power and justified its right. One democratic spokesman declared that the freemen had united their forces "to break to pieces the trammels of aristocracy, and show to the enemies of republican equality that the sons of freemen will still be free."[11]

John C. Calhoun, Abel P. Upshur,[12] and other aristocratic leaders of the South openly denied the Jeffersonian ideal of equality of all men and bitterly condemned majority rule as the tyranny of king numbers; and they had their supporters in the North among such men as James Kent, Joseph Story, and Orestes A. Brownson.[13] The less famous and little known leaders of democracy just as boldly proclaimed the doctrine of political equality. The views of the former have been given much attention by the historian; those of the latter have been generally ignored. The significant thing about the controversy, however, is that the views of the latter prevailed. The bills of rights remained unchanged and the majority forced the aristocracy to grant all white men an equal voice in the state governments. Charles James Faulkner, spokesman for the Virginia democracy in 1850, said that nothing short of a radical and fundamental change in the structure of the state constitution "could satisfy the progressive aspirations of a people who felt that their energies were held in subjugation by artificial restraints of republican freedom and equality." And, after the Virginia convention of 1850 had adjourned, he declared: "Its results was one of the proudest triumphs of popular government which the records of history attest. A revolution as decided in its results as any of those which for the last century have deluged the monarchies of Europe with blood, passed off under the influence of the acknowledged principles of popular supremacy as quietly and tranquilly as the most ordinary county election."[14]

The reform movement begun about 1800 now bore fruit in numerous constitutional conventions,[15] and these conventions rewrote the state constitutions in line with the ideals of Jacksonian democracy. Many writers have attributed the democratic reforms of the 1830's to the influence of the

[11] Salisbury *Western Carolinian,* October 22, 1822.

[12] *Proceedings and Debates of the Convention of Virginia* (Richmond, 1830), 68–71, and *passim.*

[13] For Brownson's opposition to majority rule, see his "Democracy and Liberty," in *United States Magazine and Democratic Review* (Washington, 1837–1859), XII (1843), 374–87, and his "Unpopular Government," *ibid.,* XII, 529–37.

[14] *United States Magazine and Democratic Review,* XLI (1858), 227–28.

[15] Conventions were held in Virginia in 1829–1830, Mississippi in 1832, Georgia in 1833 and 1839, Tennessee in 1834, North Carolina in 1835, and an abortive or revolutionary one in Maryland in 1836. There is a close parallel in the action of the northern states. Beginning with Connecticut in 1818, Massachusetts, New York, Delaware, Vermont, and Pennsylvania, all held general constitutional conventions by the end of the 1830's; and in Rhode Island there was an unconstitutional convention in 1842 that went beyond the extra-legal action in the southern states.

western frontier. A study of the movement in the southern states gives an emphatic denial to this assumption. The people of the southern states were cognizant of what was going on in the West, but the demands for reform grew out of local conditions and would have arisen had there been no "New West" beyond the Appalachians. In fact, it would be more nearly accurate to say that many of the ideas and motives of Jacksonian democracy were southern in origin.

To what extent was aristocracy weakened and democracy strengthened by the work of the conventions of the 1830's? In the first place, property qualifications for voting were abolished in all southern states except Virginia and North Carolina, and with Louisiana still requiring the payment of taxes.[16] The last of the religious restrictions were also abolished. In a similar manner property qualifications for office holding were wiped out except for South Carolina and Louisiana, and age and residence requirements were reduced. A large number of officers heretofore selected by the legislature or appointed by the governor were now elected by popular vote. These include civil and militia officers, justices of the peace, superior court judges, and governors in all the states except Virginia and South Carolina. Rotation in office was generally applied through short terms and restricted re-eligibility. Progress was also made in the equalization of representation. There was no uniformity in the states, however. Some used white population, some qualified voters, some federal population returns, and some a combination of population and taxation. Those states that had heretofore granted special borough representation abolished it.

In still another way these changes broadened the base of democracy. For the first time the people had been consulted as to the revision and amendment of their constitutions. The conventions were called directly or indirectly by action of the people. The revised constitutions were in turn submitted back to them for ratification or rejection. In at least one state the people twice rejected the changes, and forced the desired reforms through by legislative amendments. And the new constitutions provided for future amendment and revision.

In one matter there was a definite reactionary movement. This was the issue of free Negro suffrage. Virginia and North Carolina joined Maryland and Kentucky in taking from the free Negro the ballot he had heretofore possessed. In like manner all new states of the period, North as well as South, denied suffrage to free Negroes. The action of the old southern states was paralleled by that of the northern states. Delaware, Connecticut, New Jersey, and Pennsylvania took the ballot from the Negro. And New York

---

[16] Among northern states, New Jersey and Rhode Island retained property qualifications, and Connecticut, Massachusetts, Pennsylvania, and Ohio retained the tax paying requirement.

in 1821 limited Negro suffrage by requiring that he possess a freehold valued at two hundred fifty dollars over and above all indebtedness. Hence only five of the northern states granted equal suffrage to Negroes. Whether or not Jefferson, Mason, and other Revolutionary proponents of natural rights philosophy intended to include Negroes in the statement that "all men are created equal and endowed with certain unalienable rights" is a debatable question;[17] but in actual practice the American people had decided by their constitutional provisions that Negroes were not included in the *political people*. From the very day of the Declaration of Independence the race problem had caused the American people to make an exception to the doctrine that "all men are created equal." But the partial exclusion of the Negro from the promises of democracy did not impair the faith of the whites in those promises.

The influence of the democratic reforms of the Jacksonian period were far-reaching. Evidence of this is to be seen in many phases of southern life —social, intellectual, economic, and political. But the people were not satisfied with their partial victory, and the signs of progress only made them more determined to complete the democratization of their state governments. Their increased political power made the task of securing additional amendments and revision of their constitutions easier than had been that of calling the conventions of the 1830's. In the first case, they had threatened extra-legal action; in the second, they simply used the powers already possessed to put through additional reforms. This time they determined to take from the aristocratic class its last remnants of special political privileges. Important amendments in Georgia, Missouri, and North Carolina, and revision by convention in Louisiana, Kentucky, Maryland, and Virginia,[18] brought those states in line with the most democratic ones. Virginia in 1851 was the last state to provide for popular election of governor; and North Carolina in 1856 abolished the fifty-acre freehold required to vote for members of the state senate. The three new states, Arkansas, Florida, and Texas, all established complete equality of the whites in political affairs, and made all officials elective by popular vote. *The United States Magazine and Democratic Review,* analyzing the progress of constitutional reform in the nation, declared that the constitution of Louisiana showed "more political insight, and a more absolute reliance upon the principle upon which popular governments are based, than appears in the fundamental law of any other state in the Union." But the Missouri constitution "affords more

---

[17] Samuel E. Morison and Henry S. Commager, *The Growth of the American Republic,* 2 vols. (New York, 1937), I, 82, state that "Jefferson did not mean to include slaves as men."

[18] Louisiana in 1844 and 1852, Kentucky in 1849, and Maryland and Virginia in 1850.

efficient guarantees to individual rights, and leaves fewer opportunities for political corruption and for intercepting the fair expression of the wishes of the people" than that of any other state.

These changes left South Carolina the one remaining stronghold of the landed aristocracy in the South. While she had granted manhood suffrage in 1810, she continued to require her governor to possess a freehold until after the Civil War; the governor and presidential electors were chosen by the legislature; and representation was apportioned on a combination of white population and taxation. But among the northern states, Massachusetts continued to apportion representation in her senate on property until 1853; and Rhode Island continued to require voters and office holders to possess real estate valued at one hundred thirty-four dollars over and above all incumbrances, or with a rental value of seven dollars, until 1888.

The establishment of white manhood suffrage, the abolition of property qualifications for office holders, the election of all officers by popular vote, and the apportionment of representation on population rather than wealth, with periodic reapportionment, dealt a death blow to the political power of the landed, slaveholding aristocracy of the Old South. No longer could the members of that class dictate to the great majority of free white men. The aristocracy still had influence, as the wealthy merchant and industrialist of the northern states had influence, and as men of property in all times and places have influence, but they did not possess that influence because of special political privileges. Some southern planters possessed baronial wealth but this wealth no longer gave them political control. They constituted a social not a political aristocracy. "Such an aristocracy, although it may confer personal independence, cannot create political authority."[19]

If the landed aristocrat wished to sit in the seat of power and administer the affairs of state he must seek the support of the voter, his master. He must recognize every voter, however poor, as his political equal. And in the political hustings landlord and squatter, wealthy planter and poor white, did mingle as equals.[20]

The political revolution also meant that large numbers of the small farmer and yeoman classes began to enter politics, and win seats in legislature, Congress, and the governor's office. The first governor chosen by popular vote in Virginia, in 1851, was Joseph Johnson, whose childhood had been spent in abject poverty without the opportunity for formal schooling.

[19] Frederick Grimke, *Considerations upon the Nature and Tendency of Free Institutions* (Cincinnati, 1848), 311, 314; Camp, *Democracy*, 220–21.

[20] For descriptions of the equality of all classes at the polls, see Hamilton W. Pierson, *In the Bush; or, Old-Time Social, Political, and Religious Life in the Southwest* (New York, 1881), 131–46, and Lester B. Shippee (ed.), *Bishop Whipple's Southern Diary, 1843–1844* (Minneapolis, 1937), 22–23, 52.

Despite these handicaps he had served in the legislature and Congress, beating some of the most wealthy men of his district.[21] Indeed six of the eight men who served Virginia as governor in the years just prior to the Civil War came from the plain people; two began life as farm hands, one as a tailor, one as a mill hand, and another as a mail contractor. Henry County, Virginia, had the second highest percentage of large slaveholders in the state, yet only two justices of the peace, chosen between 1853 and 1858, possessed as many as ten slaves, while seven owned none and five owned only two each.[22]

Few studies of southern leadership have been made, but preliminary investigations suggest that a majority of the political leaders of the Old South between 1830 and 1860 came from the plain people rather than from the large planter class. Many such men received aid from wealthy planters to secure their education, as did George McDuffie and Alexander H. Stephens. The literary societies at the University of North Carolina paid all expenses of one "penniless student" each year. Several of these students rose to high rank in the state, one becoming a United States senator.[23] Dozens of the men who rank at the very top in political leadership began as poor boys, and became planters and men of wealth by their own efforts. Let one of these men tell his own story. "When I was a boy—a very little boy—an honest but poor man settled (squatted is a better word) in a country where I yet reside. . . . Day by day he might have been seen following his plough, while his two sons plied the hoe. . . . The younger [of the sons] studies law and . . . was drawn into politics. He was elected to the State Legislature, to Congress, Judge of the Circuit Court, Governor of his State, to Congress again and again, but he never forgot that he was a squatter's son. He stands before you today."[24] Like Albert Gallatin Brown, many of the leaders of the Old South grew up on the frontier where free men could not and did not recognize any political superior. In fact much of the South was only one generation removed from frontier society in 1860. Aristocracy takes more time to establish itself than one generation.

One test of the effectiveness of democracy is the exercise of the suffrage by those qualified to vote. The southern states met this test to about the same degree that the northern states did. There was considerable variation from state to state in both the North and the South, but the percentage of votes cast, according to the voting population, in the southern states ex-

[21] "Joseph Johnson," in *Southern Historical Magazine* (Charleston, W. Va., 1892), I (1892), 185–87.

[22] Gustavus W. Dyer, *Democracy in the South before the Civil War* (Nashville, 1905), 80–82.

[23] Kemp P. Battle, *Memories of an Old Time Tar Heel* (Chapel Hill, 1945), 93.

[24] Albert Gallatin Brown, *Speech of . . . in the House of Representatives* (Washington, 1852).

ceeded that of the North as often, and to about the same degree, as it failed to reach it. For instance, in the presidential election of 1828, Georgia with a white population of 296,806 cast 18,790 votes and Connecticut with a white population of 289,603 cast 18,277 votes; Alabama, however, with a white population of 190,406 cast 19,076 votes. Thus the vote of Georgia and Connecticut was 6.3 per cent of the voting people, but that of Alabama was 10.1 per cent. In the same election, Massachusetts with 603,351 free people cast 35,855 votes; Virginia with 694,300 whites cast 38,853 votes; but Tennessee with only 535,746 whites cast 46,330 votes. The percentages of these states were 5.9, 5.5, and 8.2, respectively. In the presidential election of 1860, Georgia with a white population of 595,088 cast 106,365 votes; Connecticut with 406,147 white people cast 77,146 votes; and Alabama with 529,121 whites cast 90,307 votes. The percentages for the three states were 18.0, 16.7, and 17.0, respectively. In this election, Massachusetts had 1,231,066 free people and cast 169,175 votes; Virginia had 1,105,453 whites and cast 167,223 votes; and Tennessee with 834,082 whites cast 145,333 votes. The percentages were 13.7, 15.1, and 17.4, respectively. A comparison of all the southern with all the northern states shows a white population of 7,614,018 casting 1,260,509 votes and 18,736,849 people casting 3,369,134 votes, or a percentage of 16.6 for the South and 17.9 for the North. The western states gave the North the advantage in the over-all comparison. But if one uses adult white male population, which is more accurate for voting percentages, then the South had a percentage of 69.5 and the North of 69.7.[25]

The vote of the southern states was almost equally divided between the Whig and the Democratic parties in the presidential elections from 1836 to 1852 inclusive. In the five elections the total popular vote of the Whig candidates was 1,745,884, that of the Democratic candidates was 1,760,452, or a majority for the Democrats of only 14,568. The Whigs had a majority in three elections, but in 1836 it was only 1,862 votes and its biggest majority was in 1840 with 52,851. The Democratic majority in 1844 was only 23,766, and in 1852, when the Whigs were weakened by the Compromise issue, it was 79,690. There was a total of twenty-seven states in the Whig column and thirty-seven in the Democratic column for the five elections, but except for the election of 1852 there was no overwhelming majority for either party; and in 1848 the parties divided the states equally. Such an equal division of party strength prevented any one group from dominating

[25] White population is used as a basis for all these calculations except that free population is used for the six states that permitted Negroes to vote. South Carolina is excluded, since the presidential electors of that state were chosen by the legislature. Population figures are taken from the United States Census reports; the votes from Thomas H. McKee. *The National Conventions and Platforms of All Political Parties, 1789–1900; Convention, Popular, and Electoral Vote* (Baltimore, 1900).

the political situation in the South. The states were shifting back and forth between the two parties so rapidly that no one could hope to retain power long enough to consolidate party, much less planter class, control. This situation also enabled the southern states to exert popular control over the United States senators who were elected by the state legislatures. With party changes in the states the senators were often instructed by the legislature how to vote on major issues in Congress. While the purpose of instruction was partisan it nevertheless resulted in the senators being made responsible to the majority will as expressed in state elections for many senators voted according to instructions and others resigned rather than do so.

With the coming of manhood suffrage came the demand for popular education so that the voter might cast a more intelligent ballot. It was recognized that democracy and republicanism could work effectively only with an educated electorate. Since "The chief object of constitutions and laws" is "to render its citizens secure in their lives, liberty and prosperity," the importance of "a good education to each individual, to every community, and to the State, cannot be too highly valued," declared a report of the Louisiana constitutional convention of 1844.[26] Popular education, wrote James M. Garnett of Virginia, "is of most importance in all governments. But it is indispensable in ours where all political power emanates immediately from the people, who must be themselves both intelligent and virtuous, or it will rarely happen that their public functionaries will be any better than themselves."[27] Even the aristocratic element recognized the principle that they must now educate their masters, although many did not wish to support education by taxation. One of them declared "that in adopting universal suffrage, we took necessarily the consequences that would flow from it were any portion of the people ignorant and debased. ... Without you enlighten the sources of political power, we shall have no government. ... You have adopted the principle of universal suffrage, but the basis is public education."[28]

Recognizing the need every southern state, with the exception of South Carolina where a system of poor schools existed, provided for the establishment of a public school system of education before 1860. North Carolina led off in 1839; the question had first been submitted to popular vote and carried by a large majority. In some states, Louisiana for instance, the constitution required the legislature to provide a state system and to support it

[26] *Proceedings and Debates of the Convention of Louisiana, Which Assembled at the City of New Orleans, January 14, 1844* (New Orleans, 1845), 316–19.

[27] James M. Garnett, "Popular Education," in *Southern Literary Messenger* (Richmond, 1834–1864), VII (1842), 115.

[28] *Proceedings and Debates of the Convention of Louisiana* (1844), 909.

by taxation. All the states except Virginia and South Carolina provided for a state superintendent of public instruction; in most states the superintendent was elected by popular vote. The systems of public education in the southern states, in provisions for administration, support, and general results, compare favorably with those in the northern states in 1860.[29]

In like manner, popular control of southern state governments brought measures designed to minister to the economic wants of the people. In fact some leaders of democratic reform boldly proclaimed that this was one of the major purposes of government.[30] Boards of public works, popularly elected, were created to supervise internal improvements and to further the economic progress of the states. They were interested also in the public utilization of the natural resources of the states. Imprisonment for debt was prohibited; banks were brought under state control; provision was made for chartering corporations; monopolies were prohibited; and provisions were made for uniform and equal taxation of property according to value. All these measures were included in the state constitutions. The states, too, safeguarded the rights and interests of the unfortunate classes. State asylums for the insane and schools for the deaf, the dumb, and the blind were established at state expense.

The history of the southern state constitutions and governments from 1776 to 1860 reveals a progressive expansion in the application of the doctrine of political equality. By 1860 the aristocratic planter class had been shorn of its special privileges and political power. It still gave tone and color to political life but it no longer dominated and controlled the political order. On the other hand, the great mass of the whites had been given more and more authority, and majority rule had been definitely established. The interpretation of the southern states as "political aristocracies of the sternest and most odious kind" had no basis in fact. With the exceptions already noted the southern state governments were as democratic in 1860 as their northern sister states. They had not attained the ideal goal of absolute equality, but in spirit and administration as well as in form they had progressively become more and more concerned with the rights and interest of the people.

[29] Edgar W. Knight, *The Influence of Reconstruction on Education in the South* (New York, 1913), 94, 98.

[30] See, for instance, Charles J. Faulkner, "Speech," in *United States Magazine and Democratic Review*, XLI (1858), 218.

7

Who Were the Southern Whigs?

Charles G. Sellers, Jr.

The political reality of the Old South has proven as difficult to assess as the nature of its myth-bound social structure. The tendency has been to project the concept of a "solid South" back into the shadows of an antebellum Eden, and to argue that by 1830 the South found itself politically unified and indomitably resolved in opposition to the nationalistic, anti-slavery, capitalistic North. In the view of Charles G. Sellers, Jr., of the University of California, Berkeley, such a historical portrait has catered to what he aptly describes as "the myth of a monolithic South." Also to be corrected, says Professor Sellers, are the related assumptions of John C. Calhoun's pervasive political leadership after 1830, and the notion that the southern wing of the Whig party consistently aligned itself in support of the state rights position of the great planters. In attempting to redress these well-worn antebellum stereotypes, Mr. Sellers notes the vigorous two-party system which prevailed in the pre–Civil War South, and fashions an array of evidence clearly demonstrating that a correlation between the Whigs and the state rights position never in fact existed. Rather, the unifying strength of the Whig party, South as well as North, lay in the area of banking and financial policy. The major clientele of the Whig party comprised merchants, bankers, and lawyers. Planters, when members, were so for economic reasons, since the Whig party at no time either represented or articulated a blind devotion to state rights. It took more than the leadership of a John C. Calhoun for most southern Whigs to abandon their stance as economic capitalists.

From Charles G. Sellers, Jr., "Who Were the Southern Whigs?," *American Historical Review* (1954). Reprinted by permission of the author.

Students of the Old South have spent much of their time in recent years dispelling myths about the fabled land of moonlight and magnolias. Our understanding of the social, intellectual, and economic life of the ante-bellum South has been considerably revised and immeasurably widened by the work of a large number of able scholars.

Political history, however, has been unfashionable, and one of the results has been the survival of a series of myths about the political life of the South in the 1830's and 1840's. The key myth may be called the myth of a monolithic South: a section unified as early as the 1820's in its devotion to state rights doctrines and its hostility to the nationalistic, antislavery, capitalistic North. The result of approaching ante-bellum history by way of Fort Sumter and Appomattox, this point of view found its classic statements in the apologias of Jefferson Davis[1] and Alexander H. Stephens,[2] but it was made respectable in the first generation of professional scholarship by such historians as Herman Von Holst[3] and John W. Burgess.[4] It colored such early monographs as U. B. Phillips' "Georgia and State Rights"[5] and H. M. Wagstaff's *States Rights and Political Parties in North Carolina, 1776–1861*,[6] and is to be seen in most of the more recent works on the pre–Civil War South.[7] It has also given rise to the corollary myths that Cal-

---

[1] *The Rise and Fall of the Confederate Government*, 2 vols. (New York, 1881).

[2] *A Constitutional View of the Late War between the States*, 2 vols. (Philadelphia, 1868–70).

[3] *The Constitutional and Political History of the United States*, 8 vols. (Chicago, 1876–92).

[4] *The Middle Period, 1817–1858* (New York, 1905).

[5] *Annual Report of the American Historical Association*, 1901, II, 1–224.

[6] Johns Hopkins University Studies in Historical and Political Science, Series XXIV (1906), Nos. 7–8.

[7] See particularly Jesse T. Carpenter, *The South as a Conscious Minority, 1784–1861* (New York, 1930); Robert S. Cotterill, *The Old South* (Glendale, Calif., 1939); and Charles M. Wiltse, *John C. Calhoun*, 3 vols. (Indianapolis, 1944–51). Charles S. Sydnor, in what is, in many respects, the finest work on the ante-bellum South, presents a persuasive restatement of the traditional sectional–state rights interpretation. His chapter headings on politics from the Panic of 1819 to nullification describe a developing sectionalism: "From Economic Nationalism to Political Sectionalism," "End of the Virginia Dynasty," "The Lower South Adopts State Rights," and "Bold Acts and Bolder Thoughts." The 1830's and 1840's, however, present a paradox. Professor Sydnor finds a growing "Regionalism in Mind and Spirit," but a "decline of sectionalism in politics." This he explains as a result of the fact that "major Southern hopes and fears found no champion in either party," so that "party conflict south of the Potomac . . . had the hollow sound of a stage duel with tin swords." "The agrarian South felt little interest," writes Professor Sydnor, in that conflict between the "wealthier and more conservative segments of society" and the liberal, democratic elements "which formed a major issue between the Democratic and Whig parties" in the nation as a whole. *The Development of Southern Sectionalism, 1819–1848* (Baton Rouge, 1948), especially p. 316. Notable for their freedom from overemphasis on sectionalism are Thomas P. Abernethy, *From Frontier to Plantation in Tennessee: A Study in Frontier Democracy* (Chapel Hill, 1932); and Roger W. Shugg, *Origins of Class Struggle in Louisiana* (University, La., 1939).

houn was the representative spokesman and political leader of the South after about 1830, and that the Whig party in the South mainly reflected the state rights proclivities of the great planters.

These myths have been strengthened by Frederick Jackson Turner's sectional analysis of our early national history. Turner's approach has been extremely fruitful, but its sweeping application has tended to exaggerate differing sectional tendencies into absolute sectional differences. The application of geographic sectionalism to individual states, moreover, has fostered the further myth that political strife within the Old South was confined largely to struggles over intrastate sectional issues between upcountry and low country, hill country and "black belt."[8]

All of these myths have some basis in fact. They are, however, the product of a misplaced emphasis which has permeated nearly all the studies of pre–Civil War southern politics. Sectionalism and state rights have been made the central themes of southern political history for almost the entire ante-bellum period. Southern opposition to nationalistic legislation by Congress has been overemphasized. And the social, economic, and ideological lines of political cleavage within the slave states have been obscured. The early history of the Whig party below Mason and Dixon's line shows the character of these distortions.

It is too often forgotten that in the ante-bellum period the South had a vigorous two-party system, an asset it has never since enjoyed. Until at least the later 1840's, the voting southerner was much more interested in the success of his own party and its policies than in banding together with southerners of the opposite party to defend the Constitution and southern rights against invasion by the North. The parties were evenly matched, and elections were bitterly contested. It was rare for any southern state to be regarded as absolutely safe for either party. Of the 425,629 votes cast in the slave states at the election of 1836, the Whigs had a majority of only 243 popular votes. In this and the three succeeding presidential elections, a total of 2,745,171 votes were cast, but the over-all margin, again in favor of the Whigs, was only 66,295, or 2.4 per cent of the total votes. In these four elections the Whigs carried a total of twenty-seven southern states and the Democrats twenty-six.[9]

An equally close rivalry is evident in congressional representation. In the five congressional elections between 1832 and 1842, southern Democrats won an aggregate total of 234 seats, while their opponents captured 263. Whigs predominated among southern representatives in three of these five

[8] See especially William A. Schaper, "Sectionalism and Representation in South Carolina," *Annual Report of the American Historical Association*, 1900, I, 237–463; and Charles H. Ambler, *Sectionalism in Virginia from 1776 to 1861* (Chicago, 1910).

[9] Edward Stanwood, *A History of the Presidency* (Boston, 1898), pp. 185–88, 203–204, 223, 243. *Cf.* Fletcher M. Green, "Democracy in the Old South," *Journal of Southern History*, XII (1946), 20–21.

Congresses, and Democrats in two. In three of them the margin between the southern wings of the parties was five or less.[10] We have then a picture of keen political competition, with a vigorous Whig party maintaining a slight ascendancy.

What did this Whig party stand for? The pioneer account of the southern Whigs was the essay by U. B. Phillips which, significantly, appeared in the *Festschrift* to Frederick Jackson Turner.[11] This study shows Phillips' characteristic tendency to generalize about the entire South on the basis of conditions in his native Georgia. "The great central body of southern Whigs," he declares, "were the cotton producers, who were first state-rights men pure and simple and joined the Whigs from a sense of outrage at Jackson's threat of coercing South Carolina."[12]

Two years after Phillips' essay appeared, Arthur C. Cole published his exhaustive monograph on *The Whig Party in the South*.[13] Less than a third of the Cole volume is concerned with the period before 1844, when Whiggery was of greatest importance in the South, and he generally follows the Phillips interpretation of its origins. His account of the birth of the party devotes three pages to early National Republicanism in the South, twenty to the anti-Jackson sentiment aroused during the nullification crisis, and only four and a half to the fight over the national bank and financial policy.[14] "Various interests," he says, "linked in political alliance with the few

[10] Party affiliations of members of Congress have been determined largely from election returns in *Niles' Register* up to 1837, and from the *Whig Almanac* for the subsequent years. These sources have been supplemented by information from: *A Biographical Congressional Directory* (Washington, 1913); Charles H. Ambler, "Virginia and the Presidential Succession, 1840–1844," in *Essays in American History Dedicated to Frederick Jackson Turner* (New York, 1910), pp. 165–202; Ambler, *Sectionalism in Virginia;* Henry H. Simms, *The Rise of the Whigs in Virginia, 1824–1840* (Richmond, 1929); J. G. de Roulhac Hamilton, *Party Politics in North Carolina, 1835–1860,* James Sprunt Historical Publications, XV (1916); Clifford C. Norton, *The Democratic Party in Ante-Bellum North Carolina, 1835–1861,* James Sprunt Historical Studies, XXI (1930); Phillips, "Georgia and State Rights," *loc. cit.;* Paul Murray, *The Whig Party in Georgia, 1825–1853,* James Sprunt Studies in History and Political Science, XXIX (1948); Theodore H. Jack, *Sectionalism and Party Politics in Alabama, 1819–1842* (Menasha, Wis., 1919); Cleo Hearon, "Nullification in Mississippi," *Mississippi Historical Society Publications,* XII (1912), 37–71; James E. Winston, "The Mississippi Whigs and the Tariff, 1834–1844," *Mississippi Valley Historical Review,* XXII (1937), 505–24; James B. Ranck, *Alfred Gallatin Brown: Radical Southern Nationalist* (New York, 1937); Joseph G. Tregle Jr., "Louisiana and the Tariff, 1816–1846," *Louisiana Historical Quarterly,* XXV (1942), 24–148; and Wendell H. Stephenson, *Alexander Porter: Whig Planter of Old Louisiana* (Baton Rouge, 1934).

[11] "The Southern Whigs, 1834–1854," *Essays in American History Dedicated to Frederick Jackson Turner,* pp. 203–29.

[12] *Ibid.,* p. 209.

[13] Washington, 1913.

[14] Cole, pp. 2–30.

southerners whose interests and inclinations led to the support of latitudinarian principles, a still larger faction made up of those who supported constitutional doctrines on the opposite extreme and whose logical interests seemed to point against such an affiliation."[15]

An analysis, however, of the record of the Twenty-second Congress (1831–1833) leads to somewhat different conclusions. It was this Congress which dealt with the tariff, nullification, and national bank questions, and it was during this Congress that the groundwork for the Whig party was laid. Of the ninety southerners in the House of Representatives, sixty-nine had been elected as supporters of Andrew Jackson, while twenty-one, nearly a fourth, were National Republicans. Of the sixty-nine Democrats, twenty-five were subsequently active in the Whig party. Eighteen of the latter were state rights Whigs, while seven were not identified with the state rights wing of the opposition. These twenty-five men then, together with the twenty-one National Republicans, may be regarded as representative of the groups which formed the Whig party in the South.[16]

These incipient Whigs voted twenty-four to twenty-one in favor of the tariff of 1832, a measure denounced by state rights men and nullified by South Carolina.[17] They also voted twenty-four to nineteen for the Force Bill, which was designed to throttle the nullifiers.[18] This backing of administration measures was hardly a portent of an opposition state rights party. The real harbinger of Whiggery was the vote on the national bank bill, which this group supported twenty-seven to seventeen.[19]

The Whig party actually took shape during the Twenty-third Congress (1833–1835), in which it gained the allegiance of fifty-two of the ninety-nine southern members of the House. They voted twenty-nine to sixteen in favor of rechartering the national bank[20] and unanimously in favor of restoring the government deposits to Biddle's institution.[21] By a closer vote of twenty-two to twenty they supported repairing and extending the Cumberland Road.[22] In the Twenty-fourth Congress (1835–1837) the forty-eight Whig Representatives from the South divided thirty-eight to three in favor

[15] *Ibid.*, p. 2. E. Malcolm Carroll, in his scholarly *Origins of the Whig Party* (Durham, N. C., 1925), pays almost no attention to the southern states and follows Cole where southern developments have to be mentioned. In his one general statement about the southern Whigs, he takes the position that they were men of property, who turned instinctively to an association with northerners of similarly conservative interests. *Ibid.*, pp. 190–91.

[16] See note 10 above.

[17] *House Journal*, 22 Congress, 1 session, pp. 1023–24.

[18] *House Journal*, 22 Cong., 2 sess., pp. 453–54.

[19] *Register of Debates*, 22 Cong., 1 sess., p. 3852.

[20] *House Journal*, 23 Cong., 1 sess., pp. 483–85.

[21] *Ibid.*, pp. 485–86.

[22] *Ibid.*, pp. 758–59.

of Clay's bill to distribute the proceeds from sales of public lands to the states.[23] Other votes showing similar tendencies might be cited, but enough has been said to suggest that, even in the beginning, a majority of southern anti-Jackson men were far from being state rights doctrinaires.

In the light of this record it is not so surprising that only a handful of southern Whigs followed Calhoun when he marched his supporters back into the Democratic household during Van Buren's administration.[24] The record also prepares one for the increasing manifestations of nationalism among southern Whigs which Phillips and Cole found so difficult to explain.[25] The southern wing of the party backed Clay almost unanimously for the Presidential nomination in 1840.[26] Tyler's nomination for Vice President was more a sop to the disappointed Clay men, of whom Tyler was one, than a concession to the state rights proclivities of southern Whiggery, the reason usually given for his choice.[27]

[23] *House Journal,* 24 Cong., 1 sess., pp. 1023–24.

[24] Senator William C. Preston and Representative Waddy Thompson of South Carolina refused to leave the Whig party with Calhoun, and three other Representatives from the state took the Conservative, or anti-Subtreasury, position. Outside his own state Calhoun carried with him only seven members of Congress: Dixon H. Lewis of Alabama; Edward J. Black, Walter T. Colquitt, and Mark A. Cooper, of Georgia (in 1839–40); Samuel T. Sawyer and Charles Shepard of North Carolina; and Robert M. T. Hunter of Virginia (in 1839–41). The Georgia apostates were defeated for the next Congress by the regular Whigs, who made a clean sweep of the congressional elections under the general ticket system. In North Carolina Sawyer was displaced by a loyal Whig at the next election, and Shepard met the same fate two years later. In the Presidential election of 1840 the southern Whigs, far from being weakened, had a majority of 58,675, as compared with 243 four years earlier. See Murray, *Whig Party in Georgia,* pp. 90–95; Hamilton, *Party Politics in North Carolina,* pp. 55, 79; Stanwood, *History of the Presidency,* pp. 165–203.

[25] Phillips, "The Southern Whigs," *loc. cit.,* pp. 216–17; Cole, *Whig Party in the South,* pp. 65–89.

[26] Cole, pp. 53–54.

[27] George R. Poage, *Henry Clay and the Whig Party* (Chapel Hill, 1936), pp. 13, 34–35. Tyler's most recent biographer, Oliver P. Chitwood, maintains that "Tyler was given the second place on the ticket mainly because he was from the South and had been a strong advocate of States' rights," or, in another passage, that "he was put up partly to placate the Clay faction but mainly to satisfy the States' right element of the Whig party." Chitwood bases his position on the ground that it "is the explanation usually given." *John Tyler, Champion of the Old South* (New York, 1939), pp. 172, 194. In taking this position, Chitwood has to discount completely Henry A. Wise's story of an arrangement with Clay leaders in 1839, whereby Tyler was to withdraw as a competitor with W. C. Rives for the Senate but was to receive the Vice Presidential nomination. Chitwood is probably correct in denying that Tyler himself had any part in such an understanding, but he fails to explain why Tyler was expected to be Clay's running mate before the convention met and why the Clay men were so confident of their ability to control Tyler just after he succeeded Harrison. *Ibid.,* pp. 172–73, 210, 215. Chitwood also finds it necessary to try to disprove persistent reports that Tyler intimated during the campaign that he was friendly to a national bank. It cannot be denied that his campaign statements were highly equivocal. *Ibid.,*

The nature of southern Whiggery had its real test when Tyler challenged Clay for leadership of the party. Of the fifty-five southern Whigs in the lower house of the Twenty-seventh Congress (1841–1843), only three stuck by the Virginia President and his state rights principles, whereas Mangum of North Carolina presided over the caucus which read Tyler out of the party, and southern Whig editors joined in castigating him unmercifully.[28] Southern Whigs supported Clay's legislative program—repeal of the Subtreasury, a national bank, distribution, and tariff—by large majorities.[29] Even the Georgians, Berrien, Toombs, and Stephens, defended the protective features of the tariff of 1842.[30]

Having said so much to the point that the Whig party in the South did not begin as and did not become a state rights party, it is necessary to add that neither was it consciously nationalistic. State rights versus nationalism simply was not the main issue in southern politics in this period. It is readily apparent from the newspapers and correspondence of the time that, except for Calhoun and his single-minded little band, politicians in the South were fighting over the same questions that were agitating the North —mainly questions of banking and financial policy.

It is hard to exaggerate the importance of the banking question. State and federal governments, by their policy in this sphere, could cause inflation or deflation, make capital easy or difficult to obtain, and facilitate or hinder the marketing of staple crops and commercial activity generally. And by chartering or refusing to charter banks, they could afford or deny to the capitalists of the day the most profitable field of activity the economy offered.

The banking issue is the key to an understanding of southern as well as northern Whiggery. Merchants and bankers were most directly concerned in financial policy, but their community of interest generally included the other business and professional men of the towns, especially the lawyers, who got most of their fees from merchants, and the newspaper editors, who were dependent on the merchants for advertising revenues. The crucial

---

pp. 188–94, 171–77. On one occasion Tyler endorsed Harrison's contention that "There is not in the Constitution any express grant of power for such purpose [a national bank], and it could never be constitutional to exercise the power, save in the event the power granted to Congress could not be carried into effect without resorting to such an institution." *Ibid.,* p. 190.

[28] Cole, pp. 92–93.

[29] Southern Whigs in the House voted forty-four to four in favor of Clay's original bank bill. *House Journal,* 27 Cong., 1 sess., pp. 409–10. They supported the tariff of 1842 by a vote of twenty-nine to eleven. *House Journal,* 27 Cong., 2 sess., pp. 1440–41.

[30] Murray, *Whig Party in Georgia,* p. 109; Rudolph Von Abele, *Alexander H. Stephens* (New York, 1946), pp. 86–87.

point for southern politics, however, is that the large staple producers were also closely identified economically with the urban commercial groups.[31] These were the principal elements which went into the Whig party.

The Whigs generally defended the national bank until its doom was sealed, then advocated a liberal chartering of commercial banks by the states, and finally, after the Panic of 1837, demanded a new national bank. The Democrats fought Biddle's institution and either favored state-operated banks to provide small loans for farmers, as distinguished from commercial banks, or tried to regulate banking strictly or abolish it altogether.[32]

Much of the misunderstanding about the Whig party in the South may be traced to the technique of plotting election returns on maps. Such maps tell us much, but they may also mislead. They show, for example, that the "black belts" of the lower South were the great centers of Whig strength. This has led scholars to reason: (1) that the Whig party was a planters' party *par excellence,* (2) that planters were necessarily rigid state rights men, and (3) that the Whig party was, therefore, a state rights party. *Q. E. D.!*

What the maps do not illustrate, however, is the dynamics of the political situation—the elements of leadership, impetus, financing, and propaganda, which are the real sinews of a political organization. In the case of the Whig party, these elements were furnished mainly by the commercial groups of the cities and towns, with their allied lawyers and editors. Lawyers were the practicing politicians for both parties, but the greater incidence of lawyers among the Whigs is an indication of the commercial affiliations of the party. Seventy-four percent of the southern Whigs who sat in Congress from 1833 to 1843 are identified as practicing attorneys, as compared with fifty-five percent of the Democrats.[33] In the lower house of the Ten-

---

[31] Ralph C. H. Catterall, *The Second Bank of the United States* (Chicago, 1903), pp. 140–44; Thomas P. Abernethy, "The Early Development of Commerce and Banking in Tennessee," *Mississippi Valley Historical Review,* XIV (1927), 316–19; Thomas P. Govan, "Banking and the Credit System in Georgia, 1810–1860," *Journal of Southern History,* IV (1938), 164, 178–84.

[32] Charles H. Ambler, *Thomas Ritchie: A Study in Virginia Politics* (Richmond, 1913), pp. 176–78; Ambler, *Sectionalism in Virginia,* pp. 237–39; George T. Starnes, *Sixty Years of Branch Banking in Virginia* (New York, 1931), pp. 71–103; William K. Boyd, *The Federal Period, 1783–1860,* Vol. II of *History of North Carolina* (Chicago, 1919), pp. 274–75; Norton, *Democratic Party in North Carolina,* pp. 54–59, 188–92; Hamilton, *Party Politics in North Carolina,* pp. 80, 88; Govan, "Banking in Georgia," *loc. cit.,* pp. 164–84; Jack, *Sectionalism in Alabama,* pp. 61–63; William O. Scroggs, "Pioneer Banking in Alabama," in *Facts and Factors in Economic History: Articles by Former Students of Edwin Francis Gay* (Cambridge, Mass., 1932), pp. 421–23; Abernethy, "Banking in Tennessee," *loc. cit.,* 321–24; Eugene I. McCormac, *James K. Polk: A Political Biography* (Berkeley, 1922), pp. 88, 169–70, 190; Shugg, *Class Struggle in Louisiana,* pp. 134–38.

[33] Based on vocational identification in *Biographical Congressional Directory.*

nessee legislature of 1839, farmers predominated, but a fourth of the Whigs were lawyers, as compared with only a tenth of the Democratic membership.[34]

The size and importance of the urban middle class in the Old South has yet to be fully appreciated. As early as 1831, Nashville, for example, contained twenty-two wholesale houses and seventy-seven retail stores, not to mention numerous other businesses, such as the sixty taverns and tippling houses.[35] Even the little county seat town of Gallatin, Tennessee, boasted in 1840 ten mercantile firms, a grocer, a merchant tailor, three hotels, five lawyers, five doctors, a paper and grist mill, and eighteen artisans' establishments of one kind or another.[36]

Businessmen dominated the towns socially, economically, and politically, and the towns dominated the countryside.[37] This was particularly true of the "black belts" of the lower South, since the great cotton capitalists of this region were especially dependent on commercial and credit facilities for financing and carrying on their extensive planting operations.[38] In recognition of the urban influence on politics, congressional districts were commonly known by the names of the principal towns in each—as, for example, the Huntsville, Florence, Tuscaloosa, Montgomery, and Mobile districts in Alabama.

Other evidence points in the same direction. A large majority of the stockholders in Virginia banks in 1837 lived in the areas of heaviest Whig voting. The principal commercial towns of the state—Richmond, Petersburg, and Norfolk—gave unbroken Whig majorities throughout the period 1834–1840.[39] In North Carolina twenty of the twenty-one directors of the

[34] Vocational identification from "List of Members of the House of Representatives of the Tennessee Legislature," broadside (Nashville, 1839). Party affiliations from a memorandum by James K. Polk in the Polk Papers (Library of Congress), First Series, placed at end of November, 1839.

[35] Nashville *Republican and State Gazette,* Oct. 20, 1831.

[36] Gallatin *Republican Sentinel,* Jan. 28, 1840.

[37] Lewis E. Atherton, *The Southern Country Store, 1800–1860* (Baton Rouge, 1949), especially pp. 191–92. This study is of great significance in indicating the importance of commercial interests and of even the smaller interior merchant in the life of the ante-bellum South. Atherton does not deal with the political activities of merchants in this volume, but in a similar study for Illinois, Missouri, and Iowa, he found the merchants active in politics. Seventy per cent of a sample for whom political affiliation could be determined were Whigs. *The Pioneer Merchant in Middle America,* University of Missouri Studies, XIV (1939), No. 2, pp. 23–26.

[38] Clanton W. Williams, "Early Ante-Bellum Montgomery: A Black-Belt Constituency," *Journal of Southern History,* VII (1941), 510–11, 515; Shugg, *Class Struggle in Louisiana,* p. 138; Stephenson, *Alexander Porter,* pp. 33–35; J. Carlyle Sitterson, "Financing and Marketing the Sugar Crop of the Old South," *Journal of Southern History,* X (1944), 188–99.

[39] Simms, *Whigs in Virginia,* pp. 13, 167–92.

two principal banks in 1840 were Whigs.[40] The first Whig governor of North Carolina was a railroad president; the second was a lawyer, cotton manufacturer, and railroad president; and the third was one of the wealthiest lawyers in the state.[41]

Similar party leadership obtained elsewhere. In Virginia, younger men of the type of John Minor Botts of Richmond and Alexander H. H. Stuart of Staunton actually directed the party of which Tyler and Tazewell were nominal leaders. Senators George A. Waggaman and Judah P. Benjamin were typical of the New Orleans lawyers who guided Louisiana Whiggery. Poindexter and Prentiss in Mississippi were intimately associated both personally and financially with the bankers and businessmen of Natchez. The Tennessee Whigs were led by John Bell, Nashville lawyer and iron manufacturer, who had married into the state's leading mercantile and banking house; Ephraim H. Foster, bank director and Nashville's most prominent commercial lawyer; and Hugh Lawson White, Knoxville lawyer, judge, and bank president.[42]

This commercial bias of the Whig party did much to pave the way for the industrial development of the South after the Civil War. It was no accident that former Whigs provided a large part of the leadership for the business-minded Conservative-Democratic parties which "redeemed" the South from Republican rule and then proceeded to make the conquered section over in the image of the victorious North, often in the interest of northern capital.[43]

Commercial considerations and the banking question did not, of course, determine political alignments in the Old South by themselves. Pro-tariff sentiment made for Whiggery among the sugar planters of Louisana, the

[40] Boyd, *Federal Period*, p. 274.

[41] Hamilton, *Party Politics in North Carolina*, pp. 36, 57, 92–94.

[42] Lawyers provided much of the leadership for the Democratic party also, but they tended to be from the smaller towns rather than the big commercial centers—as, for example, James K. Polk, Cave Johnson, and Aaron V. Brown, in Tennessee. There were also a goodly number of "Democrats by trade"—men like James K. Polk's merchant-banker-mail contractor brother-in-law, James Walker—who were active in Democratic politics for personal profit. The top Whig leadership, however, contained few men of the decidedly noncommercial backgrounds of such Democrats as Andrew Johnson, the Greenville tailor; Bedford Brown, the upcountry small planter who inherited Nathaniel Macon's mantle in North Carolina; Richard M. Johnson, the ebullient Tecumseh-slayer, who continued to wait on customers in his Great Crossings inn while Vice President of the United States; David Hubbard, the self-educated carpenter who championed the poor whites of northern Alabama; Franklin E. Plummer, the picturesque loco-foco from the piney woods of eastern Mississippi; and General Solomon W. Downs, who led the "Red River Democracy" of northern Louisiana in the fights for suffrage extension and bank reform. Davy Crockett was, of course, the exception among the Whigs that proved the rule.

[43] C. Vann Woodward, *Origins of the New South, 1877–1913* (Baton Rouge, 1951), pp. 1–50.

hemp growers of Kentucky, and the salt and iron manufacturers of western Virginia and Maryland. The more liberal policy of the Whigs toward internal improvements by both the state and federal governments won them support in landlocked interior sections and along the routes of projected transportation projects. And the fact that the Democrats generally championed a broadened suffrage, apportionment of congressional and legislative seats on the basis of white population, and other measures for extending political democracy, inclined propertied and conservative men to rally to the Whig party as a bulwark against mobocracy.

These factors, however, merely reinforced the commercial nature of southern Whiggery. The business orientation of the Whigs and the relative unimportance of their state rights wing become quite apparent if the party is described as it actually developed in the various states, rather than on the basis of general assumptions about southern politics.

A state by state analysis would indicate that, in the four border slave states and Louisiana, Whiggery was simply National Republicanism continued under a new name. The National Republicans were also strong in Virginia, but here they were joined in opposition to the Democrats by a body of state rights men alienated from Jackson by his attitude toward nullification. The National Republican and commercial wing of the party, however, was the dominant one, especially after the business-minded Conservative Democrats joined the Whigs on the Subtreasury question.[44] In North Carolina and Tennessee, the Whig party was formed by the secession of pro-Bank men from the Democratic party, aided in Tennessee by the local popularity of Hugh Lawson White as a Presidential candidate in 1835–1836.[45]

[44] Ambler, *Sectionalism in Virginia*, pp. 219–50, especially p. 222; Simms, *Whigs in Virginia, passim*.

[45] Boyd, *Federal Period*, pp. 181–84; Burton A. Konkle, *John Motley Morehead* (Philadelphia, 1922), p. 127; Lawrence F. London, "George Edmund Badger in the United States Senate, 1846–1849," *North Carolina Historical Review*, XV (1938), 2–3; Powell Moore, "The Political Background of the Revolt against Jackson in Tennessee," *East Tennessee Historical Society's Publications*, No. 4 (1932), 45–66; Thomas P. Abernethy, "The Origin of the Whig Party in Tennessee," *Mississippi Valley Historical Review*, XII (1927), 504–22; Joseph H. Parks, *John Bell* (Baton Rouge, 1950), pp. 58–133. The difficulty historians have had understanding why the North Carolina planters perversely remained in the Democratic party arises from the initial error of regarding the Whig party as primarily a planter group. The basic explanation is that the Old Republican planters of North Carolina, unlike the agricultural capitalists of the lower South, were antagonistic toward the commercial-financial group, rather than identified with it. With a smaller investment in land and slaves than his Mississippi counterpart, with little chance to make large profits by further investment, and relying less on a single cash crop, the average North Carolina planter was much less dependent on the town merchant and banker. For some years before the Jackson era, the planters had been resisting demands for banks and internal improvements, while simultaneously trying to stem the tide of democratic discontent with planter rule. It was the union of these two anti-planter forces, commer-

The state rights element was more conspicuous in the four remaining states of the lower South. But it was by no means the majority wing of the Whig party in all of them. Both Alabama and Mississippi had an original nucleus of pro-Clay, anti-Jackson men, and in both states the nullification episode caused a substantial defection from the Jackson ranks. In Mississippi, however, a greater defection followed the removal of government deposits from the national bank. The state rights men were clearly a minority of the opposition party, which elected an outspoken foe of nullification to the governorship in 1835 and sent the ardent Clay partisan, Seargent S. Prentiss, to Congress two years later.[46]

The state rights defection seems to have been more important in Alabama, where it was led by the able Dixon H. Lewis. The Lewis faction, however, maintained only a tenuous connection with the regular Whigs, and in 1837 Lewis and his supporters followed Calhoun back into the Democratic party. The significant fact is that in neither Alabama nor Mississippi were the Whigs greatly weakened by the departure of Calhoun's admirers.[47]

Only in South Carolina and Georgia did avowed state rights men make up the bulk of the anti-Jackson party. When the real nature of the new party alignments became apparent, the politicians of Calhoun's state gave proof of their sincerity (and of the Presidential aspirations of their chief) by moving back to the Democratic ranks at the first decent opportunity.

The principal Whig leader in Georgia was John M. Berrien, a Savannah lawyer and attorney for the United States Bank who had been forced out of Jackson's cabinet by the Peggy Eaton affair. At the time of the election of 1832, Jackson's Indian policy was so popular in Georgia that Berrien did not dare oppose the President openly. Instead, he went about stirring

---

cial and democratic, which produced the Whig party in 1833–1835. Businessmen controlled the new party, but they retained popular support by championing constitutional reform and by progressive legislation in the fields of internal improvements and public education. There is no adequate account of the North Carolina Whigs in print. The situation in Virginia was somewhat similar, in that a majority of the planters, Phillips and Cole to the contrary notwithstanding, remained Democrats. In the period 1833–1843, the twelve congressional districts of plantation Virginia, lying east of the Blue Ridge and south of the Rappahannock, were represented thirty-eight times by Democrats and twenty-two times by Whigs or Conservatives, with nine of the Whig elections being won in the commercial Norfolk, Richmond, and Fredericksburg districts. The Democratic party of Virginia differed from that of North Carolina, however, in having a much larger popular element.

[46] Hearon, "Nullification in Mississippi," *loc. cit.,* pp. 37–77; Winston, "Mississippi Whigs and the Tariff," *loc. cit.,* pp. 505–24; James E. Winston, "The Mississippi Whigs and the Annexation of Texas," *Southwestern Historical Quarterly,* XXIX (1926), pp. 161–80; Ranck, *Alfred G. Brown,* pp. 4–15; Dallas C. Dickey, *Seargent S. Prentiss: Whig Orator of the Old South* (Baton Rouge, 1945), pp. 45–266.

[47] Jack, *Sectionalism in Alabama,* pp. 21–85.

up anti-tariff and state rights sentiment, while secretly trying to prevent anti-Bank resolutions by the legislature. Immediately after Jackson's re-election, however, Berrien and his allies managed to reorganize the old Troup political faction as an openly anti-Jackson state rights party. In view of Berrien's pro-Bank attitude and his subsequent staunch support of Clay's policies, it seems probable that he was merely capitalizing on state rights sentiment to defeat Democratic measures which he opposed on other grounds. At any rate, the Georgia Whigs were soon arrayed against the Jackson financial program, and they held their lines nearly intact in the face of the desertion of state rights Whigs to the Democrats on the Sub-treasury issue. By 1840 Berrien had brought his Georgia followers into close harmony with the national party.[48]

This summary sketch of southern Whiggery raises, of course, more questions than it could possibly answer definitively. It has attempted to suggest, however, that preoccupation with the origins and development of southern sectionalism has led to distortions of southern political history in the 1830's and 1840's. Specifically, it is suggested:

That only John C. Calhoun and a small group of allied southern leaders regarded state rights as the most important issue in politics in this period.

That the southern people divided politically in these years over much the same questions as northern voters, particularly questions of banking and financial policy.

That the Whig party in the South was built around a nucleus of National Republicans and state rights men, but received its greatest accession of strength from business-minded Democrats who deserted Jackson on the Bank issue.

That the Whig party in the South was controlled by urban commercial and banking interests, supported by a majority of the planters, who were economically dependent on banking and commercial facilities. And finally,

That this alliance of the propertied, far from being inherently particu-laristic, rapidly shook off its state rights adherents and by 1841 was almost solidly in support of the nationalistic policies of Henry Clay.

There is a great need for intensive restudy of southern politics in the 1830's and 1840's, and particularly for critical correlation of local and national developments. The story as it comes from the contemporary sources is full of the resounding clash of solid interests and opposing ideol-

---

[48] Thomas P. Govan, "John M. Berrien and the Administration of Andrew Jackson," *Journal of Southern History*, V (1939), pp. 447–67; Phillips, "Georgia and State Rights," *loc. cit.*, pp. 113–50; Murray, *Whig Party in Georgia, passim*. Despite the defection of three congressmen to the Democrats on the Subtreasury issue, the Georgia Whigs won the subsequent congressional election and carried the Presidential election of 1840 by three times their majority in 1836.

ogies, hardly having "the hollow sound of a stage duel with tin swords" which one historian seems to detect.[49] And recent events should make the student wary of state rights banners, especially when raised by conservative men against national administrations not conspicuously devoted to the interests of the propertied.

[49] Sydnor, *Development of Southern Sectionalism,* p. 316.

8

Romance and Realism in Southern Politics

T. Harry Williams

A sense of history, soil, climate, and race have all, at various times, served as a basis for explaining the distinctiveness of the southern past. But assuming that a successful formula for the uniqueness of the southern experience has yet to be proven sufficiently persuasive, T. Harry Williams, Boyd Professor of History at Louisiana State University, offers the "romance" of southern politics as a possible alternative. Anticipating later emphasis on the mythological content of southern history, Professor Williams deciphers the codes of southern political conduct during the pre–Civil War decades in terms of its affinities for image-building. The interchange of issues with the North, he argues, forced the South to react defensively, signaling a retreat into the less hostile confines of the southern mind. Southern political behavior was clearly tinged by its penchant for failing to grasp the essence and reality of key political issues. As such, the South unknowingly came to compromise the possibility of eventual victory in the intersectional struggles by virtue of this rather basic flaw in its political character. As the crisis of civil war approached, the South exhibited an inability to sustain natural political affiliations with the West, and proved unwilling to shape critical issues in accordance with anything other than the defense of slavery. In lieu of coming to terms with political realities—construed as "the puny inadequateness of fact"—the South became a cultural prisoner of its psychological impulse for the romantic. Indeed, given this proclivity toward romanticism perhaps the "lost cause" was predestined.

From "The Distinctive South" in *Romance and Realism in Southern Politics,* by T. Harry Williams. Athens, Georgia: The University of Georgia Press, 1961. Reprinted by permission of the publisher.

We are accustomed to saying that there is a place called the South and that it is inhabited by an identifiable people known as Southerners. We know that this is so, but many of those who most often tell us about it, including natives of the section, would have trouble defining their phrases if pressed for a formula. Even the specialists, the scholars who study the structure of Southern society—historians, sociologists, political scientists—have had trouble in deciding what made the South distinctive or what elements determined the pattern of Southernism. Ironically enough, in attempting to ascribe reasons for coherence, they have come up with diverse analyses. They have pointed to the South's agrarian economy and its staple crops, its rural society and English gentry ideals, its plantation system and institution of slavery, its conservative way of thought and stable way of life, and its consciousness of race and fixation on race relations. And these are not all the formulas advanced to explain the South. The literary artists, sometimes more perceptive in social analysis than the social scientists, have had their go at the problem. As we might perhaps expect, they have seen the land itself as a powerful factor. The physical environment was such that it sustained life without too much expenditure of energy. Not having to conquer his environment, the Southerner was free to exploit its pleasures. "Soil, scenery, all the color and animation of the external world tempted a convivial race to an endless festival of the seasons," wrote Ellen Glasgow. "In the midst of a changing world all immaterial aspects were condensed for the Southern planter into an incomparable heartiness and relish for life. What distinguished the Southerner . . . from his severer neighbors to the north was his ineradicable belief that pleasure is worth more than toil, that it is even worth more than profit."

The most recent attempts by historians to explain what is distinctive about the South have got away from the older formulas of race, economics, or ruralism. Now the purpose is to show in what ways the South has not shared in or has stood apart from the common American tradition. Thus Professor Vann Woodward, who has done so much to illumine our understanding of the region, points out that the South has not participated in three of the great national legends and that its experience in these areas is quite un-American. In a land of plenty the South was from the Civil War and until recent times a region of poverty. In a nation whose history has been an unbroken success story the South has known "frustration, failure, and defeat." Their heritage affords Southerners no basis for the American conviction that there is nothing beyond the power of humans to accomplish. In a society bemused with innocence and optimism the South has lived with evils—slavery and the aftermath of emancipation—and it does not believe that every evil has an easy cure. "In that most optimistic of centuries in the most optimistic part of the world, the South remained basically pessimistic in its social outlook and its moral philosophy," Woodward concludes. "The experience of evil and the experience of tragedy are parts of the Southern heritage that are as difficult to reconcile with the American legend of innocence and social felicity as the experience of poverty and defeat are to reconcile with the legends of abundance and success."

Professor Woodward is also responsible for another current notion— that more than any other Americans Southerners have a sense of history. This is not to be taken in a literal sense as meaning that the people below the Potomac have an unusual devotion to a full and objective record of their past or that, happily, they read a large number of history books or honor history professors above other savants. Rather, it is, to borrow a phrase that Woodward borrowed from Toynbee, that Southerners know history has happened. They know this because Southern history has been compounded of tragedy and many of the elements of that tragedy are still apparent today. More poignantly than other Americans, they realize that the past impinges on the present, and more often than their fellows in other sections they relate the present to something in the past. Indeed, one commentator, Henry Savage, has suggested that this sense of history is the thing that has made the South an entity. "With the exception of what their history did to them, Southerners are much like Americans anywhere in the country," Savage writes. He adds that outsiders would understand the South better if they realized that Southern differences are solely the products of history.

Although most observers admit the existence of this attachment to the past, not all view it with affection or even amusement. Some have found it irritating and have easily proceeded to the conclusion that it is dangerous. Thus Marshall Fishwick explodes: "How can people who know and intuit so much not know that a constant posture of looking backward is the hallmark of stagnation? Very few of us who purport to be historians know much about history. But everything we do know indicates that history is incapable of running backward."

It may be that the critics on both sides are exaggerating the Southerner's consciousness of history. All of this alleged identification with the past may be only another demonstration of his undoubted great ability to deceive himself as well as to spoof the outsider. And this may be the quality that makes him unique among Americans. Far beyond any native competitors, he is marvelously adept at creating mind-pictures of his world or of the larger world around him—images that he wants to believe, that are real to him, and that he will insist others accept. This is another way of saying that the Southerner is likely to be a romantic and that in many situations he almost certainly will refuse to recognize reality. It is an attitude that has fascinated and frustrated beholders. Harry Ashmore, who admits to both reactions, speaks of the Southerner's "remarkable capacity for unreality, which still enables him to hold out against the logic of arguments and of events." W. J. Cash, in *The Mind of the South,* that brilliant book which has been so praised and so damned but which is always quoted by critics from both sides, dealt caustically with the Southerner's capacity for self-deception: "To say that he is simple is to say in effect that he necessarily lacks the complexity of mind, the knowledge, and above all, the habit of skepticism essential to any generally realistic attitude. It is to say that he is inevitably driven back upon imagination, that his world-construction is bound to be mainly a product of fantasy, and that his credulity is limited only by his capacity for conjuring up the unbelievable."

If we admit here at the beginning that the Southerner is, more than other Americans, a romantic, it is pertinent to ask at this point of departure: What are the factors or forces that have made him what he is? The question is by nature a slippery one, and the answers perforce must be elusive. Nor will the vast apparatus of scholarship be of much help to us. The historian with all his documents and the social scientist with all his data cannot throw appreciable light on this problem. But we may with some, but not complete, confidence turn for possible clues to the literary artists who have depicted the Southern scene. There fortunate folk have not been inhibited by the scholar's proper caution in dealing with the inner nature of man. On the contrary, as is proper with them, they have felt impelled to explain man in terms of their art. It would seem significant that in interpreting man, or any other manifestation of the Southern scene, they give great weight to the physical environment. Some have believed that the very nature of the Southern world—the climate, the colors, the odors, the foliage—militates against reality. That "subtle, murky, slumberous clime . . . swart hot land of pine and palm . . . the sweet and sensuous South," wrote James Maurice Thompson. Cash, in one of his most impressionistic passages, contended that the environment constituted "a sort of cosmic conspiracy against reality in favor of romance." Describing the land as a pattern of blurred softness, Cash spoke of the mood it induced: "It is a mood, in sum, in which directed thinking is all but impossible, a mood in which the mind yields almost perforce to drift and in which the imagination holds unchecked sway, a mood in which nothing any more seems improbable save the puny inadequateness of fact, nothing incredible save the bareness of truth."

More quotations from the literary community could be introduced, but if the more mundane-minded suspect the validity of observations from this source we may summon a colder witness, a New England Adams. Henry Adams attested the effect the South first had on him in words that might have come from a Southern poet: "The May sunshine and shadow had something to do with it; the thickness of foliage and the heavy smells had more; the sense of atmosphere, almost new, had perhaps as much again; and the brooding indolence of a warm climate and a negro population hung in the atmosphere heavier than the catalpas. The impression was not simple, but the boy liked it: distinctly it remained on his mind as an attraction, almost obscuring Quincy itself." If the Southern scene could almost obscure the stark reality of Quincy in the mind of an Adams, it must have been powerful indeed. With this, let us be content and assume that something in the Southern background produced a tendency toward romanticism in thought and politics.

Of all the mind-pictures created by the romantic Southerner, the greatest, the most appealing, and the most enduring is the legend of the Old South. The minute investigations of the historians, the political scientists, and even the sociologists have not succeeded in destroying it or even seriously modifying it. Even those Southern writers who have believed that the legend was bad for the South, when they have come to write about it, expended their most eloquent passages, so in a perverse way testifying to its attraction.

Cash seems carried away despite himself in describing the image of the South that was, "shimmering there forever behind the guns of Sumter.... Perpetually suspended in the great haze of memory, it hung, as it were, poised, somewhere between earth and sky, colossal, shining, and incomparably lovely...." Depicting the growth of the legend after 1865, Henry Savage, who thinks it has held the South in a bondage of prejudice, nevertheless can write: "But in the past, the sky was yet still bright with a shining glory. Although it was but afterglow of the glorious sunset of a magnificent day which was done, it was still something with which Southerners could identify themselves to relieve the terrible gloom of their contemporary lot."

This cherishing of an ideal dream-world in the past was both a reflection of the Southerner's capacity for unreality and a cause of his continuing reluctance to face the realities of the modern world; for obviously the myth of a perfect society was a powerful argument against change, against even considering whether there was any need for change. And here we may observe that if the Southerner were as aware of history as some of the writers suppose, he would have pursued a different course in some of the social conflicts of modern times. Presumably a people that have experienced evil, defeat, and repression would realize the advantage of adjustment and accommodation in political relations, techniques not noticeably present in the recent South.

But the legend of the Old South is only one demonstration of the Southern talent for fantasy. We see it in many areas of Southern life and in almost every segment of Southern history. It is in the writings of intellectuals like Donald Davidson, who could declare that the cause of the

South in the 1920's was "the cause of civilized society against the new barbarism of science and technology controlled and directed by the modern power state." It was in the speeches of politicians in the depression-ridden 1930's, speeches that ignored the harsh economic realities while harking back to old glories that had been destroyed by alien persecutors. It first appeared when the South emerged as a section, when Southern leaders chose to stake the destiny of a whole people on one issue to be fought for with one strategy.

Historians differ as to the exact date when the South became an entity, recognized by itself and other areas as a distinct section. Although some scholars claim that the states below the Potomac realized they had separate interests as early as the Constitutional Convention, most put the time much later. There is pretty general agreement that the phenomenon we know as the South was at least taking shape by the 1830's. Certainly Southerners were then becoming aware, and often bitterly so, that they were in some way different from people in the rest of the country. These years witnessed the beginning of the abolitionist attack on slavery, the nullification crisis, and the first burgeoning of the Northern industrial order. Suddenly the Southern states were thrown on the defensive—morally, politically, economically. And it was at this moment, exclaims Henry Savage, that the South was born, "the old South of book and song, romance and tragedy, of adulation and castigation." Essentially the same conclusion was reached by the most thoughtful historian of the region in the 1830's, Charles S. Sydnor. By the close of the decade, Sydnor decided, Southerners had come to have a feeling of "oppression, of defeat, and even of desperation." "From this time onward," he wrote, "it is not always possible to explain Southern actions and attitudes by a rational analysis of the facts in each new episode." To Sydnor the salient development was that for the first time Southerners realized they were different. Although they had possessed a distinctive social system, they had not known it until outsiders told them so. Now and rather abruptly "the Southern mind was turned inward to a consideration of its own society."

Unquestionably the South was under attack in the 1830's. But a people whose institutions are being criticized may react in a number of ways. They may, if they are sure of themselves and their security, disdain the criticisms. They may concoct defenses of various kinds, political and polemical, and of varying intensity. Or they may, if they are adept at accommodating themselves to power, which no Americans are, prepare to accept adjustments in their system that will involve a minimum of dislocation. But the Southern response was none of these. Instead, Southerners assumed the position that their society, lying under the disapproval of not just the North but of the whole Western world, was the highest example of civilization to be found on the planet. Other peoples have looked forward or backward to a golden age, but those of the antebellum South proclaimed that they lived in one. "Surely, Southerners had come a long way from Jefferson and a long way out of reality," Sydnor concluded with apparent sadness. "Fighting to defend their way of life, they had taken refuge in a dream world, and they insisted that others accept their castle in the sky as an accurate description of conditions in the South."

Whatever the precise movement when the South passed from a geographic region to a political section, it is evident that the transition was an ominous one, both for the South and the nation. We cannot say with certainty that the change was inevitable. Given all the factors in the situation—the nature of Northern and Southern opinion, the convulsing currents working in the political system, the transforming upheavals occurring in the economic sphere—it probably was. But one of these factors was particularly important in driving the South into a mood of insecurity and isolation. Then, as in later crises, external attacks would have the effect of solidifying internal divisions in a region that naturally was one of great contrasts. And then, as later, the North would show little understanding of or sympathy for the problems of the South.

Many of the condemnations flung against the South went far beyond the bounds of legitimate social criticism, and were, whether or not mischievously conceived, calculated to inflame Southerners to extreme reaction rather than to calm examination of their society. Witness these examples. From the New York *Tribune:* "The Southern plantations are little less than Negro harems. . . . Of all the Southern presidents hardly one has failed to leave his mulatto children. . . . The South is a perfect puddle of amalgamation." From the New York *Times:* "The Southern character is infinitely boastful, vainglorious, full of dash, without endurance, treacherous, cunning, timid, and revengeful." From a Northern minister: "A foaming fountain of insecurity and alarm, of violence and crime and blood, the institution of slavery is." From *Harper's Weekly:* "Their civilization is a mermaid—lovely and languid above, but ending in bestial deformity."

Under almost constant assault after the 1830's, in its response the South committed almost every political error in the book. First, it permitted the opposition to define the issue, slavery, thus putting itself at an immediate disadvantage. Second, it identified every other issue and, indeed, its whole way of life with the defense of slavery. Finally, as Woodward writes: "Because it identified the internal security of the whole society with the security of its labor system, it refused to permit criticism of that system. To guarantee conformity of thought it abandoned its tradition of tolerance and resorted to the repression of dissent within its borders and the forcible exclusion of criticism from outside."

There had been a time when some of the most intelligent social criticism in vogue emanated from Southerners. Indeed, the South had furnished the most informed critics of the institution of slavery itself. But by 1850 this atmosphere of free inquiry and free expression was gone. No longer could Southerners, as in the days of Jefferson and Mason, disapprove of aspects of life in their sections or agree with the strictures of outsiders and remain honored at home. Now most Southerners refused even to view slavery as a discussable question or to consider its relation to their or man's future. A taboo on the subject, unofficial but the more stringent and repressive because it represented the feeling of the community, a kind of folk-enforcement, enveloped all of Dixie. The taboo extended to subjects related to slavery even indirectly—to, in fact, anything that could be considered un-Southern. Nor was it enough for men merely to observe the taboo, to remain silent. They must, if they were not to be suspect, speak out in glorification of slavery, and align themselves actively with its defenders. If this was not enforced conformity of thought, it was close to it. Certainly that freedom of the spirit that Jefferson had said was necessary to the good society did not exist in the South before the Civil War. There is a grim irony in the situation. Inevitably one wonders what would have happened to the Sage of Monticello if he had returned to his native section in the 1850's.

It may be objected that in this presentation of the South there is an apparent glaring paradox. Strait-jacket conformity does not seem to fit in with the tradition of Southern individualism. And we know that Southerners, particularly those of the ruling class, were as individualistic a set of men as America has produced. Mrs. Chesnut has left us an unforgettable picture of a representative of the aristocratic order, her father-in-law: "Partly patriarch, partly *grand seigneur,* this old man is a species that we will see no more; the last of the lordly planters who ruled this Southern World. His manners are unequalled still, but underneath this smooth exterior lies the grip of a tyrant, whose will has never been crossed. . . . If a lady's name is given, he uncovers and stands hat in hand until she passes. He has still the Old World art of bowing low and gracefully. He came of a race that would brook no interference with their own sweet will by man, woman, or devil; but then such manners would clear any man's character, if it needed it." Mrs. Chesnut, ordinarily so perceptive in her judgment, was in this case perhaps misled by mere exterior attractiveness. She was writing at the end of the Civil War when the whole Southern world was about to crash after military defeat, a defeat that in part had been brought about by the very traits in the Southern character that she depicted in her father-in-law. Too many Southerners, and often those in high places, had simply refused to impose on themselves the discipline that modern war demands.

And here we have the resolution of the paradox. Southern individualism was of a particular type. It expressed itself in matters of speech and conduct, in self-assertion, sometimes for its own sake, and in self-will, sometimes just to prove somebody had a will. It could not express itself in other areas because dissent in thought was not generally permitted. Could it be that the conformity of the slave system bred an individualism that helped to destroy the Confederacy? If this be true, we have another irony to add to a long list in Southern history.

Perhaps the greatest error committed by the South in the political battles of the antebellum years was in alienating its natural ally, the West. On a number of issues, primarily economic in nature, the two sections had worked together, often to the South's advantage. There was a strong probability that the alliance might have continued. It did not, and largely because again the South insisted on identifying everything with the one issue of slavery. The South demanded that the West accept its position on the status of slavery in the territories. Now people in the West might have varying feelings about the morality of slavery, some being much agitated on the question and others very little, but they were united on one conviction: they did not want to meet the competition of slave labor in the national domain. And so the South lost the West to the Northeast—by insisting on the acceptance of a system utterly unadapted to the needs of the West.

If this seems like unrealistic strategy, we may point to other examples. To the student of politics it is a matter of marvel that Southerners would let their stand on many issues be determined not by political requirements or realities but by the stand of "the enemy," the Northern antislavery elements. Thus at the time of the debate on the Kansas-Nebraska Bill it was freely admitted all over the South that the measure would be of no practical value to the section and might even injure it. Yet Southerners supported it. The Charleston *Mercury* explained why: "Can the South stand listlessly by and see the bill repealed, when this is made the direst issue against her . . .? There is no alternative for the South. When the North presents a sectional issue, and tenders battle upon it, she must meet it, or abide all the consequences of a victory easily won, by a remorseless and eager foe."

The final and tragic climax to the one-issue strategy came at the Democratic national convention at Charleston in 1860, when Southerners demanded that the party adopt a platform on slavery in the territories that they admitted would bring defeat in November. The Western Democrats refused, the party split into two wings, Lincoln won the election, and the South was left standing alone.

When the Southerners could not get what they wanted at Charleston, they walked out. They departed, says Avery Craven, "under the impression that they were upholding a principle," but in reality most of them did not know what to do and only followed an aggressive few who pretended to know the answer. Hitherto in this review of developments since the 1830's we have stressed that the South had a certain latitude of choices as to the course it would take and that because of certain factors in the Southern situation and psychology it took the wrong course, wrong in the sense that the strategy decided on defeated its purpose. We can believe this to be true, and at the same time agree with Craven that in the successive crises before 1860, or in the one of that year, most Southerners simply acted out of a feeling of apprehension or frustration. That is, although they may have had the possibility of choice they were also, to an extent, controlled by circumstance.

Humans do not always have the freedom of decision that later scholars may think. There is an element of inevitability in many episodes of history, and the one present in antebellum America may have been particularly puissant. Much of what happened was not planned or plotted by anybody. Great changes occurred, but they were the result of impersonal rather than personal forces. The North moved ahead into the modern world, while the South remained static, its economy and society not greatly different from the colonial period. The South fell to the status of a minority and blamed the North or, more accurately, men in the North for its reduction. But no men had done it, Craven points out. "The Industrial Revolution was the real culprit."

What the Industrial Revolution did was epitomized in the career of the ablest man to come out of the South since Jefferson. Nobody has described the tragedy of John C. Calhoun more eloquently than Craven. By circumstance *and* choice, Craven emphasizes, Calhoun was forced into a position "from which he had to defend slavery when all the rest of the Christian world was leaving it behind; he had to defend the political rights of the locality when all the forces of modern technology and business were producing interdependence and the need for centralized efficiency; he had to uphold strict construction of the Constitution when the forward sweep of the whole modern social-economic order demanded a broader view; he had to speak for an agricultural interest and way of life just as industry and the city were about to take over; he was forced to be a voice out of the past while he yet lived. . . ."

Whether it was choice or circumstance or both that impelled the South along the course to secession and the Civil War, we cannot with certainty say. We do know that the course was taken and we know what the results were for the South. The war did many things to the section. Among other things, it ensured that the South would remain a section for a long time to come. History provides a number of examples of civil conflicts between classes or factions diffused throughout a country but few in which the contestants faced each other over some kind of geographical line. In the

Civil War it was not just a people that had been defeated but also a distinct region. Even if the South had wanted to forget that it was a section, the North hardly would have permitted it to do so. The South, of course, did not want to forget. Rather, it wanted to remember, perhaps had to remember. "Defeated on the actual ramparts of Virginia," wrote Clarence E. Cason, "the Southerners retired to the ramparts of the mind. Here the glories of the old South became an impregnable castle over which was flown the invincible banner of 'the Lost Cause.' Since reality was unbearable, mythology became supreme." It was now that the legends of the Old South of the golden age before Sumter and of the Lost Cause destroyed in the guns after Sumter came to fullest fruition. Perhaps the legend-making was necessary in the conditions prevailing immediately after Appomattox. We are accustomed to saying that the war set the South back economically, but we forget that it also did something perhaps more serious—it threw the South back culturally and socially a century. This being so, Southerners could hardly be expected to respond to all situations in contemporary terms. But we shall have occasion to note that they would cling to the legends long after the circumstances existing in the postwar years had changed if not disappeared.

We have stressed that in the politics of the Old South there was a theme —others, of course, could be developed—and in treating it we have used words like romance and unreality. That is, we have tried to say that in large part politics did not operate in its normal or proper sense to resolve and compromise class and group differences while at the same time maintaining that plurality of opinion ordinarily found in democratic societies. There was a singular oneness about Southern politics—by the 1850's, for all practical purposes, only one party existed; the defense of the section against outside attack was identified with one issue; and the defense was pitched to one strategy.

It has been argued that all of this indicates a tendency to lose reality, to live in a Never-Never land. But after 1865 the South would emerge into a new world. Many of the forces that had molded it had gone with the war. Would the politics of this new South be different from that of the old? Would Southerners learn something from the tragic past that would change their future?

9

The South and the Myth of the Garden

Henry Nash Smith

Basic affiliations and political relationships between South and West date at least from the time of early colonial western land claims. Such associations were reinforced by the fact that, with "the roll of frontier upon frontier—and on to the frontier beyond," settlement of the great interior of virgin land was invariably in flux. Settlement patterns of West and South became, over time, almost inextricably intertwined. Observing that this kinship between South and West has often been reflected in the mirror of national politics, Henry Nash Smith, Professor of English, University of California, Berkeley, seeks to isolate the factors responsible for the sections' gradual disaffection. Despite southern efforts to the contrary, the potent South-West political coalition fell victim to developing technological and economic realities. The Erie Canal, steamship traffic on the Great Lakes, and the implementation of an east-west railway line worked together to overcome the "natural" alliance of geography and political sentiment which southerners had sought to cultivate with the developing West. In addition, the process of political disenchantment was abetted by psychological and philosophical contentions based on contrasting and conflicting images of their shared frontier experience. As the West became increasingly enamored with the ideal of the yeoman farmer and the "myth of the garden," the South was undergoing the psychological process of enshrining the plantation legend. As the one celebrated the industrious and free yeoman farmer as a cultural model, the other mentally applied an aristocratic veneer to the slave system. In the end, it was conflicting visions of Eden which prompted and reinforced the prewar isolation of the South.

Reprinted by permission of the publishers from Henry Nash Smith, *Virgin Land: The American West as Symbol and Myth*, Cambridge, Mass.: Harvard University Press. Copyright 1950, by the President and Fellows of Harvard College.

By the 1850's the South had become actively hostile to the yeoman ideal which had been developed as a rationale of agricultural settlement in the Mississippi Valley. But this break with the Northwest came only after a long struggle on the part of the Southern leaders to maintain economic and political ties with all the interior basin.

The first advance beyond the Alleghenies, in the last quarter of the eighteenth century, had been decidedly Southern in coloring. Virginia and North Carolina had been the bases for the settlement of Kentucky and Tennessee. Even the earliest Anglo-American penetration north of the Ohio, in the wake of George Rogers Clark's expedition during the Revolution, was largely a Southern venture. The history of Western exploration is filled with Southern names, from Boone and Lewis and Clark to James Clyman of Virginia and John Charles Frémont of South Carolina. Through Jefferson, Virginia had provided the geographical insight and the strategic planning for the first half-century of westward advance. So marked was the Southern dominance of this process that as late as 1846 the Pennsylvanian William Gilpin could, to be sure with an element of exaggeration, ascribe the entire impulse to the South. "The progeny of Jamestown," he declared, "has given to the Union twelve great agricultural States; has created that mighty production and generating capacity on which are based the grand power and prosperity of the Nation." Among Southern accomplishments he listed not only the settlement of Kentucky, Tennessee, Missouri, and the Southwest, but also that of Ohio, Indiana, Illinois, and Iowa.[1] Even after the Civil War Whitman declared in his poem "Virginia—The West" that Virginia had given to the nation the stalwart giant of the West whose plenteous offspring had put on uniforms of blue and preserved the Union against the rebellious Confederacy.[2]

The association between South and West had been reflected in national politics. Many representatives of the Middle States and New England had feared from the beginning that the development of the trans-Allegheny would unduly strengthen the South. In August, 1786, James Monroe wrote to Patrick Henry from New York, where Congress was sitting, that the Northerners meant to break up the settlements on the western waters in order to "keep the States southward as they now are."[3] In the Constitutional Convention of 1787 Gouverneur Morris of Pennsylvania proposed inserting into the Constitution a provision "That the number of representatives in ye first branch from the States hereafter to be established

[1] 29 Cong., 1 Sess. Senate Report No. 306. Committee on the Post Office and Post Roads (April 20, 1846), pp. 28–29.

[2] *Leaves of Grass,* inclusive edition, ed. Emory Holloway (Garden City, New York, 1931), pp. 248–249.

[3] *The Writings of James Monroe,* ed. Stanislaus M. Hamilton, 7 vols. (New York, 1898–1903), I, 150.

shall not exceed the representatives from the States already confederated."[4] Delegates to the Convention regarded this proposal as a clear test of strength between North and South. It was rejected by the close vote of four states to five, with Pennsylvania divided. The states favoring the measure were Massachusetts, Connecticut, Delaware, and Maryland (which, having no claim to Western territory, was jealous of Virginia). Those opposing it were New Jersey, Virginia, North Carolina, South Carolina, and Georgia.[5]

During the next twenty years the alignment of South and West against North and East persisted through a series of crises, of which the most spectacular arose from Federalist opposition to the Louisiana Purchase in 1803 and to the War of 1812, especially in its Western phase. As Benton picturesquely summarized the attitude of New England Federalists, the cry was, "The Potomac the boundary; the negro States by themselves! The Alleghanies the boundary, the western savages by themselves! The Mississippi the boundary, let Missouri be governed by a Prefect, or given up as a haunt for wild beasts!"[6] The alliance of West and South continued into the 1850's as a political force to be reckoned with. It was the basis of the careers of Jackson, Benton, Douglas, and other Democratic leaders; and even after the Northwest had been won for the Republican Party in the election of 1860, Western sympathy with the South found expression in the powerful Copperhead movement of disaffection during the Civil War. But the changes in the structure of American society recorded in the Republican victory of 1860 had begun soon after the War of 1812. Although the introduction of steamboats on the western waters for a time strengthened the sway of New Orleans throughout the Mississippi Valley, the Erie Canal, steam transportation through the Great Lakes, and the east-west trunk line railways eventually tied the Northwest to New York rather than to the Gulf of Mexico.

The changes which had begun to take place in the relations among the sections were fully explored in the famous Webster-Hayne debate of 1829–1830, noted in the history books for its bearing on constitutional theory, but originating in a Southern bid for Western support. The doctrine of nullification which Hayne, acting as the mouthpiece for Calhoun, announced in the course of this debate, and which South Carolina put into effect two years later in its declaration that the tariff of 1832 would not be enforced in ports of the state, expressed the Southern fear that a coalition

[4] Max Farrand, ed., *The Records of the Federal Convention of 1787*, 4 vols. (New Haven, 1911–1937), I, 533.

[5] *Ibid.*, II, 2.

[6] *Speech of Mr. Benton, of Missouri, in Reply to Mr. Webster: The Resolution Offered by Mr. Foot, Relative to the Public Lands, Being under Consideration. Delivered in the Senate, Session 1829–1830* (Washington, 1830), pp. 53–54.

of North and West would soon outweigh the strength of the South within the Union. From this time on the South wavered between two strategies. One was to surrender its long-standing but now weakening dominance of the West and fall back on constitutional minority rights. The other was to try to regain control of the West through development of trade routes from the south Atlantic coast to the Ohio Valley. Southern spokesmen in Congress resisted federal aid in the construction of canals and other means of bringing the Northwest and New England closer together, and tried to protect the position of New Orleans as queen of the trade on the western waters.

Benton stated the doctrine underlying such efforts: ". . . every canal, and every road, tending to draw the commerce of the Western States across the Alleghany mountains, is an injury to the people of the West." His desire for a continued economic alliance of South and West clouded his vision of the impending revolution in transport. Here, as in his discussion of a transcontinental trade route, he insisted that the steamboat would always outweigh the railway in importance. The bulky products of Western farms and packing houses would continue to make their way to market downstream through New Orleans. "As to the idea of sending the products of the West across the Alleghanies, it is the conception of insanity itself! No rail roads or canals will ever carry them, not even if they do it gratis!" Commercial routes from East to West could be useful only for carrying manufactured goods of relatively small bulk. If Westerners bought these goods they endangered their own market at New Orleans; for New Orleans could not buy if she were not allowed to sell. Besides, decline of the trade with New Orleans threatened to destroy the immensely important steamboat system of the West, which already, in 1829, had grown to three hundred thousand tons.[7]

The desire to strengthen economic ties with the West accounts for one of the strangest moments in the career of Calhoun, archchampion of the strict construction of the Constitution which most Southerners believed forbade federal aid for internal improvements. Having reluctantly accepted an invitation to attend the Memphis Commercial Convention of November, 1845,[8] Calhoun was elected president of the meeting and delivered the

---

[7] *Ibid.*, p. 65.

[8] James Gadsden, urging Calhoun to accept the invitation, wrote: "Now is the time to meet our Western friends at Memphis—to set the ball in motion which must bring the Valley to the South: and make them feel as allies of the Great Commercial and Agricultural interests—instead of the Tax gathering and Monopolizing interests of the North" (J. Franklin Jameson, ed., *Correspondence of John C. Calhoun* [Washington, 1900], p. 1062). Calhoun's attitude is discussed in Herbert Wender, *Southern Commercial Conventions 1837–1859,* Johns Hopkins University Studies in Historical and Political Science, Series XLVIII, No. 4 (Baltimore, 1930), p. 54.

opening address. This discourse shows what a strong attraction was being exerted by the West on Southern constitutional theory. Calhoun begins with the assumption that the Western and the Southern states occupy a single physiographic region, consisting of the Mississippi Valley and the Gulf Plains from the Atlantic to the Rio Grande—a patent translation of political desire into geographical terms. He dwells on the need for free and ready transit for persons and merchandise among the various portions of this vast region of the world. Integration of the South with the West obviously depended upon the utmost possible development of the river systems, especially of the Mississippi, whose current drew the produce of every part of the valley to the Southern metropolis of New Orleans.[9]

The crucial importance to the South of maintaining this commercial connection along the channels of the inland waterways demanded every effort to foster navigation, including federal appropriations to remove snags, dredge channels, install lighthouses, and so on. Calhoun Democrats had opposed such appropriations for twenty years as unconstitutional. But before an astonished and delighted audience Calhoun himself now proceeded to perform the mental gymnastics necessary to reach the conclusion "that the invention of Fulton has in reality, for all practical purposes, converted the Mississippi, with all its great tributaries, into an inland sea. Regarding it as such," he continued, "I am prepared to place it on the same footing with the Gulf and Atlantic coasts, the Chesapeake and Delaware Bays, and the Lakes, in reference to the superintendence of the General Government over its navigation."[10] Indeed, under the influence of this new exaltation, Calhoun even found himself celebrating the passage to India. In words that might almost have come from the lips of William Gilpin he announced in conclusion:

you occupy a region possessing advantages above all others on the globe, of the same extent, not only for its fertility, its diversity of climate and production, but in its geographical position; lying midway between the Pacific and Atlantic Oceans, in less than one generation, should the Union continue, and I hope it may be perpetual, you will be engaged in deliberations to extend your connection with the Pacific, as you are now with the Atlantic; and will ultimately be almost as intimately connected with the one as the other. In the end, you will command

[9] *Reports and Public Papers of John C. Calhoun,* being Volume VI of *Works,* ed. Richard K. Crallé (New York, 1856), pp. 273–274.

[10] *Ibid.,* p. 280. Benton had called the Mississippi and its tributaries *"mare nostrum"* in his speech during the Webster-Hayne debate fifteen years before (*Speech of Mr. Benton . . . in Reply to Mr. Webster,* p. 66). An anonymous contributor to the *Southern Quarterly Review* of Charleston, more orthodox than the Pope, greeted Calhoun's "inland sea" doctrine with the cry, *"Et tu, quoque, Brute?"* (IX, 267, January, 1846).

the commerce . . . of the world, as well as that of our greater Union, if we preserve our liberty and free popular institutions.[11]

But Calhoun's effort was in vain. The South failed in the end to maintain its hold on the developing Northwest, and the failure was a turning point in American history. When the break between North and South came in 1860, the Northwest went along with the Union. The weakening of the South's hold on the area north of the Ohio can be traced in the history of the now familiar symbols which expressed the ultimate purposes of the two sections. The richest vein of Southern materials bearing on this subject is the file of *DeBow's Review*, established in New Orleans in 1846 and devoted to the promotion of commercial relations between the South and the West along the lines endorsed by the Memphis Convention. DeBow and his contributors constantly urged the development of trade routes connecting New Orleans with the upper Mississippi Valley. They warned the South of the ominous increase in trade from the Great Lakes through the Erie Canal.[12] They urged New Orleans to waken from her complacent reliance on the Mississippi and build railways.[13] In accordance with the geographical conception advanced by Calhoun, which regarded the South and the Mississippi Valley as forming one region, DeBow celebrated the progress of the Great West as enthusiastically as Benton himself.[14] This policy led him to publish contributions from Western spokesmen developing the theme of the garden of the world. As late as 1858 DeBow included in his *Review* two characteristic essays by William Gilpin.[15] He also published articles by Jessup W. Scott of Ohio, who had long been a contributor to *Hunt's Merchants' Magazine* of New York on the development of the West. Scott, who will come up for fuller discussion in another connection, elaborated for DeBow's readers the familiar ideas of manifest destiny, predicting that the Star of Empire would "shine for ages and ages from the zenith on our central plain."[16]

DeBow's commitment to the theme of Western progress, which implied national unity if it was to benefit the South, early came into conflict with

[11] *Works*, VI, 284.

[12] Buckner H. Payne, "New Orleans—Her Commerce and Her Duties," *DeBow's Review*, III, 39–48 (January, 1847).

[13] Thomas B. Hewson, "Thoughts on a Rail-Road System for New Orleans," *ibid.*, X, 175–188 (February, 1851).

[14] "Progress of the Great West in Population, Agriculture, Arts and Commerce," *ibid.*, IV, 31–85 (September, 1847).

[15] "Hemp-Growing Region of the United States," *ibid.*, XXIV, 56–58 (January, 1858); "The Great Basin of the Mississippi," *ibid.*, XXIV, 159–165 (February, 1858).

[16] "The North American Plain," *ibid.*, XXVI, 564 (May, 1859). Scott also contributed "Westward the Star of Empire," *ibid.*, XXVII, [125]–136 (August, 1859).

his enthusiastic support of slavery. As early as 1851 he was speaking of secession as a step the South might have to take if Northern attacks continued.[17] Southern leaders were eventually forced to recognize that the notions of the course of empire and of the coming dominance of the West were implicitly free-soil. By 1860 Senator Louis T. Wigfall of Texas could put this awareness into words in an attack on Andrew Johnson's expansionism:

> The Senator from Tennessee [declared Wigfall] supposes that we have a sort of blatherskiting Americanism that is going to spread over the whole continent, and cross the Pacific, and take in the Sandwich Islands; and that, in the area of freedom, we are going to take in the whole world, and everybody is going to benefit us. The whole of that is false doctrine. I think it is a doctrine that no Democrat should ever entertain.

There was no manifest destiny, Wigfall insisted, in the Kentucky and Virginia Resolutions. "We ought to begin and repudiate and trample on this national idea," he exclaimed. The notion of colonizing and extending the area of freedom was nothing but "Red Republicanism; it is Federalism; it is nationalism; it is an ignoring of history."[18] Wigfall's instinct was sound. The very men to whom DeBow turned in the late 1850's for celebration of the imperial destinies of the Mississippi Valley were free-soilers, soon to enter the Republican party. The hero of their expansionism was Gilpin's soldier of the pioneer army, the axe man, the industrious farmer, the independent yeoman of the Western agrarian tradition. And this man was free.

Nothing could stand in greater contrast to the symbols which had meanwhile been created to express the ideal ends of the slave system. These symbols were grouped in the powerful and persuasive myth of the Southern plantation. Originating within the nostalgic and sentimental mode of Washington Irving, and first applied to the South in John P. Kennedy's *Swallow Barn* (which was published in 1832 at the turning point of Southern history), the picture of aristocratic masters, brilliant and charming heroines, and devoted slaves reached full development in the historical fiction of the Virginian John Esten Cooke in the middle 1850's. So compelling to the imagination was this group of symbols, bathed as they were in the charm of pastoral tradition and feudal romance, that they long survived the destruction of the plantation system itself. In the hands of such Southern

---

[17] "The Cause of the South," *ibid.*, X, 107 (Janaury, 1851).

[18] 36 Cong., 1 Sess., *Congressional Globe*. Senate (March 22, 1860), pp. 1303–1304.

writers as Thomas Nelson Page after the Civil War the idealized image of the plantation proved to have a strong appeal to Northern as well as to Southern audiences, and indeed to this day forms an apparently indestructible part of the national store of literary themes.[19]

But the briefest glance at the plantation in literature shows why it could not compete with the myth of the garden of the world as a projection of American experience in the West, and therefore why men like DeBow had no imaginative weapons to supplement their geographical and economic arguments for maintaining the Mississippi Valley under the hegemony of the South. The fiction dealing with the plantation emphasizes the beauty of harmonious social relations in an orderly feudal society. It presupposes generations of settled existence and is inimical to change. Literary plantations are almost always in the older South, and when they are situated in the new, developing Southwest, they are unhistorically depicted as duplicates of the Virginia and Carolina estates on which the convention was first based. Such symbols could not be adapted to the expression of a society like that of the West, either South or North, where rapidity of change, crudity, bustle, heterogeneity were fundamental traits.

It is true that during this same period the Southwest produced its own striking symbols, embodied in the newspaper sketches and oral tales which were called, collectively, Southwestern humor. These symbols were also destined to survive the Civil War and to have important consequences for American literature. They formed the tradition out of which developed Mark Twain. But Southwestern humor was of little or no use politically because while it depicted a society containing slaves, it dealt with slavery only incidentally and had no case to make for the institution. The boisterous mood of this writing veers toward satire rather than toward apologetics; it makes no appeal to sentiment, which proved to be the most powerful weapon of both defenders and attackers of slavery.

During the 1830's and early 1840's the case for westward expansion of the plantation system was the case for the annexation of Texas. The fertility of this enormous region beyond the Sabine, the mildness of its climate, its unexampled resources of every kind were presented so enthusiastically by travelers and settlers that an epidemic of "Texas fever" raged in the South.[20] Despite Mexican laws, slavery had been established in Texas from the earliest days of Anglo-American settlement, and it was generally recognized that the region offered a vast area suitable for the

[19] Francis P. Gaines, *The Southern Plantation. A Study in the Development and Accuracy of a Tradition* (New York, 1925).

[20] Lewis C. Gray, *A History of Agriculture in the Southern United States to 1860*, 2 vols. (Washington, 1933), II, 906–907.

cultivation of cotton and other plantation crops. Yet pro-slavery advocates of annexation failed entirely to create symbols comparable to the free-soil symbol of the yeoman. They were prepared to defend slavery as such with the standard doctrines, and to state the familiar propositions of manifest destiny, but they were not able to endow the westward expansion of the slave system with imaginative color. One of the most celebrated statements of the case for annexation is a letter written by Robert J. Walker of Mississippi for circulation as campaign literature in 1844. Asserting that the reannexation of Texas is "the greatest question, since the adoption of the constitution, ever presented for the decision of the American people,"[21] Walker makes the standard appeal to the need for restoring the integrity of the Mississippi Valley. The Creator, he declares,

> has planed down the whole valley, including Texas, and united every atom of the soil and every drop of the waters of the mighty whole. He has linked their rivers with the great Mississippi, and marked and united the whole for the dominion of one government and the residence of one people; and it is impious in man to attempt to dissolve this great and glorious Union.[22]

The oratory moves with assurance toward the images that had become a part of the folk heritage:

> Who will desire to check the young eagle of America, now refixing her gaze upon our former limits, and repluming her pinions for her returning flight? ... Who will oppose the re-establishment of our glorious constitution, over the whole of the mighty valley which once was shielded by its benignant sway? Who will wish again to curtail the limits of this great republican empire, and again to dismember the glorious valley of the West? ... Who will refuse to heal the bleeding wounds of the mutilated West, and reunite the veins and arteries, dissevered by the dismembering cession of Texas to Spain?[23]

[21] *Letter of Mr. Walker, of Mississippi, Relative to the Annexation of Texas: In Reply to the Call of the People of Carroll County, Kentucky, to Communicate his Views on That Subject* (Washington, 1844), p. 5.

[22] *Ibid.*, pp. 8–9. The prevalence of this argument is indicated by Albert K. Weinberg, *Manifest Destiny. A Study of Nationalist Expansionism in American History* (Baltimore, 1935), pp. 52–56. It should be pointed out that many proslavery Southerners were opposed to the annexation of Texas (Chauncey S. Boucher, "In Re That Aggressive Slaveocracy," *Mississippi Valley Historical Review*, VIII, 27, June–September, 1921).

[23] *Letter of Mr. Walker*, p. 9.

But in his treatment of the problem of slavery Walker falls back upon the defensive, picturing the economic ruin of the North and the social chaos of the South that would follow emancipation.[24] The annexation of Texas, he argued, would drain Negro population away from the older Southern states. A large and increasing number of Negroes, attracted by a congenial climate, would cross the Rio Grande and mingle with the population of the Latin-American republics to the South on a basis of social equality. Indeed, this process would eventually bring about universal emancipation. Slavery, announced the prophet with the emphasis of italics, "will certainly disappear if Texas is reannexed to the Union. . . ."[25] Providence would open Texas "as a safety valve, into which and through which slavery will slowly and gradually recede, and finally disappear into the boundless regions of Mexico, and Central and Southern America."[26]

Although this is ingenious, it is not an ideology of slavery expansion. The only Southern expansionist dream which had imaginative depth led in a different direction. This was the notion of a Caribbean slave empire, which found its most spectacular expression in the Ostend Manifesto of 1854. The Southern diplomats who in this remarkable document threatened forcible conquest of Cuba if Spain refused to sell the island to the United States, were trying to put into effect a geopolitical conception developed in part from the general notion of manifest destiny and in part from the idea of the passage to India. The oceanographer Mathew F. Maury, leading Southern scientist of his day, had called the Gulf of Mexico the American Mediterranean. Into this sea emptied the Mississippi, and the archaic Southern tendency to emphasize the primacy of natural waterways allowed Southern thinkers to conceive of the Gulf as dominating the whole interior valley. On the east the Gulf merged into the Caribbean, which touched the Isthmus of Panama, gateway to the Pacific; control of the Gulf was said to mean mastery of the dominant commercial route to the Indies. Southward the Caribbean led to South America, where the slave empire of Brazil in the fabulous basin of the Amazon offered the world's most promising theater for expansion of the plantation system.[27] The key to all this potential empire was Cuba: ". . . if we hold Cuba," wrote an editorialist in the Richmond *Enquirer*, "in the next fifty years we will hold the destiny of the richest and most increased commerce that ever dazzled the cupidity of man. And with that

---

[24] *Ibid.,* p. 11.

[25] *Ibid.,* p. 14.

[26] *Ibid.,* p. 15.

[27] Mathew F. Maury, "Gulf of Mexico," in James D. B. DeBow, ed., *The Industrial Resources, Etc., of the Southern and Western States,* 3 vols., (New Orleans, 1852), I, 365–373.

commerce we can control the power of the world. Give us this, and we can make the public opinion of the world."[28]

Well might a Southerner point out that the South had a manifest destiny different from that of the North.[29] The conception of a tropical empire occupying the basins of the Amazon and the Mississippi and controlling the trade of the Pacific, populated by Negroes brought from Africa through a reopened slave trade—"the purple dream," as Stephen Vincent Benét calls it,

> Of the America we have not been,
> The tropic empire, seeking the warm sea,
> The last foray of aristocracy,—*[30]

offers a glaring contrast with the myth of the garden of the world which expressed the goals of free-soil expansion into the Mississippi Valley. But the dream was powerful enough to inflame a young printer and newspaperman in Keokuk, Iowa, Sam Clemens by name, who set out down the Mississippi in 1856 on his way to found a coca plantation on the Amazon.[31]

---

[28] Reprinted in *DeBow's Review,* XVII, 280–281 (September, 1854). The Democratic platform in 1856 demanded that the United States maintain its ascendency in the Gulf of Mexico to protect the mouth of the Mississippi, and that American "preponderance" in the Interoceanic Isthmus be guaranteed also.

[29] "J. C.," "The Destinies of the South," *Southern Quarterly Review,* N. S. XXIII, 201 (January, 1853).

* Copyright, 1927, 1938, by Stephen Vincent Benét.

[30] *John Brown's Body* (Garden City, New York, 1928), p. 374.

[31] Albert Bigelow Paine, ed., *Mark Twain's Letters,* 2 vols. (New York, 1917), I, 34–35. Mark Twain mentions the report by Lieutenants William L. Herndon and Lardner Gibbon (*Exploration of the Valley of the Amazon, Made under Direction of the Navy Department,* 2 vols. and volume of maps, [Washington, 1853–1854], 32 Cong., 2 Sess. Senate Executive Document No. 36). Herndon was a Virginian and the brother-in-law of Maury, whose views about the development of the Amazon valley as a slave empire he shared (I, 193, 281). The expedition was ordered by John Pendleton Kennedy, Secretary of the Navy, and bore an obvious relation to Southern policy. Coca, in which Mark Twain was interested, is mentioned at I, 88–89, 249; II, 46–47.

10

Cavalier and Yankee: Synthetic Stereotypes

William R. Taylor

By 1859 the plantation legend and its complement the southern cavalier had become the dominant images shaping southern social psychology. Though critical to the development of incipient southern nationalism, the South's psychological construction of the "cavalier image" was to be but one of a cluster of images which were eventually to emerge supporting the view that southerners were a distinct people. The important void yet to be filled on the historical landscape was a counter-image—the "yankee" stereotype. William R. Taylor, Professor of History at the University of New York, Stony Brook, delineates the political and psychological forces responsible for the emergence of Cavalier *and* Yankee as contending symbols of alien cultures North and South. Following a coalition of historical circumstances—particularly John Brown's raid at Harper's Ferry in October of 1859 and the election of Abraham Lincoln as President in November of 1860—the "incompatability of temper" evident in political matters now began to manifest itself psychologically. John Brown's "private war" served to reinforce the predatory Yankee image, thus maximizing psychological and political tensions. Lincoln's election, given the South's erroneous image of him as a tool of the abolitionists, worked to the same end. The quest for an independent and uncontaminated South was now largely completed. A whole new set of assumptions had emerged and taken hold, so forcefully in fact that even after the war images of Cavalier and Yankee would continue to engage the imaginations of southerners and northerners alike.

By the summer of 1861 the subdued, candid and reasonable exchange of views which had taken place between Jefferson and John Adams some 45 years before seemed to belong to another, faraway age.[1] Early that year, as every schoolboy knows, a separate Southern government had been organized in Montgomery, Alabama. Fort Sumter had fallen in April, a peace conference in Washington had collapsed and by July the United States were at war with themselves. Historians agree that the vast majority of people in the North and South had not wanted secession, to say nothing of war, but events swept them up in a whirlwind of excitement and precipitant action over which no one, finally, could exercise control.

In the South the move to separate had at first received massive support. Of those who hung back, some, perhaps most, were genuinely undecided, others confused or indifferent, and still others afraid to acknowledge their secret convictions. Little recourse was left open for moderation. The choice, to use the language of the time, lay between "secession" and "submission." The insurgents, capitalizing on the fears inspired by Lincoln's election and emboldened by their confidence in the invincibility of the united South, had moved ahead, heedless of dissenting views.

One by one the "erring sisters" had departed "in peace"—South Carolina on December 20; Mississippi, Alabama, Georgia, and Louisiana during the month of January, and Texas on February 1. Not until late spring or early summer did Tennessee, North Carolina, and Arkansas finally secede. Only on April 17, and after Lincoln had called upon her for her militia, did Virginia, the historical leader of Southern opinion, pass an ordinance of secession. Missouri, Maryland, and Kentucky, although tragically divided, chose to remain with the Union.

Along this middle tier of states, which separated New England and the Northwest from the lower South, a resolution of conflicting loyalties was arrived at only after agonizing and prolonged reflection and debate. Lincoln correctly gauged the mood which existed in these still uncommitted parts of the South when he inserted into his Inaugural Address, delivered in March of that year, a pointed reference to Hamlet's Third Act soliloquy. Was the South, he asked, contemplating suicide?

> Will you hazard so desperate a step while there is any possibility that any portion of the ills you fly from have no real existence? Will you, while the certain ills you fly to are greater than all the real ones you fly from, will you risk the commission of so fearful a mistake?[2]

[1] [For an interesting letter on secession] See Representative David Clopton of Alabama to Senator Clement C. Clay, Dec. 13, 1860, in Clement Eaton, *A History of the Southern Confederacy* (New York, 1954), p. 12.

[2] Richard Hofstadter (ed.), *Great Issues in American History: A Documentary Record* (New York, 1958), p. 392.

In the state capitals, county seats, in village assemblies and in individual families, anguishing, seldom unanimous, decisions were made, and by midsummer the peoples of the North and South, sometimes with reluctance and sometimes in a fever of excitement, were beginning to array themselves on opposite sides of the battle lines. In a poem written that year, one of the Union's warmest advocates caught the sense of the moment in a few lines of verse.

> Beat! beat! drums!—blow! bugles! blow!
> Make no parley—stop for no expostulation,
> Mind not the timid—mind not the weeper or prayer. . . .[3]

The most memorable war in American history was about to begin.

Historians have long debated the causes which precipitated this rapid series of events, and doubtless they always will. Much has been learned about the subtle shifts of opinion which occurred within various Southern states between John Brown's raid on Harper's Ferry in October, 1859, and Lincoln's fateful decision in April, 1861, to send supplies to the beleaguered garrison at Fort Sumter. Careful studies have been made of the parochial political circumstances which heightened the sensitivity of parts of the South to sectional issues and made the election of Abraham Lincoln, as the Northern President backed by a Northern party, a nightmarish prospect. The list of Southern grievances against the federal government, it has been made clear, had been growing since the debates over Missouri in 1819–20; and the constitutional arguments employed at the time of secession have a history almost as long as the Union itself. The growth of the Southern movement for independence has been traced back to the statements of its earliest proponents in the thirties. It is the importance of this idea of Southern nationality, the popular supposition that Southerners and Northerners were distinct and different peoples, which has prompted the present study. If this idea had not been firmly embedded in the consciousness of extremists on both sides and vaguely present in the thinking of countless others, it seems doubtful that secession and Civil War would have taken place at the time and in the way that they did.

No one, of course, will ever be able to recapture in their totality the elusive feelings of individual Southerners in the face of these bewildering events, but it is clear that a significant shift in attitude took place after 1859. For a time during the early fifties the threat of open rebellion seemed to have disappeared. Problems there were, and some of them very grave, but concessions had been made. The South was enjoying flush times with

---

[3] Walt Whitman, "Beat! Beat! Drums!" *Complete Poetry and Selected Prose and Letters* (ed.), Emory Holloway (London, n.d.), p. 260.

cotton and slave prices at an all-time high, and Democrats responsive to Southern opinions were in control of the government in Washington. Then came the brief rehearsal for civil war, between Northerners and Southerners fighting over the corpse of "bleeding Kansas," the appearance on the scene of a sectional party with growing strength, a sudden and disastrous economic depression and Lincoln's highly publicized "House Divided" speech, made during his senatorial campaign in 1858. Lincoln himself conceded that some kind of crisis lay ahead, and a great many people who saw eye to eye with him on little else were inclined to agree. Then, in quick succession, came two events which shattered what little complacency remained in the South. Miscalculation of the significance of these dramatic moments was in the spirit of the times, rumors consciously launched grew rapidly out of control and genuinely conciliatory gestures on the part of the North slipped by unnoticed.

The first shock was provided by John Brown's Private War, as C. Vann Woodward has called it. This brief but highly publicized skirmish began near Harper's Ferry on the night of October 16, 1859, when Brown and 18 cohorts captured a federal arsenal. The struggle was of short duration, and it collapsed in a matter of hours. It left in its wake some 15 dead, a great mass of documents compromising Brown's supporters in the North and one of the most controversial prisoners ever to be arrested and executed by an American state. For many Southerners who took the documents at face value and let their imaginations play over the potential consequences of a massive conspiracy of this kind, John Brown personified Northern predatory intentions which they all along had suspected lurked behind the reasonable and accommodating gestures of Northern statesmen. His name evoked almost everything hateful about the Yankee character: destructiveness, conspiracy, and hypocrisy. Upon this one man for a time were focused the emotions which for close to 30 years had been gathering around the figure of the Yankee. Brown's defense by a few New Englanders such as Emerson and Thoreau, who looked upon him as a saint and a martyr, only quickened Southern response. The possibility that he may have been mad was dismissed by his attackers and supporters alike. The fact that certain of his defenders, like the Reverend Theodore Parker of Boston, were actively implicated in his conspiracy led to gross exaggerations of his real support in New England and the magnitude of his enterprise generally. Although not a single slave rose in rebellion and Brown's action was deplored in Washington by all but a few extremists in the North, the South in a matter of weeks was thrown into a state of panic and one of the worst witch-hunts in American history occurred as eccentrics and "suspicious characters" of all kinds, many of them innocent strangers passing through, were mobbed, beaten, and tarred and feathered in a vigilante effort to root out Yankees and potential Southern subversives.

No relaxation of tension followed. Rumors of slave insurrections swept the South during the next year. Finally, the election of Lincoln, who was popularly believed to be the pawn of abolitionists, and the anticipated prominence in his coming administration of William Seward of "Irrepressible Conflict" fame provided the finishing touches to the picture of a Northern conspiracy about to be launched against the South.[4]

The state of feeling that existed in the South during these fateful months can be suggested in a series of brief tableaux. In Washington Southern congressmen, and in the South, federal judges, began to resign their offices; some like Senator James H. Hammond with hesitation, some with feelings of vindictiveness and triumph. Northerners who happened to be stranded in the South were threatened, mistreated, and even mobbed, and most of them rapidly headed for home. Daniel Hundley, a Southerner living in Chicago, fled the city under cover of night out of fear for his life. There was in fact a general exodus of Southerners from Northern cities. On December 22, 1859, a trainload of students from Philadelphia arrived in Richmond, marched past the stately capitol designed by Jefferson, and assembled before the governor's mansion to hear a speech from Governor John A. Wise on Southern self-sufficiency. "Let Virginia call home her children!" the governor told them, and he went on to advocate self-sacrifice and austerity. "Let us," he said, "dress in the wool raised on our own pastures. Let us eat the flour from our own mills, and if we can't get that, why let us go back to our old accustomed corn bread."[5] Troops of "Minute Men" wearing the blue cockade drilled before admiring Negroes who caught only the holiday spirit of color and display. Everywhere the hated Yankee became a figure of ridicule and contempt. He was a conspirator and a hypocrite, but he was also a coward. He would never fight, and he could certainly never win.

The move to dissociate the South from every contaminating northern influence had reached almost hysterical proportions by the time of Lincoln's inauguration. The capital was almost empty of its former official occupants. Southern politicians and their ladies, including many of the city's most prominent hostesses, had departed for home, leaving the incoming Northern administration to run the country and—such as it was—Washington society. It was all a little mad, Senator Hammond, himself once an ardent secessionist, frankly conceded—and suicidal too. "It is an epidemic and very foolish," he wrote in December, 1860. "It reminds me of the Japanese who when insulted rip open their own bowels."[6]

    [4] C. Vann Woodward, "John Brown's Private War," *The Burden of Southern History* (Baton Rouge, 1960), pp. 41–68.

    [5] Eaton, *Confederacy*, p. 1.

    [6] *Ibid.*, pp. 9–10.

By the following summer, then, communications between North and South had broken down—even the mail had stopped moving across the Potomac—and many leading spokesmen of both sections now regarded one another suspiciously and hostilely as symbols of alien cultures. To Mrs. Chesnut, who was inclined to see things somewhat melodramatically and—like Lincoln—in familial terms, it was also a question of a divided household and a marriage gone bad. "We separated," she wrote in her diary, "because of incompatibility of temper; we are divorced, North from South, because we have hated each other so."[7] "And for so long a time," she might have added without greater exaggeration than she had already employed, since the hatred to which she referred had been slowly intensifying for over 30 years, and along with it the awakening sense of a divided culture.

Two English astronomers, Charles Mason and Jeremiah Dixon, in an effort to settle a boundary dispute, had run a line between Pennsylvania and Maryland in the 1760s, but no one had then conceived of such a boundary as dividing a North from a South. Jefferson had seen the danger of such a distinction at the time of the Missouri Compromise, but a popular belief in a precise demarcation between North and South was a development of the decades which followed, and the frontier was still indistinct even after secession. Maryland, immediately south of the line, remained loyal and other so-called slave states like Missouri and Kentucky, both of them in some measure Southern in their traditions and style of life, remained officially in the North. If there was a line, and increasingly Americans agreed that there was, it possessed no geographical definition. It was a psychological, not a physical division, which often cut like a cleaver through the mentality of individual men and women everywhere in the country.

The shift in attitude which occurred during the fifties and the alignment which rapidly appeared during the tense months following Lincoln's election in 1860, much as they owe to particular contemporary events, are deeply rooted in an equally significant but much less easily defined reorientation of American mentality which had been taking place at least since the thirties. If separation as a political and social fact was the immediate result of the political pressures, miscalculations and excited activism of these tumultuous months, the idea of a coherent South, of a distinct and different Southern civilization was not new in 1850, to say nothing of 1859; yet it was an idea which would have startled both Jefferson and Adams in 1816, and did in fact alarm Jefferson when he caught the first intimation of it in 1820.

[7] Mary Boykin Chesnut, *A Diary from Dixie* (Boston, 1949), p. 20; cited by Eaton, *Confederacy*, p. 17.

Neither Jefferson nor Adams, furthermore, had thought of the natural aristocrat—their choice for the republican leader—as possessing any particular regional traits. Neither, certainly, would have localized either lower-class villainy or aristocratic honor and virtue in any North or South which they knew. Adams, with his alertness to the danger of a false aristocracy in New England and with his keen sense of fallibility, saw evil and ambition lurking in every man's heart. He probably would have found the fully developed idea of the Yankee laughable and yet a little appealing, but he scarcely would have looked for better human materials south of the Potomac. Jefferson would have looked upon the full-blown Cavalier ideal with something like loathing and seen in its currency the undoing of much that he had worked to accomplish. Yet some three decades were sufficient to bring about these changes and to usher in a whole new set of assumptions concerning the history, cultural background, and racial composition of the two regions from which these two men had sprung— and for which they had made themselves the spokesmen. The nature of these changes is implicit in the preceding chapters, but the pattern of change is a somewhat complicated one and perhaps deserves brief reiteration.

The Southern Cavalier Redivivus

The first quarter of the nineteenth century had not passed before a significant number of Americans in both the North and the South had begun to express decided reservations about the direction progress was taking and about the kind of aggressive, mercenary, self-made man who was rapidly making his way in their society. In everyone's eyes this type of parvenu came to express a worrisome facet of the national character, to symbolize, in fact, both the restless mobility and the strident materialism of new world society. In the face of the threat which seemed to be posed by this new man, Americans—genteel and would-be genteel—began to develop pronounced longings for some form of aristocracy. They longed for a class of men immune to acquisitiveness, indifferent to social ambition and hostile to commercial life, cities, and secular progress. They sought, they would frankly have conceded, for something a little old-fashioned.

Writers like Cooper, Sarah Hale, and Paulding, themselves representative spokesmen of a much larger group, were particularly attracted by the idea of a conservative country gentry such as England possessed—or, at least, had possessed—only purer and better. The equalitarian character of life in the North provided an unsuitable terrain in which to locate, even in fantasy, an aristocracy of this kind. By the 1830s the legendary Southern planter, despite reservations of one kind or another, began to seem almost perfectly suited to fill the need. His ample estates, his spacious style of life, his Cavalier ancestry and his reputed obliviousness to money matters gained him favor in the eyes of those in search of a native American aristocracy. More and more, he came to be looked upon *the* characteristic expression of life in the South. Meanwhile, the acquisitive man, the man on the make, became inseparably associated with the North and especially with New England. In the end, the Yankee—for so he became known—was thought to be as much the product of the North as the planter-Cavalier of the South. By 1850 these two types—the Cavalier and the Yankee—expressed in the popular imagination the basic cultural conflict which people felt had grown up between a decorous, agrarian South and the rootless, shifting, money-minded North.

No such absolute division, of course, ever really existed between the North and the South. Southerners engaged in business, speculated on real estate, sought profits, lived in towns and cities, voted for the same national parties and subscribed to many of the same ideals and values as other Americans. What differences they developed, as over the issue of Negro slavery, did not lead many of them to formulate a totally different set of social objectives; these differences simply complicated their response to objectives which they already in large measure had accepted. Thus, in crying out against the Yankee North, Southerners who did so were, in a sense, striking out at part of themselves. By 1860 they had become self-divided, frustrated in their hopes and wishes, increasingly unrealistic in their social aspirations and ripe for some kind of bloody showdown.

The problem for the self-conscious South finally lay in the need which it felt to isolate—to quarantine—itself from the contaminating influence of the Yankee North, which it both feared and envied—and which, finally, was so much a part of itself. The result was the creation of an exclusively Southern historical, and even racial, heritage. Outvoted or overruled in national affairs, outgrown in population, outproduced and, as many Southerners at least secretly felt, outraged on the justice of slavery, the South in 1860 sought some kind of redemption in separateness, only to set up a Confederate government which was not essentially different, even in its constitutional details, from the federal republic from which it had just seceded.

The "Southern" problem was, then, for these men a condition of paralysis brought on by conflicting loyalties—they finally could not believe in either their own regional ideals or those of the country as a whole. Belief in the one conflicted with belief in the other; the result was confusion, indecision, and a kind of gnawing dispiritedness. By the 1850s, certainly, they no longer believed wholeheartedly in the effectiveness of the Cavalier gentleman, since they, too, came to measure achievement by financial success and the gentleman planter was, almost by definition, born to fail. But neither could they worship success, since it was measured in dollars and cents rather than in honor and cultural elevation. The improvident, generous-hearted gentleman planter for them became increasingly a symbol of a Lost Cause—an insurgent, a dueler, a fighter against overwhelming odds—in short, a figment of a utopian social world which was doomed to be submerged under a tide of middle-class materialism.

Without quite acknowledging it, many Southerners during these years had been waging a kind of war with themselves. Increasingly their ideal of a stable social order came into conflict with the social and political realities with which they were confronted. The lowly, whether white or black, gave clear evidence that they did not wish to remain lowly and feudally dependent upon the planter's goodwill. Even women were beginning to speak out in their own names, and some of the things they said represented a distinct challenge to the patriarchal role which the planter had assumed for himself and to many of the values which he thought of himself as embodying. Meanwhile, in the larger sphere of political events, the planter class in the Southern states, divested of the support of the West and challenged at home by its own yeomanry, found its power threatened both in Washington and in state legislatures. And what was an aristocrat who did not possess the power to order his own home, to say nothing of ruling over the national councils, especially when he was beginning to question some of the sanctions upon which his power had been based?

The Alabaman, Daniel Hundley,[8] for example, expressed his ambivalent attitude toward the force of the Cavalier ideal in his *Social Relations in our Southern States,* the book which he published on the eve of the war. In it he drew an ominous picture of the aristocrat in the South surrounded by predatory, or at least more forceful, social types, who seemed destined to overthrow his cultural and political domination. His book contained chapters devoted to the Southern Yankee, the southern bully, the poor white, and the enterprising and forward-looking representative of the new middle class. While he argued for the aristocratic ethos of the Southern gentleman, his confidence in his effectiveness clearly wavered before the vision of a rising Southern bourgeoisie.

Few figures in Southern history exemplify better than Edmund Ruffin the tensions and frustrations felt by those who had long battled for the Lost Cause. Ruffin, for years one of the South's leading agricultural scientists and an advocate of a diversified farm economy, was never reconciled to the defeat of the Cavalier ideal. Toward the end of his life, weary and partly deaf, he became obsessed by the idea of an independent, uncontaminated South and fought every inroad of what he regarded as Yankeeism. Dressed—rather conspicuously—in coarse Southern homespun; or,

[8] Hundley is discussed at greater length in another section.

in 1859, at the age of 63, attending John Brown's hanging clad in the uniform of a VMI cadet; or, as a volunteer in the Palmetto Guards, pulling the lanyard that sent one of the first shells toward Fort Sumter, he became a kind of Lanny Budd of the Old South, his every act a symbolic repre- sentation of Southern intransigeance before the Yankee North.

Few men more keenly sensed or more deeply resented the obstacles with which true Southernism was confronted within the South itself; no one, certainly, lashed out at the Yankee with greater bitterness or, finally expressed his feelings of frustration and self-defeat more melodramatically. As an agitator he repeatedly faced indifferent Southern audiences and, poor speaker that he was, he constantly reproached himself for his failure to bring the South to a boil. Virginia he early abandoned as reprobate; he was appalled to find the large planters in Kentucky holding strong Unionist views; and even South Carolina constantly disappointed him by her unwillingness, as in 1850, to take deliberate action. On a visit to White Sulphur Springs in August, 1859, he was astonished to find himself virtually alone among some 1600 Southern guests in calling for secession. For a time after John Brown's raid he hoped "the sluggish blood of the South" would be stirred,[9] and he personally sent pikes with which Brown had intended to arm the slaves to the governors of all the Southern states; but once again he was disappointed in his expectations. Even when con- fronted with the virtual certainty of Lincoln's election, no state except South Carolina expressed a willingness to take the initiative in seceding. The election of 1860, in which the more moderate Bell triumphed over Breckinridge within the South by a majority of 136,875, only confirmed his fear that the South would never act.

Then, as Southern states began to pass ordinances of secession, his hopes soared one final time. After a lifetime of ceaseless struggle, his dream of an independent South seemed about to become a reality. Once the exciting days of Fort Sumter were over, even these hopes were dashed as Jefferson Davis neglected former secessionists and formed a government dominated by moderates and men Ruffin regarded as would-be reunionists. Davis himself, furthermore, seemed slow to move and indecisive, and left South- ern extremists generally dissatisfied with his leadership. But for Ruffin—as for most Southerners—the most crushing blow, one which destroyed for all time the myth of Southern invincibility, was the military defeat of the South by the Northern armies that swarmed across his beloved Virginia, destroying his plantation "Beechwood" and leaving obscene graffiti scrawled on the walls of his house. His plantation a shambles, deserted

[9] Avery Craven, *Edmund Ruffin Southerner: A Study in Secession* (New York, 1932), p. 171.

by his slaves, his hearing gone, and the alien North on his very doorstep, he had little left to him that he valued save his sense of honor, his bitterness, and his pride, to which he regularly gave expression in a diary kept through these trying years.

On June 17, 1865, after he had digested the news from Appomattox, he made this entry in the diary:

I here declare my unmitigated hatred to Yankee rule—to all political, social and business connections with the Yankees and to the Yankee race. Would that I could impress these sentiments, in their full force, on every living Southerner and bequeath them to every one yet to be born! May such sentiments be held universally in the outraged and downtrodden South, though in silence and stillness, until the now far-distant day shall arrive for just retribution for Yankee usurpation, oppression and atrocious outrages, and for deliverance and vengeance for the now ruined, subjugated and enslaved Southern States! . . . And now with my latest writing and utterance, and with what will be near my latest breath, I here repeat and would willingly proclaim my unmitigated hatred to Yankee rule—to all political, social and business connections with Yankees, and the perfidious, malignant and vile Yankee race.[10]

Almost before the ink of this entry had dried the old man performed his most symbolic act. Seating himself erectly in his chair, he propped the butt of his silver-mounted gun against a trunk at his feet, placed the muzzle in his mouth and, as his son reported in a letter to members of the family, "pulled the trigger with a forked stick."[11]

Coda

With Edmund Ruffin's suicide and the collapse of the Confederacy which it symbolized, the Old South as a concrete entity passed beyond history and into legend. One prolonged attempt to establish and sustain an aristocratic ideal in the face of obstacles of the kind invariably thrown up by American circumstances had ended. It was not the first such attempt, as colonial historians have shown,[12] nor was it to be the last, as those

---

[10] *Ibid.,* p. 259. The information about Ruffin, except for the details of his death, derives entirely from Professor Craven's biography.

[11] Edmund Ruffin, Jr., to his sons, June 20, 1865, in "Death of Edmund Ruffin," *Tyler's Quarterly Historical and Genealogical Magazine,* V (January, 1924), 193.

[12] Bernard Bailyn, "Politics and Social Structure in Virginia," *Seventeenth-Century America: Essays in Colonial History* (ed.), James Morton Smith (Chapel Hill, 1959), pp. 90–115.

familiar with elitist groups at the end of the century can testify;[13] but perhaps, because of its bearing on the course of American history before 1861 and because of its more general consequences for the development of our cultural self-awareness, it has been the most important.

The Cavalier ideal was predestined to fail, as some of its earliest proponents secretly knew. The men who originated it were not aristocrats in any sense which Europeans would have recognized. Often they themselves were self-made men, provincial in their outlook and historically naïve, who possessed no sure sense of any cultural tradition. I have spoken, principally as a matter of convenience, of "the South" and "the planter class" in assigning a specific locus to the kind of thinking which I have been describing; but at no time, I suspect, was the Cavalier ideal as it was defined by Beverley Tucker, for example, widely understood or embraced by Southern planters in general, to say nothing of other people living within the South. Such an ideal was significant because it exemplified an important American cultural problem and because it defined a tendency in Southern thought which ultimately affected political events.

· As it moved toward implementation, of course, the ideal was repeatedly and necessarily compromised. The constitution of no Southern state, not even that of South Carolina, provided for anything more than a kind of modified planter oligarchy; most of the older states within the South yielded to democratic pressures before the war; and the newer states of the Southwest were no more exclusive in their political arrangements than comparable states in the North. The Confederate constitution, finally, despite its explicit recognition of slavery, was in no sense meant to set up an aristocracy, and in certain ways it provided more assurance of popular government than the federal Constitution.

The legacy left behind by the Cavalier ideal is a little difficult to define; a careful consideration of it would require a study in itself. The close of the war did not mean, certainly, that some kind of aristocratic ideal ceased to form a part of Southern thinking, nor did it mean, once Reconstruction was over, that some kind of planter class ceased to dominate Southern politics. Quite the contrary. The century had virtually ended before the old dominant groups in the South and their new business allies received any substantial challenge from the majority of Southerners, whose affairs they had historically directed. After the war, as everyone knows, the legend, far from dying away, was given a new lease on life and, in the North, probably enjoyed greater popularity and evoked more interest than at any other time. Its vitality, it seems apparent enough, has not yet

[13] Barbara Miller Solomon, *Ancestors and Immigrants: A Changing New England Tradition* (Cambridge, Mass.; 1956); Arthur Mann, *Yankee Reformers in The Urban Age* (Cambridge, Mass., 1954).

exhausted itself today after more than a century of discussion and dramatic reembodiment. The nostalgia felt by Americans for the antebellum South and for the drama of the Civil War is a phenomenon which continues to startle those unfamiliar with our culture, with our collective anxieties about the kind of civilization we have created, and with our reservations concerning the kind of social conformity which, it appears, it has been our destiny to exemplify before the world. Some of our greatest writers—Henry Adams and Henry James within the nineteenth century—have employed the Cavalier legend as a means of defining and measuring the failures and limitations of our culture at large. It seems scarcely necessary to add that this same concern has characteristically engaged the imagination of William Faulkner. But for the great mass of Americans, even those who take their impression exclusively from popular novels, television plays, and Civil War centennials, the Old South has also become an enduring part of our sense of the past. At odd moments probably even the most skeptical of us allow our thoughts to play over this lingering social image, and to concede with mingled pride and wonderment: "Once it was *different* down there."

11

The Confederate Myth

Frank E. Vandiver

To the minds of most, the War Between the States represents the greatest watershed and psychodrama of the national experience. It represents as well the most acute trauma in southern historical consciousness. The southern mind and its mystique are clearly wedded in the Civil War. To Frank E. Vandiver, Professor of History and Provost at Rice University, Houston, the impact of the war and the consequent emergence of the Confederate States of America had been debilitating as regards the social imagination of the South. It was the war experience that reinforced the "pseudo-past" of the Old South. It was by virtue of "the crusade of the planters" that a related, but nonetheless new, mythical edifice began to emerge from the ashes of Shiloh, Vicksburg, and Chattanooga. Ironically, however, it was not the mythologized Confederate leadership which functioned as principle architects of the "Confederate Myth," but rather future idolaters with an appetite for historical romance. In the wake of civil war, Confederate political and military leaders continued at the cutting edge of historical change. They stood in the vanguard of a New South, a redeemed South based on economic progress. It would be subsequent generations who would function as the mythmakers and falsifiers of history—seeing the revolutionary generation as strict state righters, blind patriots to a "lost cause," and preservers of southern racial integrity. As has often been the case in other political circumstances, it was "enterprising conservatives" who led a historical pilgrimage to the shrine of dead radicals.

From Frank E. Vandiver, "The Confederate Myth," *Southwest Review,* 46 (Summer 1961), 199–204. Reprinted with permission of the publisher and author.

In the states of the old Confederacy the Centennial celebration of the Civil War is to be largely a refurbishing of the Confederate myth. The Confederate myth is a vital part of life in the South. According to this legend, sanctified southern ancestors fought valiantly against virtually hopeless odds to sustain a "way of life" peculiar to the section of long, hot summers, and Negro field hands. This "way of life" never seemed to be wholly understood, but it found description in various paeans of nostalgia and in the self-image of all southerners. Key elements in the southern mode of living were tradition, dedication to the protocols of lineage, land, cotton, sun, and vast hordes of blacks. Tending southern life were a special breed represented by the planters. Not everybody by any means was a planter, but the myth holds that everybody wanted to be and that all had the same chance to rise to that pinnacle of grace—all save the noncitizens with dark skin. The planters came to hoard their status with a certain grim zeal. Under increasing pressure throughout the 1830's, 40's, and 50's, they turned to all types of protection—censorship, intimidation, propaganda, open hostility to fellow-Americans.

But their tactics were glossed by myth into a creditable struggle for self-determination against a tide of urban nationalism which threatened extinction of the "way of life" so happy and so alien to the time.

The crusade of the planters spread to a campaign for Southern Rights, and hence the small farmer, the town merchant, the southern clergy found themselves sharing the planter's war. What was good for the planter was good for the South.

War, according to the myth, may not have been the only way to save the social and economic order, but it showed how deeply dedicated were the southerners to their inarticulated "rights." Against forces most formidable the southerner pitted himself, his small fortune, his Lilliputian industry, his life, and his girded honor. He lost, but lost magnificently. He lost wholly, utterly, but out of the ashes of his homes, his cities, his broken generation, he salvaged his sacred honor. And with this scrap of victory he could build the myth that has sustained him, has shackled him to a false image, and has convinced him of a lasting difference between himself and the rest of the United States.

Marshall Fishwick, in a brave and controversial essay, "Robert E. Lee: The Guardian Angel Myth" (*Saturday Review,* March 4, 1961), points out that Lee's noble virtues, peerless leadership, and heroic acceptance of defeat fixed in the southern mind the meaning of the Lost Cause. That cause represented the true acme of southern achievement: for it died the flower of the South, and those who yielded up their blood were such southerners as all those who came since would like to be. They were the shining model, the marble image, the men above men who lived a brief moment as destiny's chosen. They were the South.

They still are the South, for they stand above, around, and beyond what the South now is, and loom as silent prophets to lesser men in troubled times. And so they are God and curse, inspiration and death. Their stone faces look from countless shafts to the past, and their sons, grandsons, and great-grandsons look with them. They are different from the present; they were alien to their time. So, too, the modern southerner who points to difference, to his ageless "white man's burden" and his genteel poverty. His ancestors lurking from musty picture frames stood against the leviathan state and its leveling tendencies. He, too, stands with his own perception of past obligations and future duties. If the rest of the nation has lost its agrarian innocence, the southerner remembers. He, at least, is faithful to a dim Jeffersonian image and to a Greek democracy ideal which came, was fleetingly touched by life and sustained by blood, and faded to the pantheon of lost glories. But the brief blood bath lent a strange endurance and gave hope to generations held tight in inertia, fear, poverty, and the horror of a lost dream and a shattered mirror. The broken image had to be conjured again, and when it came it was twisted into a grotesque sort of plaster beauty which satisfied its designers and doomed the past it seemed to limn to a hundred years of distortion.

Distorting Civil War southerners was not easy. They lived larger than most, fought, raged, cowed, bled, spoke, and died with the nobility of desperation. They were, like their northern brethren, touched with timeless animation. They were unique and so should have been immune to the myth-makers and falsifiers of history. But myth-makers are determined and their works often approved by necessity. So the Confederate changed from a human, striving, erring being to something much different. All Confederates automatically became virtuous, all were defenders of the rights of states and individuals, all were segregationists, all steadfast, all patriotic. .

Like all lasting myths, this one had enough validity to sound good. The Lost Cause came on to the present as the last American resistance against the Organization State, against racial indistinction, against mass and motor.

And while post-Civil War southerners were pushing as fast as they could into the New South, were grasping Yankee dollars with enthusiasm, they purified their motives in the well of Lost Causism. Politicians found it a bottomless source of bombast and ballots, preachers found it balm and solace to somewhat reluctant middle-class morals, writers found it a noble and salable theme. What the South had been could be the touchstone for the future, could be the fundament of a section going into the industrial age with part of its heart and holding firm to the past with the other.

Lost Causism came to fulfil a role similar to that of the pro-slavery argument in ante-bellum times. It offered justification for resistance to the leveling tendencies continued by harsh Reconstruction measures. It cloaked the lawless Klansman and lent license to the segregating Christian. It was, finally, the cornerstone of the New South.

The tragedy is that the Confederate myth is so wrong. That the Confederacy could come to represent in the present things it never represented in its lifetime is an irony of the present southern dilemma.

What, then, are some of the axioms of the Confederate myth?

First: The Confederate States represented the unified nationalistic yearning of all the state rights advocates in the South.

Wrong. State righters were not unified and there is considerable doubt that they were in the majority when the Confederacy took form in February, 1861. Certain it is that they failed to gain control of the government under Jefferson Davis, and although they did much to impede the Confederate war effort, they did not dominate the high councils.

Second: The Confederacy was defended to the last by gaunt gray heroes who went with Lee and Johnston and others to the bitterest end.

Wrong again. There was probably more per capita desertion from Confederate ranks than from the ranks of the Union. Far more Rebel troops were absent from roll call at the end of the war than were with the colors. Much bravery, even shining, incredible heroism the southern men did display, but that they were all blind patriots is demonstrably untrue.

Third: Any Confederate could lick ten Yankees.

Possibly, but in the end the Rebels were "overwhelmed."

Fourth: Everyone behind the Confederate lines showed the same dauntless dedication to oblivion as the soldiery. Men, women, and children all served the cause to the last shred of cloth, the last window weight, the last crust of bread.

Not so. While there were many magnificent examples of fate-defying loyalty by southern civilians, there were also many examples of petty speculation, wanton brigandage, Unionism, criminal selfishness, and treason. Defection behind the lines, open resistance to Confederate laws, became a matter of national scandal before the conflict ended.

Fifth: All Confederate leaders were unswervingly dedicated to the cause and would have preferred to perish rather than survive under a despised and crushing victor.

Still wrong. Many Confederate leaders, including Davis, Stephens, Lee, and Stonewall Jackson, looked on secession with a jaundiced eye. Legal they thought it to be, but they doubted its practicality. And when the war ended only a few of the leaders who survived buried themselves in the past. Davis did, and so did lasting disservice to the section he strove to defend. Lee, on the other hand, put the war behind him and worked unsparingly for a prosperous New South sharing fully the destiny of a re-United States. His example set the tone for most veterans. Numbers of former generals, to be sure, used their combat records to gain some personal advantage, but most wanted that advantage to further a career in business or politics and hence partook of the new industrial age.

Sixth: The Confederacy fought not only for state rights, but also and especially to preserve racial integrity. The government and the people of the embattled southern states were solidly against letting down racial barriers and understood that a northern victory would mean abolition. The Negro was kept in his place in the Confederacy, was used only for agricultural and menial tasks, and what was good enough for the Confederates is good enough for us.

False, and this is false on two levels. During the war the South did attempt for a time to shore up the bonds of servitude, but when the pressure of defeat grew grim, various southern leaders, including Lee and Davis, came to advocate the use of slaves in the army; some even suggested freedom in return for service. And after the war, on the level of special pleading, the South engaged in a long paper conflict with northern historians about the causes of the fighting. A point which the southerners strove staunchly to sustain was that the war had not been fought to preserve slavery, but to preserve the "Southern Way of Life," of which slavery was only an aspect. Finally some argued that the war had been fought solely to gain independence, and cited the offer to England in March, 1865, of total freedom in exchange for recognition as proof.

Seventh: The Confederate government was a supreme, unsullied example of a state rights organization that remained loyal to the principles of Calhoun, even in the face of defeat.

This is the wrongest of all assumptions. Davis and his administration tried for a while to do what seemed constitutional under the narrow southern view of law, but war and a curiously unnoticed strain of mind in the South changed the course of governmental conduct.

Union sentiment, long-standing in many parts of the South, united with conservative Democratic sentiment and with latent Whiggery to introduce a new element in southern politics. Men who looked on violent change with repugnance banded together to prevent the secessionists from carrying the Confederacy to revolutionary excesses. These men, including Davis himslf, kept the Montgomery Convention in hand, saw to it that the trend toward vast, ruinous upheaval was halted by moderate counsel. The result of moderate control at Montgomery was a Confederate constitution much like that of the Union, a government based on established and familiar federal principles, and a president who had not camped with the fire-eaters. Many with these cautious views were elected to the various Confederate congresses and so held some authority through the war.

Caution and the natural conservatism of some Democrats and Whigs did not mean that these members of the Confederate Congress were unwilling to fight a hard war. Most of these southern moderates were men dedicated to strong central government as the main bulwark of law and order. They hated disturbance and resisted disruption of the Union. But when it came, they "went with their state," they stayed with family and land. They stayed, too, with principles of steady government, strong law, and established order. Consequently they stood for power in the hands of the executive, power in the federal government, and a stern war effort.

It was these Whiggish moderates who came to represent the Confederate "left" and to urge big government to fight a big war. They knew something of the corporate state, saw that it had virtues for organization, and urged Davis and his cabinet to centralize and command. These neo-organization men supported the growth of a large army, strict taxation (in keeping with sound Whig monetary views), conscription, impressment of private property, and finally the use of Negro slaves in the ranks—even to the point of manumission in return for service. When the war ended, these same "leftists" of the Confederacy moved into the New South.

Many became leaders in new southern industries, some went into politics and supported the coming of northern capital, most stood for sound finances, restoration of order, and the onward march of business. These moderates, these quiet men who abhorred revolution but used it when they had to, were the ones who brought about the greatest revolution of the South. They changed the Confederacy right under the eyes of the rabid secessionists from a localistic community into a small industrial power run along centralized lines. They aroused resistance from the Confederate "right"—state righters and fire-eaters—but kept control and forced their opponents to adopt modern centralist measures to resist them. When their attempt to remake the wartime South ended in defeat, they continued their efforts with the aid of Radical Republicans and ultimately achieved their goal. The Old South disappeared in the smoke of Chattanooga's and Birmingham's iron furnaces, in the dust of Alabama's coal pits, in the busy marts of Atlanta, Houston, Memphis, and New Orleans. These quiet, soft action men were the ones who set the base for the rise of a new industrial giant south of Mason and Dixon's Line, a giant whose future, according to Professor Walter Prescott Webb, is limitless because of its natural resources.

But in one salient° respect these Whiggish gentlemen failed to remold their native section: this boundless potential painted by Webb and many chambers of commerce is sharply restricted by the Confederate myth. Although the moderate businessmen of the Confederate and New South were willing and partially able to set the black man free, and did break the bonds of southern agriculture, they could not unshackle the mind of the South—the Negro became a symbol of all troubles, and the Confederacy lingered as the herald of the South's greatness. The myth holds that the South was so great when it fought with piteous ardor for a twisted past and for principles aged and vestigial, that there was no future left for it. Its future lay buried with its gray dead.

This stultifying acceptance of decline is the wages of the Confederate myth. What was, was pure and better than what is, and in what was lies a sort of self-realization. While the South was transformed by Confederates into a moderately modern, progressive nation, the myth twists the achievement of the rebellious generation and dooms descendants to cheating themselves. Acceptance of the illusion of rabid Confederate racism, for instance, leads the modern Confederate to waste a vast source of manpower—a source which could be of inestimable value if the South is to move into the rosy future that some have predicted for it.

The Centennial years could best be devoted to revising the Confederate myth and bringing it up to date. Instead of standing for a pseudo-past, for false traditions and sham virtues, it should be repaired by the reality of perspective into what it has always been. Lee, Davis, members of the Confederate Congress, many soldiers who fell gallantly on scores of fields, were alert, forward-looking southerners. They were willing, for the sake of their cause, to abandon old shibboleths, to change the very nature of their body politic and body social. Instead of looking back and making war with weapons withered by age, they looked at the new ones their enemies used and copied, improved, progressed. The Confederate States of America did not have America in the name for nothing. Confederates were Americans, too, and so had no fear of challenge. The Rebels accepted challenge and almost met it. Most of them surely would regard with scorn their descendants who look backward in frustration.

12

Dawn without Noon:
The Myths of Reconstruction

Carl N. Degler

With the afterglow of the sectional conflict still firing their imaginations, southerners and northerners collectively began the arduous
process of reshaping the social and political configuration of the
Southland. The desire to "bind up the nation's wounds," to re-
direct the frenetic energy of the Civil War into reconstructive
channels, was a major compulsion of post–Civil War America.
Indeed, the war for the Union had settled many issues, but had
left as many outstanding. Unfortunately for "posterity," the historical record of the dozen years of Reconstruction—in fact, that
of the total postwar experience from 1865 to 1900—has been
extremely difficult to assess. An important challenge to the resultant
legends of the Reconstruction era has been sounded by Carl
Degler, Professor of History at Stanford University. Since the so-
called "tragic era," Americans North and South have become
addicted to a view of the postwar era depicting corruption and
graft, military despotism, black political control, and white disfranchisement—all, of course, arranged by a vengeful and vindictive Congress. After examining the major deficiencies of such
a view, Professor Degler concludes that black disfranchisement and
de jure segregation did not ensue upon the withdrawal of federal
troops in 1877. Rather, the southern attempt to keep the freedman
"in his place" is a late nineteenth, indeed a turn of the century,
phenomenon. In important ways, then, the southerner's image of the
Negro as forged by the legacy of slavery continued in a recon-
structed but largely undiluted biracial form into the twentieth century.

From pp. 217–232 in rev. ed., *Out of Our Past* by Carl N. Degler. Copyright © 1970
by Carl N. Degler. By permission of Harper & Row, Publishers, Inc. (Footnotes have
been renumbered.)

There is a myth of Reconstruction history to which most Americans, Northerners and Southerners alike, give credence. In brief outline it goes something like this. In 1867, a vengeful Congress placed the southern states under a military despotism which supported by its bayonets an alien regime in each of the states, composed of white adventurers—the carpet-baggers and scalawags—and their ignorant Negro allies. For a decade thereafter, the story continues, these regimes looted the treasuries of the southern states, impoverished the region with high taxes, denied the southern white people any say in their own governance, and spread terror through-out the Southland. Not until the withdrawal of federal troops in 1877, it is said, did this nightmare end and decency in government return to the South. As in most myths, there is some truth in this one; but a balanced picture of Reconstruction is quite different.

For one thing, though it is common to think of Reconstruction as lasting the ten years from 1867 to 1877, the actual duration of the military and Radical regimes varied considerably from state to state. Democratic or conservative governments came to power in Virginia and North Carolina as early as 1870 (in fact, Virginia never experienced a true Radical civilian government at all); in Georgia in 1871; in Texas, Arkansas, and Alabama in 1874; in Mississippi in 1876. Only South Carolina, Florida, and Louisiana depended upon the withdrawal of federal troops in 1877 for the overthrow of their Radical government. In brief, Radical Recon-struction, including the military phases as well as the civilian, lasted as short a time as three years in two states and as long as ten years in only three.

Because it is so often assumed that Radical Reconstruction was synonymous with military rule, the role of the Army in the South during this period must be precisely understood. Under the congressional plan of Reconstruction as set forth in the acts of 1867, the South was divided into five military districts, each under a major general. It was the responsi-bility of these generals to oversee the establishment of registration lists for voters for the constitutional conventions and the election of new gov-ernments in the states of their districts. Once this was accomplished, civil governments based on the new constitutions would assume power. Gen-erally, the ending of military rule roughly coincided with the date at which Congress admitted the state to the Union. Thus military rule ended in 1868 in all of the southern states except Virginia, Texas, and Mississippi, and in those states it was over in 1869 or 1870. (Only in Georgia was military rule ever imposed again.) Often, it must be admitted, the Radical civil governments required or utilized the aid of militia and sometimes the federal troops to support their regimes, but this does not mean that an extraconstitutional government was in power. For the greater part of Radical Reconstruction, then, the southern states were under civil, not military, government, and, in most cases, these were governments which conservative white Southerners could influence with their votes. Indeed, it was by losing elections that many of the Radical governments fell into conservative hands before 1877.

But even when the southern states were under the military, it should not be assumed that the government was corrupt, oppressive, or unfair toward the whites. Contrary to the usual conception of the military occupation of the South, the number of troops actually stationed in the whole region was very small. No more than 20,000 men were involved in the whole "occupation," of whom fully 7,000 were concentrated in the two states of Louisiana and Texas. No garrison, except those in Richmond and New Orleans, which contained 1,000 each, numbered more than 500 men. The relative weakness of the military force, of course, is a measure of the southern acceptance of northern control.

Though weak in manpower, the military was supreme in law. In fact, the whole machinery of government and law was at the disposal of the Army; its authority was final. But the acquiescence in this on the part of the Southerners—for there was no organized opposition—is weighty testimony to the relative fairness of the administration. "It would be hard to deny that, so far as the ordinary civil administration was concerned," William A. Dunning, the authority on Reconstruction and no friend of the Radicals, has written, "the rule of the generals was as just and efficient as it was far-reaching. Criticism and denunciation of their acts were bitter and continuous; but no very profound research is necessary in order to discover that the animus of these attacks was chiefly political. . . ." There is good reason for believing, he continued, "that military government, pure and simple, unaccompanied by the measures for the institution of Negro suffrage, might have proved for a time a useful aid to social readjustment in the South, as preliminary to the final solution of political problems."

Even later, when the federal troops intervened in the South, it was with care and with a concern for fairness to the whites. President Grant in 1871, much disturbed by the attacks of the Ku Klux Klan upon Negroes, prevailed upon Congress to pass an act to aid in the suppression of the violence. Only once, however, did the President invoke the broad powers which Congress granted; this was in the famous incident of the nine counties of South Carolina in 1871. But even in this instance, Grant was careful enough to have the Attorney General investigate the situation in the area before he acted, and the President withdrew his order for one county when he found he was mistaken as to the disorders and conditions there.

In the prosecution of Southerners for infractions of the so-called enforcement acts, passed in 1870–71 to assist in the suppression of opposition to Negro suffrage, the federal courts tried hard to be fair. Out of the hundreds of cases against whites for infringements of these laws, there were relatively few convictions. One authority, William W. Davis, a Southerner, has estimated that only about 20 percent of the cases under the acts resulted in conviction; and about 70 percent of them were dismissed or nolle-prossed. "The Federal courts," Davis has written, "insisted on reasonable testimony, and the judges, with some notorious exceptions, were generally fair in their rulings." Moreover, he added, "White judges were inclined toward leniency in judging the white man prosecuted under the force acts on the testimony of black men." In summary, then, it would seem that justice was obtainable for the white man even during the grimmest days of so-called Black Reconstruction.[1]

Perhaps the explanation most commonly offered for the ascendancy of the Radicals and the Negroes in southern state governments is that the conservative whites were disfranchised at the same time the Negroes were enfranchised. As a literal and nonquantitative statement, this is true, but as an explanation it will not hold water. At no time were sufficient whites deprived of the ballot to permit the Negroes and Northerners to take over the governments of the southern states by default.

Before the numbers involved can be discussed, the two different kinds or phases of disfranchisement must be understood. The first was during military rule, when Congress stipulated that those who had deserted federal office for the Confederacy or had voluntarily given aid to that cause were to be denied the suffrage and officeholding. Though it is impossible to obtain a completely accurate record of the number disfranchised under this rule (thousands of whites, for example, refused to register as a form of protest, but they are sometimes counted as disfranchised), the figure usually accepted is 150,000 for the whole South. This is to be compared with a total registration for whites in 1868 of about 630,000. Regardless of the size of the figure, under this disfranchisement only two elections were held, one for the choosing of the delegates to the state constitution conventions and the other for the selection of the officers of the new governments created under the constitutions. After that, the qualifications for voting would be those decided upon in the conventions and written into the new constitutions. And that was the second phase of disfranchisement.

Again, contrary to the usual opinion, the states, on the whole, in their Radical-dominated conventions were not as ruthless in disfranchisement as one might expect. And those which were, found that their disabling

---

[1] Even a work as critical and penetrating as W. J. Cash, *The Mind of the South*, published as recently as 1941, contains exaggerated presentations of what happened during Reconstruction. "For ten years the courts of the South were in such hands that no loyal white man could hope to find justice in them as against any Negro or any white creature of the Yankee policy; for twenty years and longer they continued, in many quarters, to be in such hands that such justice was at least doubtful."

clauses were removed before ratification. In the end, only Louisiana, Alabama, and Arkansas actually enforced suffrage and officeholding restrictions against whites; the other seven states placed no legal obstacle in the way of white voting. Finally, it should be noted that the number of southern leaders upon whom the disabilities of the Fourteenth Amendment were visited was greatly reduced as early as 1872. At that date no more than 750 Southerners, those who had occupied high office under the United States in 1860–61 and had deserted to the southern cause, were still barred from officeholding. The disabilities against these men were not removed until the time of the Spanish-American War.

In view of the foregoing, it is illusory to look to white disfranchisement for an explanation of the electoral successes of the Radicals in the southern states. Rather it has to be sought in the fact that many whites did not vote, either in protest or because of indifference, while many Negroes did, either from understanding of the issues or from compulsion from their white and Negro leaders. It should not be forgotten, in this regard, that the proportion of Negroes in the southern states was uniformly greater at that time than it is now. Three states, for example—Louisiana, South Carolina, and Mississippi—contained a majority of Negroes, and one would expect, everything being equal, to encounter a Negro-Radical majority in those states. Moreover, a comparison of the number of Negroes registered in 1868 in each of the southern states with the number of Negro males over twenty-one as listed in the Census of 1870 discloses that only in Alabama was the actual number of Negro registrants out of line with the potential number as counted in the census. In all the other states the registration figures are plausible and not the result of obvious padding or fraud.

This is not to suggest that fraud did not occur in Reconstruction elections any more than it is meant to convey the impression that New York City elections at this time were innocent of fraud; undoubtedly there was much in both places and on both sides of the political fence. The purpose here, rather, is to show that there is solid justification for the strong showing which the Radicals made at the polls and that it is not to be casually attributed to the "counting out" of the whites. As a matter of fact, even under military-run registration in 1868, white voters outnumbered Negro voters in Georgia, Virginia, Texas, and North Carolina, a fact which rather effectively demolishes the argument that military reconstruction disfranchised the white majorities. Yet, of the two phases of disfranchisement, this was the stricter.

Looming over all discussions of Reconstruction, whether by Southerners or Northerners, is always the question of Negro domination. Surely, in the fear-ridden mind of the South, the unforgettable evil of Reconstruction was the participation of the Negro in government. Actually, though, aside from the exercise of the suffrage, which will be left until later, the Negro played a relatively minor political role in the Reconstruction of the southern states. Indeed, so limited were the number of offices available to Negroes that some of the Negro leaders, one southern authority has written, complained to their white mentors that their race was getting too few plums of office. Often northern whites who came to the South did not look with favor upon Negroes in office, and Southerners who collaborated with the Radicals, retaining, at least in part, their southern-born attitudes on race, were chary of permitting too many Negroes to hold office.

Negroes, of course, did hold some offices under Reconstruction; in fact, outside the position of Governor, which no Negro held in any state, black men filled each executive office at one time or another. In only one state, however, was a Negro a member of the Supreme Court; that was in South Carolina. The vast majority of Negro officeholders, however, were local officials like county superintendents of education and justices of the peace.

Contrary to the legend, Negroes did not dominate the legislatures of the southern states. The popularity of James S. Pike's sensational and partisan book, *The Prostrate State,* a contemporary description of the South Carolina legislature, has fostered the erroneous conclusion that such a body was typical of Radical regimes. In truth, Negroes were a majority in the legislatures of South Carolina and Louisiana only, and even there not for all the sessions of the period. Negroes were also a minority in all of the constitutional conventions called under the military, except, again, in the instance of South Carolina, and in Louisiana, where the whites and Negroes were equally divided. (South Carolina and Louisiana stand out in this regard because each contained a large and old city in which lived numbers of free Negroes who had some education and experience outside of slavery.)

Perhaps if there had been Negro domination, Reconstruction in the southern states would have been milder, for in both the conventions and the legislatures of the states the Negro members were the opposite of vindictive toward the whites. "I have no desire to take away any rights of the white man," said Tom Lee, delegate to the Alabama Constitutional Convention in 1867, "all I want is equal rights in the court house and equal rights when I go to vote." Even in the Negro-dominated legislature of South Carolina, there was no disfranchisement of whites beyond that prescribed for officeholding in the Fourteenth Amendment. Whenever the question of amnesty for Confederates came up in the United States Congress, where several Negroes sat during Reconstruction, the Negroes were usually found on the side of leniency toward the white man.

The South Carolina convention was extreme and unrepresentative of its sister conventions when it sought to ban terms of opprobrium like "Nigger" and "Yankee." South Carolina was also out of line with the other states when it provided for racially integrated schools; only two other states followed that example. For the overwhelming majority of Southerners, Reconstruction did not involve the mixing of races in the public schools. Nor did it mean the legalization of intermarriage between the races; the ante-bellum statutes prohibiting such unions were retained by the Radical regimes. The Negroes, in the main, wanted equality, not dominance.

Among the advantages which Radical Reconstruction brought to the southern states were the new constitutions which the Negroes and Radical whites wrote in each of the states. These organic laws stand up well upon comparison with earlier and subsequent ones in the South. As E. M. Coulter of the University of Georgia, and no friend of Reconstruction Radicals, has written, "The Constitutions finally turned out were much better than the Southerners had ever hoped for: in fact, some of them were kept for many years after the whites again got control of the governments." Generally they were "more democratic than the documents they supplanted, made so by increasing the electorate through Negro suffrage, requiring the total population as the basis for representation, reducing the terms of office, and by adding such principles as homestead exemptions and non-imprisonment for debt." The constitutions also provided for "free education for all and favored the economic development of the South," Coulter concludes.

Unquestionably, the evil most often charged against Reconstruction was the extension of the suffrage to a people the overwhelming majority of whom had only recently emerged from the dependent status of slavery. It is true that Negro suffrage in the South, aside from the intense fears it stirred up in the whites, was conducive to fraud, deception, and, at the very least, thoughtless voting. But viewed through the glasses of hindsight and with the recognition that universal suffrage is fundamental to a democratic society, the enfranchisement of the Negro appears considerably less "radical" today. The insouciant manner in which the suffrage was proffered to former slaves and the universality of the extension are certainly open to question, but the elementary justice of some form of Negro suffrage cannot be denied by any sincere advocate of democratic government.[2]

---

[2] It should not be thought that illiteracy was one of the legitimate arguments against Negro suffrage. Thousands of southern whites enjoyed the franchise even though they could neither read nor write. In 1880, for example, white illiterates averaged over a quarter of the population in Georgia, Alabama, and North Carolina. J. T. Trowbridge, the journalist, who made a tour of the South in 1865–66, concluded that the Negroes should be granted the suffrage. "They are," he wrote, "by all moral and intellectual qualifications, as well prepared for it as the mass of poor whites in the South." In a good number of states of the Union at this time, even immigrants were granted the vote prior to their acquisition of citizenship. The only valid argument against universal Negro suffrage, it would seem, was the lack of independent experience which was inherent in the Negro's former slave status.

Unfortunately, on the matter of suffrage, neither white Southerners nor northern Radicals were prepared to adjust their conception of the Negro to reality. Though some free Negroes were obviously capable of voting intelligently in 1865, as Lincoln, for example, recognized, and most Negroes would be after the mentally crippling effects of slavery had had a chance to be outgrown, few Southerners could shed their blanket view of the Negro as an incompetent. "The fact is patent to all," a South Carolina convention of whites asserted in 1867, "that the Negro is utterly unfitted to exercise the highest functions of the citizen." The South would not change. "Left to itself," southern historian Francis Simkins has concluded, "the region would not have accorded the Negro the vote or other manifestations of equality...."

On the other hand, the northern Radicals, fearful that the South, once back in the Union, would deny the vote to all Negroes, and especially desirous of creating a large number of new Republicans, went to the other extreme and decreed universal Negro suffrage. This solution, however, overlooked the obvious disabilities which slavery had temporarily stamped upon a majority of the Negroes and seriously underestimated the tenacity of the historically ingrained racial feeling of the whites. Today the only comfort which can be drawn from the thoughtless and opportunistic policy of the Radicals is that it did provide a means for the inclusion of the Negro in the electorate, even if the means almost smothered the ideal with disrepute.

Radical Reconstruction in the South left a more permanent monument than the Negro's transient experience in public office and a nobler one than the southern white's nightmares of racial amalgamation. This was the laying of the foundation of southern free public education. Almost all of the Reconstruction conventions and legislatures erected or revived systems of free public education—a not insignificant manifestation, it might be noted parenthetically, of the Radical propensity for making over Dixie in the image of the North. In most of the southern states, these Reconstruction efforts in behalf of public education remained after 1877 to become the bases upon which post-Radical governments built their school systems. Though the South had always had some free schools and even some local public-school systems, free education as it was known in the North by the 1850's began in the South only after the War for Southern Independence.

The other educational achievement of Radical Reconstruction in the South was the conversion of the whites to the view that Negro education was not only desirable but a necessity. This was largely the work of the Freedmen's Bureau. Prior to Radical Reconstruction in Georgia, for example, as Mildred Thompson has pointed out, the postwar government provided public education only for whites. Education for the Negroes was viewed as a waste of effort and perhaps even dangerous. All over the

South in 1865–67, northern whites who attempted to instruct Negroes were subject to attack and violence. The blazing Negro schoolhouse of this period was the predecessor of the later burning cross.

Despite such opposition, the Freedmen's Bureau succeeded in establishing Negro schools before 1867. At its height, the Bureau operated over 4,000 primary schools, 74 normal schools, and 61 industrial schools for Negroes. George Bentley, a recent historian of the Bureau, concludes that by 1867 Negro and white alike in the South had come to accept the necessity for public education of the former slave. "Certainly in this respect," Bentley observes, "the Bureau had performed a commendable service for the Negroes, for the South and for the nation."

By the time the reader has gotten this far in the "other side" of Reconstruction, he is probably somewhat annoyed at the absence of references to the well-known corruption and fraud so much a part of the conventional picture of the period. He is convinced that this noisome aspect will be conveniently forgotten. There is no denying the disreputable character of all too many of the Radical state governments. Certainly the histories of Louisiana, South Carolina, Florida, and Alabama during this period provide rather painful examples of what corruption can be and what government should not be.

But again it is necessary to emphasize that the total picture is not all dark. Mississippi, for example, under Radical Republican rule enjoyed a government as administratively honest as most Democratic ones, and in some ways decidedly more honest. "The only large case of embezzlement among the state officers during the post-bellum period," writes James Garner, the historian of Mississippi Reconstruction, "was that of the Democratic state Treasurer in 1866." Mildred Thompson, writing about her native state, says that in comparison with states like Alabama and South Carolina, Georgia under Radical Reconstruction "shows a marked moderation in her government, a lesser degree of reconstruction evils, less wanton corruption and extravagance in public office, less social disorder and upheaval. In Georgia," she concludes, "Negroes and carpet-baggers were not so conspicious, and conservative white citizens were better represented."

Though Virginia escaped entirely the period of Radical Reconstruction which other southern states endured after the cessation of military rule, she did not escape extravagance. In 1869, the first and last election under military rule brought the defeat of the Radicals in a free polling. But under the conservatives who then took office, Virginia contracted as staggering a public debt as those run up in the Radical-dominated states. Even the usual stories of the high taxes imposed by the Radical governments in the various states are susceptible of a different interpretation when put into some perspective. In 1870, for instance, when the average tax rate for the southern states was 15 mills, that of Illinois was 45.

The fraudulent dealings of the Radical regimes appear less exceptional and noteworthy if they are placed within the context of the times. For instance, it is instructive to realize that after the end of Reconstruction, each of the conservative Democratic governments in Georgia, Alabama, Virginia, Mississippi, Louisiana, and Tennessee had treasurers or other officials who absconded with or embezzled state funds, the individual defalcations often running to half a million dollars. Then, of course, the years of Reconstruction also included the Tweed swindles in New York City, in which perhaps over $100 million was robbed from the public treasury. And on the national level, the frauds and stealings carried out under the unseeing eye of President Grant serve to round out the picture.

Though not at all excusing the Radical frauds, the corrupt climate of the times does make it clear that the Radical pilferings were little more than particular instances of a general postwar phenomenon. And once this fact is grasped, it becomes apparent that it is not corruption which has fastened disrepute upon these short-lived regimes, but the fact that Negroes participated in them. "Corruption and extravagance increased the intolerance with which the Negro regimes were regarded," southern historian Francis Simkins has written, "yet even if these regimes had shown exemplary statesmanship they would have been unacceptable to white Southerners as long as Negroes comprising any part of them were regarded as political equals."

The tragedy of Reconstruction is that it failed. Rather than liberating the South from its fear of the Negro, Reconstruction exacerbated it; instead of re-establishing a two-party political system, it further fastened a benumbing single party upon a region which once had led the nation in political creativity. Yet neither that section nor the North was alone responsible for the failure; both have to bear the national burden—the South for its intransigent conservatism, the North for its bungling idealism.

As is apparent today, it was imperative in those first years after Appomattox that a way be found whereby the nation and the Negro might confidently look forward to the former slave's full and equal participation in American life. But the unique opportunity of those first years was squandered. Neither Southerners nor Northerners were capable of disenthralling themselves, as Lincoln had counseled; both continued to act within their historically determined attitudinal patterns. Lincoln himself, for that matter, failed to grasp the crucial nature of the postwar era, so far as the Negro was concerned. His plan for the rapid restoration of the southern states indicated that he was quite prepared to throw away the single opportunity for realizing the equalitarian precepts of the Declaration of Independence to which he so often referred. And though the Radicals succeeded in enshrining in the Constitution their vision of equality for all, thereby illuminating the path the nation was ultimately to follow, they were woefully unequal to the complicated and delicate task of implementing their vision. Having failed to meet the problem of the black man at its inception, white Americans have been compelled to grapple with it in each succeeding generation down to our own day.

The inability of the Radicals to translate their equalitarian ideals into reality through the use of force[3] brought an end to the first phase of the search for a place for the Negro in America. During the years which followed, the South was left free to work out for itself what it considered the Negro's proper niche. Contrary to popular conceptions of Reconstruction and its aftermath, the South was neither united nor decided on what that position should be. The evolution of the region's place for the Negro would take another generation.

The southern leaders and people in 1867 had been extremely doubtful about the wisdom of Negro suffrage; but when Reconstruction came to a close, they did not move to eliminate the Negro from southern politics. Instead there was a substantial period during which the South freely experimented with Negro voting. In states like Mississippi and South Carolina, where the Negroes were a majority, a policy of bringing them into the Democratic party was tried. During the 1880's in South Carolina, for instance, several Negro Democrats sat in the legislature. A Negro was nominated by the Mississippi State Democratic Convention of 1877 for the office of secretary of state, and it was not unusual in that state for fusion tickets to be set up in black counties with Negro candidates. Such moves, however, were scattered instances, rather than general conditions; most Negroes remained in the Republican party.

As Republicans the Negroes in the South after 1877 continued to vote and to hold office, though when they threatened the supremacy of the whites, fraud, violence, and intimidation were used to right the balance.

---

[3] At the risk of seeming to condone the often cynical methods employed by the Radicals in the South, the principle behind Reconstruction deserves some attempt at a defense. It is a common argument that force cannot change ideas or dissolve prejudices, and that, therefore, from the outset Reconstruction flew in the face of experience. It is true that ideas are best changed by sincere, inner conversion, but this is not always possible; and weak as enforced conversion may be as a foundation on which to build sympathy and understanding, it is sometimes the only alternative. In both Japan and Germany after 1945, the western powers, notably the United States, undertook to impose certain concepts and forms of democratic life upon the defeated peoples. The only essential difference between these efforts to change people's minds by compulsion and that of Reconstruction was in method; the modern effort was, all things considered, intelligently and efficiently handled. The principle, however, was precisely the same as that which animated Radical Reconstruction in the South. It would seem that only those who oppose the principle of forcible democratization of Germany and Japan can consistently condemn the leaders of Radical Reconstruction for trying to solve by force, albeit ineptly, the problem of the black man in a white America.

Negroes served in the South Carolina legislature right down to 1900, usually elected, of course, from predominantly Negro districts; during the 1880's and 1890's black representatives sat in the legislatures of North Carolina, Mississippi, and Tennessee. Negroes also represented the South in Washington after Reconstruction. Between 1877 and 1900, Negro representatives and senators from the South appeared in every Congress of the United States except the Fiftieth (1887–89). The Fifty-first Congress (1889–91), for example, counted three Negroes, one each from North Carolina, South Carolina, and Virginia.[4] All this came to an end, however, at the turn of the century, a pivotal date in the nation's search for a place for the Negro.

The first permanent law for segregating Negroes from whites in railroad cars was passed as early as 1881 in Tennessee, but it is erroneous to assume, as many have done, that the so-called Jim Crow laws went onto the statute books contemporaneously with the withdrawal of federal troops. Aside from bans on intermarriage and the initiation of legal segregation on trains, the large body of discriminatory legislation that characterized race relations in the South until very recently was unknown before 1898.

Before that date the mingling of whites and Negroes in public places was often quite unrestricted. In 1878, Thomas Wentworth Higginson, scion of a prominent Boston family, abolitionist, and former officer in a Negro regiment in the war, toured South Carolina to see the results of the resurgence of white conservative rule. He found the Negroes traveling on first-class cars, serving on the police force, and generally mingling with the whites in public places. Almost twenty years later in 1897, when a move was afoot to enforce segregation on railroad cars, a Charleston editor, by implication, indicated how little segregation there was in South Carolina. "Our opinion is that we have no more need for a Jim Crow system this year than we had last year, and a great deal less than we had twenty and thirty years ago." Such a system, he said, "would be a needless affront to our respectable and well behaved colored people." One anonymous Northerner, writing in the *Atlantic Monthly* in 1882, was told by the head of a racially mixed school in the South that "mixed schools" would come to the South. The author himself became convinced "that there will soon be mixed schools, for white and colored children, in many parts of the South. There are already a few such schools." Southern leaders acknowledged this possibility, he went on, and "they are not disturbed by the prospect."

Writing in *Harper's Monthly* three years later, Charles Dudley Warner,

---

[4] All during these same years, the North sent no Negro representatives at all, though it is only fair to add that the number of Negroes in that section was then very small. Not until 1929 did the first northern Negro sit in the Congress of the United States.

on a visit to the South, noted that "In New Orleans the street cars are free to all colors; at the Exposition white and colored people mingled freely. . . . " A Negro clergyman, he reported assisted at the services of the major white Episcopal church in that city. He was told by one Negro woman that in Mobile the Negroes had their votes courted by white politicians, and served in minor municipal offices and on the police force. Even the whites' Opera House, this woman told him, was turned over to the Negroes for an exhibition which the whites also attended.

To many visitors from the North, the South in the mid-eighties seemed to be making great strides in the direction of relaxation of racial discrimination. Part of this impression was merely a reflection of increasing northern sympathy for the southern point of view now that the emotion-packed years before 1865 were receding. But a substantial part was obviously a mirroring of the true situation. The end of the Reconstruction and the restoration of white rule had not resulted in the erection of a wall between Negroes and whites in the South.

But those who thought they detected a trend toward equality were destined for disappointment. Instead of expanding the realms of equality for the Negro, the South ultimately developed a pattern of race relations which clearly marked the Negro as a second-class citizen. The 1880's was a period when the legal racial pattern was still in flux, but already there were several signs pointing in the direction the South would go. For example, though there were very few laws requiring segregation, discrimination certainly existed, particularly in hotels, theaters, and on trains. And already in the 1880's, the ugly practice of lynching was spreading ominously. Between 1882 and 1903, almost 2,000 Negroes were lynched in the southern states, as against 567 white persons.

It was the Farmers' Revolt, coming to a head in the early 1890's, which finally brought the balance down on the side of increased restrictions on the Negro. The first form this took was the legal elimination of the Negro from southern politics. Aside from the small farmer's ever-present fear and hatred of the Negro, the aroused agrarian movement had new and compelling reasons for wanting to see the Negro deprived of the vote once and for all. The farmers believed, and sometimes rightly so, that the Negro vote was often mobilized against them, corruptly or otherwise, by the conservatives and the business interests against which they were fighting. Nor were these conservative leaders reluctant, if it served their purpose, to accuse the newly formed farmers' party of splitting the white vote and thereby endangering white supremacy. The complete removal of the Negro from politics, the farmers reasoned, would permit the whites to fight out their differences untroubled by the explosive and confusing issue of white supremacy. A further impetus to the elimination of the Negro from politics was given by politicians like "Pitchfork Ben" Tillman of South Carolina and James Vardaman of Mississippi, who were eager to use the poor man's Negrophobia as a handy vehicle to power.

The movement to eliminate the Negro voter permanently and constitutionally was led by the Mississippi Constitutional Convention of 1890, and the pattern arrived at there became the model for the rest of the southern states. During the nineties and the opening years of the new century, a veritable parade of southern constitutional conventions literally wrote an end to Negro participation in southern politics. To circumvent the prohibitions of the Fifteenth Amendment and yet eliminate effectively the bulk of the Negro voters, the conventions resorted to ingenious subterfuges. Poll taxes, complicated balloting procedures, and literacy tests were among the devices employed to strike Negroes from the registers.

Because the mass of poor white farmers had always harbored deep fears of the black man, these new constitutional provisions were only a translation into law of their own emotions and attitudes. But such legal narcissism exacted a price. The procedures adopted to exclude the Negro from the suffrage also operated to disfranchise thousands of poor, untutored white men who could not surmount any of the hurdles. White registration under the new Louisiana constitution, for instance, dropped 39,000 from what it had been only three years before under the old constitution; Negro registration fell over 125,000. But even this contraction in the white electorate—the reversal of a century of uninterrupted suffrage expansion—seemed worth the candle if it meant the elimination of a threat to white supremacy.

Under the momentum of these political changes, the southern states at the turn of the century began to issue a flood of legislation narrowing the Negro's sphere of activity and carefully defining his place in southern life. Segregation of the races was decreed on street-cars (only Georgia had such a law in the nineteenth century), in waiting rooms, in hospitals, in cemeteries, in housing, in prisons, at drinking fountains, and even in telephone booths (Oklahoma, 1915). Actually, the races were already segregated in practice in many of these areas without laws as sanctions, but in some instances the new laws, in logically extending the principle of separation of the races pressed the application even into minor aspects of life, such as drinking fountains and telephone booths. Certainly no such rigid and petty segregation of the races had existed in the South before; to that extent, at least, the law was creating "custom" rather than only reflecting it.

The segregation proposals of the late 1890's came as a shock to some white Southerners. One editor in Charleston, S.C., for example, where segregation was probably the least advanced in the South, voiced his opposition to legally enforced segregation on trains. He attempted to ridicule into oblivion the principle by carrying it out to what he thought was an obvious absurdity. "If there must be Jim Crow cars on the railroads, there should be Jim Crow cars on the street railways," he wrote. "Also on passenger boats . . . if there are to be Jim Crow cars, morever, there should be Jim Crow waiting saloons at all stations, and Jim Crow eating houses. . . . There should be Jim Crow sections of the jury box, and a separate Jim Crow dock and witness stand in every court—and a Jim Crow Bible for colored witnesses to kiss. It would be advisable also to have a Jim Crow section in county auditors' and treasurers' offices for the accommodation of colored taxpayers." But, as C. Vann Woodward has dryly observed, "What he intended as a *reductio ad absurdum* and obviously regarded as an absurdity became in a very short time a reality. . . . All the improbable applications of the principle suggested by the editor in derision had been put into practice—down to and including the Jim Crow Bible."

The southern solution to the problem of the races was to be a caste system for the black man in a society "dedicated to the proposition that all men are created equal."

13

The Old South to the New

Robert S. Cotterill

It is indeed fashionable to demarcate southern history into two
segments—the Old South and the New. Fundamental to the acceptance of such a division is the belief that the Civil War represented the epitaph of the Old Order and the herald of the New.
But even though the discriminating historian uses such period
pieces and watershed events with distinct mental reservation, Robert
S. Cotterill, former President of the Southern Historical Association, argues that their acceptance has gone beyond intellectual
convenience to become hardened stereotypes. Indeed, standard
interpretations resurrect historical replicas of an Old South—an
agrarian Cotton Kingdom—replete with bluebloods, rednecks, and
blacks. In turn, the rising New Order after The War for Southern Independence is held to represent its economic antithesis—
a "new" South bent on achieving economic salvation in terms of
an entente with northern industrialism. In opposition to such views
Professor Cotterill argues that the postwar decades witnessed a re-
newal of longstanding economic energies in the South. Perhaps it
was in the New South era that the region first developed an industrial awareness; but with the possible exception of furniture production, most significant forms of southern manufacturing were rather
clearly in evidence before the war. In sum, the New South was
clearly not "barren of ancestry, destitute of inheritance." Southern
economic life in the years after civil conflict drew its vitality and
direction from a potential already present, though as yet largely unrealized. The "New South" was anything but a historical aberration.
It was instead a continuation of The South as it had always been.

Robert S. Cotterill, "The Old South to the New," *Journal of Southern History,* 15
(February 1949), 3–8. Copyright 1949 by the Southern Historical Association. Reprinted by permission of the Managing Editor.

The term "New South," if not coined by Henry W. Grady, at least first put into circulation by him, had reference originally only to the cotton manufacturing development of the 1880's.[1] To contemporary observers the name was justified since it seemed evident to them that the South was at that time altering the pattern of its economic life, turning its back on its own history, and entering upon new roads to economic salvation. In the course of years the meaning of the term was broadened to include all phases of southern life since 1865. But the very name "New" South implies an "Old" South, and this latter term now became attached to the period prior to that conflict which southern people, stubbornly and ungrammatically, insist on calling the War Between the States. Inherent in the two terms is the concept not merely of a difference in time but of a change in civilization.

This concept of discontinuity between the Old South and the New has been strengthened in two ways. One of these is the glorification of the War Between the States and the emphasizing of the ruin and devastation it brought to the South. Denied the pride of victory, the southern people developed a pride of suffering. And the thought was an inevitable one that in a tragedy so terrible and a ruin so complete no previous pattern of life could possibly have survived. Therefore, the Old South must have died. The other way in which the idea of discontinuity has been increased is by the growth of a legend of the Old South as a land of plantations, slaveowners, aristocracy, and agricultural philosophy. White people, according to the legend, disdained manual labor and refrained from any debilitating practice of it. All work was done by Negro slaves, apparently in intervals between singing the praises of the Old Kentucky Home and making metrical demands to be carried back to Old Virginny. What few common people there were in the Old South were serfs subsisting on the economic crumbs which fell from the gentry's table. Such was the Old South of legend, and since the people of the New, looking around them, saw nothing even remotely resembling it, they reasoned, quite logically, that it must have died—as the genealogists so deftly put it, O. S. P.

These, then, are the three concepts inherent in the terms "Old South" and "New South"—a legendary "Old South" that has no present counterpart, a "New South" with a pattern of life unrelated to the Old, and between them a war so devastating that it destroyed the old order making it necessary to start all things anew.

The first of these ideas may be dismissed without argument. If the Old South of legend be no longer present, it is not because it died but because it never existed. It is a figment of imagination, originating in the ignorance, or malice, of northern abolitionists and adopted by southerners suffering

---

[1] [Omitted.]

from nostalgia. It was at once a distortion and an idealization, and in neither capacity could it transmit any part of itself to later times.

But the cotton manufacturing development of the 1880's which first gave rise to the name "New South" was no hallucination. The only question about it is not whether it existed but whether it was *new*. Certainly the people of that time called it "new," and its coming was accompanied by such a rash of publicity as had not broken out on the southern body politic since the railroad building of the 1840's. Editors, orators, ministers, poets, novelists, and businessmen hymned its praises, and canny politicians hastened to cast their political bread on its waters. They proclaimed that a New South was being born. There were some people then (and there have been more since) who viewed the development of manufacturing as a surrender of southern ideals and the adoption of a low, Yankee culture. But most commentators have considered it as a beneficent dispensation which had been denied to the Old South because of the enervating effects of slavery. The most noted of these has declared in one of his books: "In the face of a freed negro population, the idea of work first seriously presented itself to the Southern white mind."[2] But since the fifteen years that had elapsed between the adoption of the Thirteenth Amendment and the supposed beginning of the manufacturing movement seemed a bit longer than should have been necessary for such a powerful regenerative force as emancipation to get into mass production, supplementary explanations had to be given. These ranged all the way from the resumption of specie payment to the psychological shock of James A. Garfield's election. They ascribed the beginning of the manufacturing movement to the poverty of the 1870's and to the prosperity of the 1880's, to jubilation over the collapse of carpetbaggery and to despair caused by war and reconstruction, to exultation over the preservation of southern ideals and to repentance for ever having had any. But although the writers differed on the origin of the phenomenon, they all agreed on the nature of it. They all agreed that it was new: it was a revolution, unrelated to the past, barren of ancestry, destitute of inheritance.

But the student of history is insistent on sequence and consequence, he demands continuity and cause. He is uncontent to find an explanation of mundane affairs in the doctrine of virgin birth. Every historical event, he considers, must have a family tree as an accessory before the fact.

The difficulty writers have experienced in explaining the origin of the "Industrial Revolution" in the South may be primarily owing to the fact that there was no Industrial Revolution to explain. The so-called Revo-

[2] Broadus Mitchell, *The Rise of Cotton Mills in the South,* in Johns Hopkins University *Studies in Historical and Political Science,* Ser. XXXIX, No. 2 (Baltimore, 1921), 57.

lution was, in fact, not a Revolution but an *evolution* from the Old South to the New. If in the Old South manufacturing was only a handmaiden to agriculture, it was not because of agricultural philosophy but of agricultural profits. By 1860 the South had 188 cotton mills, the yearly output of which was valued at $14,000,000. If it be true that it was in the face of a freed Negro population that "the idea of work first seriously presented itself to the Southern white mind," it is pleasant to reflect that all this was done without effort. The recipe seems to have been lost. Certainly the growth of manufacturing in the Old South was sufficient to excite the apprehension of northern mill-owners, apparently unaware of the fact that manufacturing was impossible in a slavery regime. And if it were not uncharitable, one might suspect that the patriotic fervor of General William T. Sherman in destroying southern cotton mills was not unadulterated by a desire to eliminate competition. But Sherman, unlike Kilroy, was here only once and some two-thirds of the southern mills escaped his evangelical efforts. It is only reasonable to suppose that the war stimulated southern interest in manufacturing. But when southern people after the war engaged in manufacturing it was neither because of prosperity during the war nor of poverty after it. It was because cotton manufacturing was one of the recognized and accepted ways of making a living. They did not *begin* manufacturing after the war: they *resumed* it; they were actuated not by novelty, but by tradition. By 1870 the losses of war were almost fully recovered: then came the seven lean years of the early 1870's, the recovery late in the decade, and then the well-trumpeted development of the 1880's. But the South in the 1880's did not become suddenly *industrial;* it only became suddenly *articulate.* The beginning was not in *manufacturing,* but in *publicity.*

The industrial inheritance of the New South from the Old was not confined to cotton manufacturing. The derivation of the Durham cigarette from Russia and of the Tampa cigar from Cuba cannot alter the fact that the paternity of southern tobacco manufacturing lies in the Old South. In the ante-bellum period it was the output of plug tobacco from southern factories that lifted expectoration in the United States to a position among the fine arts along with music and painting, and made the cuspidor standard equipment in the American home. As for iron manufacturing, even in colonial days it was important enough to be prohibited and too important to be prevented. Of the other manufactures of the New South, the only important one lacking an Old South pedigree is furniture. Even the manufacture of cottonseed oil had its beginning in the Old South, although quite a bit of it in the process of labeling seems to have undergone a metamorphosis into olive oil. The Old South discovered the coal mines of Maryland, Kentucky, Tennessee, and Alabama and exploited them so far as transportation facilities permitted. And if the petroleum industry be considered a species of mining, we may remember that Louisiana discovered oil before she discovered secession.

The only important change made by the New South in its agricultural inheritance was the substitution on its plantations and larger farms of share-cropping for slave labor and of the country store for the factorage system. Both share-cropping and the country store were Old South institutions now expanded into wider uses. Share-cropping, of course, did not originate in the Old South, but is as old as agriculture itself. The first record of it is found in Genesis 29-31 where it is told how Jacob tended on shares the flocks of his uncle Laban in the land of Pandan-aram. It may be noted, incidentally, that Jacob broke his contract, moved away secretly, and took a considerable portion of his landlord's property with him—thereby establishing a precedent that has been followed extensively to this day.

In no place of its economic life was the New South new. It was not a Phoenix rising from the ashes of the Old; not a revival; not even a reincarnation: it was merely a continuation of the Old South. And not only in its economic life: the New South inherited, also, the *spirit* of the Old. It inherited its racial pride, and if anyone wants to call it racial prejudice, there can be no objection, because pride and prejudice were inseparable companions long before Jane Austen proclaimed their union. The student of history cannot turn moralist either to exalt or to condemn this racial pride, but he must take note of its continuing existence. The New South inherited, also, a laissez-faire philosophy of living which manifested itself subjectively in an indifference to progress and objectivity in a distaste for reforming its neighbors or to confessing other people's sins. It inherited the Old South conviction that certain questions could not be surrendered to the jurisdiction of public law. The one quality of the Old South apparently uninherited by the New was self-confidence and consequent self-assertion. Says a Confederate arithmetic: If one southerner can whip twelve Yankees, how many Yankees can six southerners whip? Although the premise of this problem seems to have been somewhat unstable, it evidences a spirit of confidence that for a long time seemed lost to the New South. It may be, however, that the aggressiveness and boastfulness so characteristic of the Old South instead of dying out after the war simply followed the trail of cotton and migrated to Texas. From the time they annexed the United States in 1845 until their recent singlehanded and unaided conquest of Germany and Japan, Texans have been noted for their aversion to understatement. But it is possible that when Texans talk "big" they are speaking not as Texans but as southerners. Certainly, that Texan was speaking the language of the Old South when he rose at a banquet and gave this toast to his state: "Here's to Texas. Bounded on the north by the Aurora Borealis, bounded on the east by the rising sun, bounded on the south by the precession of the equinoxes, and on the west by the Day of Judgment."

As to the final factor in our concept, the War Between the States cannot be considered as a mighty cataclysm engulfing the Old South or as a chasm dividing the Old South from the New. The pondering of might-have-beens is normally an exercise taken in vain, but it seems clear that in no essential way did the war alter or deflect the course of southern development. It was an interruption but not a cleavage. It was, in long perspective, only an episode in a continuous southern history: a tragic episode, but even its tragedy was transient. No southerner can be tempted to belittle the war or deplore the remembrance of it. Surely it was worthy of all remembrance —a war of heroism unrewarded, of suffering uncompensated, of hopes unrealized, and of dreams that have no waking. But for the South it marked no end and no beginning: it neither buried the Old South nor brought the New to birth. There is, in very fact, no Old South and no New. There is only The South. Fundamentally, as it was in the beginning it is now, and, if God please, it shall be evermore.

Suggestions for Further Reading

The works indicated below, in addition to those from which the selections in the body of the book have been drawn, bear a particular relevance to southern history in its mythic context. The list is extensive, but certainly not all-inclusive. Acquaintance with the following materials should give the reader a basic grasp of the mythical content of the southern past. More importantly, the citations can be viewed as yet further evidence of the viability of "myth" as an approach through which the "reality" of the southern experience might better be judged.

Adams, Richard P. "Faulkner and the Myth of the South." *The Mississippi Quarterly,* 14 (1961).

Alexander, Thomas B. "Persistent Whiggery in the Confederate South, 1860–1877." *The Journal of Southern History,* 27 (1961).

Amacher, Anne Ward. "Myths and Consequences: Calhoun and Some Nashville Agrarians." *South Atlantic Quarterly,* 59 (1960).

Boorstin, Daniel J. "The Vision and the Reality." In *The Americans: The Colonial Experience.* New York: Random House, 1966.

Bradford, M. E. "What We Can Know for Certain: Frank Owsley and the Recovery of Southern History." *Sewanee Review,* 78 (1970).

Bridenbaugh, Carl. *Myths and Realities: Societies of the Colonial South.* New York: Atheneum, 1963.

Brooks, Cleanth. "Faulkner and History." *The Mississippi Quarterly,* 25 (1972).

Cann, Marvin L. "The End of a Political Myth: The South Carolina Gubernatorial Campaign of 1938." *The South Carolina Historical Magazine,* 72 (1971).

Clendenen, Clarence C. "President Hayes' 'Withdrawal' of the Troops—An Enduring Myth." *The South Carolina Historical Magazine,* 70 (1969).

Cole, Wayne S. "America First and the South." *The Journal of Southern History,* 22 (1956).

Cords, Nicholas and Patrick Gerster, eds. "The Mythology of the South." In *Myth and the American Experience.* Beverly Hills and New York: Glencoe/Macmillan, 1973.

Danoff, Clarence H. "Four Decades of Thought on the South's Economic Problems." In Melvin Greenhut and W. Tate Whitman, eds., *Essays in Southern Economic Development.* Chapel Hill: University of North Carolina Press, 1964.

Davenport, F. Gavin, Jr. *The Myth of Southern History: Historical Consciousness in Twentieth-Century Southern Literature.* Nashville: Vanderbilt University Press, 1970.

————. "Thomas Dixon's Mythology of Southern History." *The Journal of Southern History,* 36 (1970).

Davis, Michael. *The Image of Lincoln in the South.* Knoxville: The University of Tennessee Press, 1972.

DeConde, Alexander. "The South and Isolationism." *The Journal of Southern History,* 24 (1958).

Degler, Carl. "There Was Another South." *American Heritage,* 11 (1960).

————. "The South in Southern History Textbooks." *The Journal of Southern History,* 30 (1964).

Dillon, Merton L. "Three Southern Antislavery Editors: The Myth of the Southern Antislavery Movement." *Eastern Tennessee Historical Society Publication,* No. 42 (1970).

Donald, David. "The Scalawag in Mississippi Reconstruction," *The Journal of Southern History,* 10 (1944).

————. "The Confederate as a Fighting Man." *The Journal of Southern History,* 35 (1959).

Dykeman, Wilma. "The Southern Demagogue." *The Virginia Quarterly Review,* 33 (1957).

Eaton, Clement. *The Waning of the Old South Civilization.* New York: Pegasus, 1969.

Engerman, Stanley L. "The Antebellum South: What Probably Was and What Should Have Been." *Agricultural History,* 44 (1970).

Fishwick, Marshall. "Robert E. Lee: The Guardian Angel Myth." *Saturday Review* (March 4, 1961).

Floan, Howard R. *The South in Northern Eyes, 1831–1861.* Austin: University of Texas Press, 1958.

Gaines, Francis Pendelton. *The Southern Plantation: A Study in the Development and Accuracy of a Tradition.* (New York: Columbia University Press, 1924.

Gara, Larry. *The Liberty Line: The Legend of the Underground Railroad.* Lexington: The University Press of Kentucky, 1967.

Genovese, Eugene D. *In Red and Black: Marxian Explorations in Southern and Afro-American History.* New York: Vintage Books, 1971.

Govan, Thomas P. "Was the Old South Different?" *The Journal of Southern History,* 21 (1955).

Grantham, Dewey, W., Jr. "Politics Below the Potomac." *Current History,* 35 (1958).

————. "The Southern Bourbons Revisited." *South Atlantic Quarterly,* 55 (1961).

————. "South to Posterity." *Mid-West Quarterly,* 8 (1966).

————. "Regional Imagination: Social Scientists and the American South." *The Journal of Southern History,* 34 (1968).

————, ed. *The South and the Sectional Image: The Sectional Theme Since Reconstruction.* New York: Harper & Row Publishers, 1967.

Green, Fletcher M. "Listen to the Eagle Scream: One Hundred Years of the Fourth of July in North Carolina." *North Carolina Historical Review,* 31 (1954).

————. "The South and Its History." *Current History,* 35 (1958).

————. *The Role of the Yankee in the Old South.* Athens: University of Georgia Press, 1973.

Gross, Seymour L., and Eileen Bender. "History, Politics and Literature: The Myth of Nat Turner." *American Quarterly,* 24 (1972).

Hansen, Vagn K. "Jefferson Davis and the Repudiation of Mississippi Bonds (1842): The Development of a Political Myth." *Journal of Mississippi History,* 33 (1971).

Havard, William C. "The Burden of the Literary Mind: Some Meditations on Robert Penn Warren as Historian." *South Atlantic Quarterly,* 62 (1963).

Herskovits, Melville. *The Myth of the Negro Past.* Boston: Beacon Press, 1958.

Hofstadter, Richard. "Ulrich B. Phillips and the Plantation Legend." *Journal of Negro History,* 29 (1944).

Karanikas, Alexander. *Tillers of a Myth: Southern Agrarians as Social and Literary Critics.* Madison: University of Wisconsin Press, 1966.

Keyserling, Hermann. "The South—America's Hope." *Atlantic Quarterly,* 144 (1929).

Mayo, Bernard. *Myths and Men.* New York: Harper & Row Publishers, 1963.

McWhiney, Grady. *Southerners and Other Americans.* New York: Basic Books, Inc., 1973.

McWhiney, Grady and Francis Simkins. "The Ghostly Legend of the KKK." *Negro History Bulletin,* 14 (1951).

Mowry, George E. *Another Look At the Twentieth-Century South.* Baton Rouge: Louisiana State University Press, 1973.

Nash, Gary B. "The Image of the Indian in the Southern Colonial Mind." *The William and Mary Quarterly,* 29 (1972).

Noggle, Burl. "Variety and Ambiguity: The Recent Approach to Southern History." *Mississippi Quarterly,* 16 (1963–64).

Osterweis, Rollin G. *Romanticism and Nationalism in the Old South.* New Haven: Yale University Press, 1949.

Owsley, Frank L. and Harriet C. Owsley. "The Economic Basis of Society in the Late Ante-Bellum South." *The Journal of Southern History,* 6 (1940).

Potter, David M. *The South and the Sectional Conflict.* Baton Rouge: Louisiana State University Press, 1968.

Payne, Ladell. "Willie Stark and Huey Long: Atmosphere, Myth or Suggestion." *American Quarterly,* 20 (1968).

Rock, Virginia J. "The Making and Meaning of 'I'll Take My Stand': A Study in Utopian Conservatism." Unpublished Ph.D Dissertation: University of Minnesota, 1961.

Rozwenc, Edwin C. "Captain John Smith's Image of America." *William and Mary Quarterly,* 16 (1959).

Rubin, Louis D. "The Historical Image of Modern Southern Writing." *The Journal of Southern History,* 22 (1956).

————. "The South and the Faraway Country." *The Virginia Quarterly Review,* 38 (1962).

Scarborough, William K. *The Overseer: Plantation Management in the Old South.* Baton Rouge: Louisiana State University Press, 1966.

Scott, Anne Firor. "The 'New Women' in the New South." *South Atlantic Quarterly,* 61 (1962).

————. "The Progressive Wind from the South, 1906–1913." *The Journal of Southern History,* 29 (1963).

————. *The Southern Lady: From Pedestal to Politics.* Chicago: University of Chicago Press, 1970.

Sellers, Charles G., Jr., ed. *The Southerner as American.* Chapel Hill: University of North Carolina Press, 1960.

Simkins, Francis B. "The Everlasting South." *The Journal of Southern History,* 13 (1947).

————. "The South." In Merrill Jensen, ed., *Regionalism in America.* Madison: University of Wisconsin Press, 1951.

Smiley, David L. "The Quest for the Central Theme in Southern History." *South Atlantic Quarterly,* 71 (1972).

Sosna, Morton. "The South Old and New: A Review Essay." *The Wisconsin Magazine of History,* 55 (1972).

Spruill, Julia Cherry. *Women's Life and Work in the Southern Colonies.* New York: W. W. Norton & Co., 1973.

Stampp, Kenneth M. "The Tragic Legend of Reconstruction." In *The Era of Reconstruction.* New York: Alfred A. Knopf, 1965.

————. "Rebels and Sambos: The Search for the Negro's Personality in Slavery." *The Journal of Southern History,* 37 (1971).

Stephenson, Wendell Holmes. "The South Lives in History." *Historical Outlook,* 23 (1932).

Tate, Allen. "Faulkner's 'Sanctuary' and the Southern Myth." *The Virginia Quarterly Review,* 44 (1968).

Tindall, George B. *The Disruption of the Solid South.* New York: W. W. Norton & Co., 1973.

Trelease, Allen W. "Who Were the Scalawags?" *The Journal of Southern History,* 29 (1963).

Vandiver, Frank E. "The Confederacy and the American Tradition." *The Journal of Southern History,* 28 (1962).

Ver Steeg, Clarence L. "Historians and the Southern Colonies." In Ray A. Billington, ed., *The Reinterpretation of Early American History.* San Marino, California: The Huntington Library, 1966.

Ward, John William. *Andrew Jackson: Symbol for an Age.* New York: Oxford University Press, 1962.

Warren, Robert Penn. *The Legacy of the Civil War: Meditations on the Centennial.* New York: Alfred A. Knopf, 1964.

Whitridge, Arnold. "The John Brown Legend." *History Today,* 7 (1957).

Williams, D. Alan. "The Virginia Gentry and the Democratic Myth." In Quint, Albertson, and Cantor, eds., *Main Problems of American History.* Rev. ed. Homewood, Illinois: The Dorsey Press, 1972.

Woodward, C. Vann. "The Antislavery Myth." *The American Scholar,* 31 (1962).

———. "Southern Mythology." *Commentary,* 42 (1965).

———. *The Strange Career of Jim Crow.* New York: Oxford University Press, 1966.

Wright, Louis B. "Intellectual History and the Colonial South." *William and Mary Quarterly,* 16 (1959).

———. *The Dream of Prosperity in Colonial America.* New York University Press, 1965.

Zinn, Howard. *The Southern Mystique.* New York: Alfred A. Knopf, 1964.

Index

Abolitionists
  as convinced of a slaveholding aristocracy, 79, 80
  on role in development of southern myths, 6
Acton, Lord, 80
Adams, Henry, 145
  southern effect on, 112, 113
Adams, John, 138, 139
American Historical Association, meeting in Durham, N.C. (1929), 8
Aristocracy
  lack of, during Old South, 72ff.
  natural, 139
  as opposed to social aristocracy in Old South, 89
  as supposedly anti-democratic, 79ff.
Army
  during Reconstruction, 156, 157
Ashmore, Harry, on southern capacity for unreality, 111, 112
Azilia, utopian project, 25, 26, 27

Bailey, Thomas A., and definition of myth, xiv
Baxter, Richard, on Puritan ethic, 43
Benighted South, 9, 15
  on development of, during 1920s, 6
Benton, Thomas H., on economic alliance of South and West, 124
Berrien, John M., as Whig leader in Georgia, 106, 107
Bertelson, David, as author of *The Lazy South*, 34ff.
Black Codes, 52
Blacks. *See* Negroes; Slavery
Bridenbaugh, Carl, 59
Brown, Albert Gallatin, 90
Brown, John, and Harper's Ferry, 135ff.
Byrd, William II, as land promoter, 19, 20

Calhoun, John C., 58, 67, 96, 101, 107
  as Hayne's source of ideas, 123

on South's relationship with the West, 124
as spokesman for antebellum South, 118
on state rights, 151
on tyranny of the majority, 86
Whig party support for, 100
Camp, George Sidney, on democracy, 80
Carpetbaggers, 156, 163, 173
Cash, Wilbur J., xiii, xv
  on southern capacity for self-deception, 112
  on southern leisure, 33
Central theme (in southern history), xiii, xv, 13, 14, 15
  sectionalism and state rights as, 97
Charleston, S.C., 72
  as colonial trade center, 21, 22
  Democratic national convention at (1860), 117
Cherokees, during colonization, 27ff.
Chesnut, Mary, 116, 138
Clay, Henry, 100, 101, 107
Cole, Arthur C., 100
  on Whig party in South, 98
Confederacy (Confederate States of America), 148ff.
Confederate Constitution, democratic nature of, 144
Congress (United States)
  Twenty-second (1831–1833), as related to development of Whig party, 99
  Twenty-third (1833–1835), in shaping Whig party, 99
  Twenty-fourth (1835–1837), 99
  Twenty-seventh (1841–1843), 101
  Fifty-first (1889–1891), 166
Conservatism, 10
Constitution (federal), 78
  convention, 122
Cooke, John Esten, and plantation myth, 127
Copperheads, 123